AF615143

Food Policy and the Indian State

The Public Distribution System in South India

JOS MOOIJ

DELHI
OXFORD UNIVERSITY PRESS
CALCUTTA CHENNAI MUMBAI
1999

Oxford University Press, Great Clarendon Street, Oxford OX2 6DP

Oxford New York
Athens Auckland Bangkok Calcutta
Cape Town Chennai Dar es Salaam Delhi
Florence Hong Kong Istanbul Karachi
Kuala Lumpur Madrid Melbourne Mexico City
Mumbai Nairobi Paris Singapore
Taipei Tokyo Toronto

and associates in

Berlin Ibadan

© Oxford University Press 1999

ISBN 0 19564566 9

Typeset at All India Press, Pondicherry 605001
Printed in India at Pauls Press, Delhi 110020
and published by Manzar Khan, Oxford University Press
YMCA Library Building, Jai Singh Road, New Delhi 110 001

Preface

At the time that the last revisions to this book were being made, the Government of India was in the process of implementing a number of changes in the public distribution system (PDS). These changes included a considerable increase in the issue price of grain and wheat for 60 per cent of ration card holders, and a substantive reduction in the price for the 40 per cent of Indians who are estimated to live below the poverty line. These changes were introduced in 1997 and in the last chapter I briefly refer to them.

These recent revisions to the PDS made me, once again, realize how rapidly things change in India at present. In a relatively short time span of 7–8 years, the food subsidy has almost tripled, and now, perhaps, another substantial increase is under way. Proposals for restructuring or revamping the PDS follow one another quickly. The first proposal is hardly understood and/or implemented before the next one is put forward. These rapid changes make one question the potential usefulness of research. In such a fast changing world, what is the use of scholarly investigation or findings, thorough and detailed as they may be, when they are snapshots of particular moments and may be overtaken by events at the time the analysis is completed?

On the other hand, the revisions also showed me the continuity of certain dilemmas in food policy making. The subsidy burden is regarded as a problem; yet the new revisions will probably only increase the costs of the PDS. Targeting is seen as essential; yet implementation is difficult and meets with resistance. Food remains such a political issue that any policy change is always contested. In 1997, when I sent the manuscript to the publisher, the situation in this regard was no different from 1991-2, when I did the fieldwork that this book is based on, nor any other date in the past. I am also convinced that in the near and distant future, food will remain an extremely important issue on the political agenda in India. And it is for that reason that, although things may change fast, I hope a study on the politics of Indian food policy may have a wider relevance than only in relation to the relatively short time-span during which primary data collection took place.

This book is a revised version of my Ph. D. thesis, defended in November 1996 in the University of Amsterdam. While working on this project I was helped by a great many people and institutions. Financially the research has been made possible by the University of Amsterdam (which employed me as a Ph. D. researcher). Before I worked in Amsterdam, the Department of Agrarian Law (Wageningen Agricultural University) had offered me a desk and other useful facilities. The Institute for Social and Economic Change in Bangalore extended a research affiliation; the Government of India gave a research permit. The Development Policy and Practice Research Group at the Open University (Milton Keynes, UK) and the 'Fonds Landbouw Export Bureau 1916/18' in Wageningen co-financed a pilot study in 1989, and the Dutch Foundation for Scientific Research (NWO) made it possible to attend a seminar in Oxford (December 1991) and a Congress in Kerala (August 1994), where I could present some initial findings. The book was finalized when I was at the Institute of Social Studies, the Hague.

As for people, I first want to thank my colleagues and friends from the Centrum voor Landbouw Studies (Centre for Agrarian Studies; CLS): Roland Brouwer, Marina Endeveld, Kees Jansen and Peter Mollinga. They stood by the cradle of the research proposal, supported the fieldwork, and found time to comment on draft chapters, despite their busy time schedules and preoccupations with their own theses.

I had the privilege to be supervised by no fewer than three excellent scholars, each with his/her own specific background and expertise: Franz von Benda-Beckmann, Jan Breman and Barbara Harriss-White. I would like to thank them very much for their support and comments at various stages of the project.

In India I have received help from many people. First of all, I have to mention and thank all traders, government officials, politicians, consumers/card holders, lawyers etc. who were so kind in responding to my questions and queries, or in expressing opinions, sharing grievances and spending time with me. Professor M. V. Nadkarni (Institute for Social and Economic Change, Bangalore) was of great help, not only in arranging various practical matters, but also in discussing initial ideas and research plans and commenting on the draft chapters and papers. K. Jayashankara and M. R. Shashidhar provided indispensable research assistance. S. G. Shankar became my close friend. I enjoyed enormously countless discussions in his shop or in one of the Akkipura hotels. His help in finding new information and informants was invaluable, and the hospitality he and his family members offered was a great relief in my otherwise hotel-based existence. Dr Ramachandra Swamy and Sharda did their best to teach me Kannada, the language of Karnataka. I am afraid I was not a brilliant student, but I enjoyed the classes nonetheless and they proved of great help during the fieldwork. I want to thank K. S. Krishnaswamy for the many interesting discussions we had on policy and the state in India. Subash Menon and his family, and B. K. Chandrashekar were very kind and helpful friends, who greatly added to the pleasure of our stay in India. Michael Tharakan has been a source of suggestions and inspiration each time I have visited the Centre for Development Studies in Thiruvananthapuram. There were many others at the Institute for Social and Economic Change in Bangalore and the Centre for Development Studies in Thiruvananthapuram who helped me at various stages of the project. Marion Vijverberg, who stayed three months in a Karnataka village, wrote a very interesting field study report, on which part of the fifth chapter of this book is based.

Both in Amsterdam at the Centre for Asian Studies (CASA) as well as in Wageningen at the Department of Agrarian Law of the Agricultural University, I profited greatly from discussions with colleagues. I much enjoyed the bi-weekly sessions in Amsterdam as well as the evening discussions organized by Franz and Keebet von Benda-Beckmann. One of the merits of CASA is that it attracts very interesting scholars from abroad. This gave me the opportunity to discuss drafts of various chapters with Jean Drèze, K. P. Kannan, James Manor and Sudipto Mundle. The CASA secretariat provided assistance when necessary. Martin Southwold improved the English, and Erika Koldenhof was a great help with some time-consuming jobs at the end of the project. I also want to thank an anonymous referee of Oxford University Press for his/her useful comments and criticisms.

In fact, if I were fully to acknowledge my intellectual debts, I would have to go a long way back. Without trying to be exhaustive, I want to mention a few more people. My parents, of course, who have always succeeded in encouraging my sisters and me to continue our studies, in a very gentle way without exerting any pressure. Furthermore, comrades from the Wageningen *Imperialisme Kollektief.* Discussions with them greatly stimulated my just-awakened interest in political economy. The Development Policy and Practice Research Group at the Open University in Milton Keynes (UK) provided an extremely stimulating environment for developing my ideas further, which finally led to the Ph. D. research proposal. In particular, I want to mention Henry Bernstein, who helped to arrange our affiliation with DPP, and who has been a good friend since. And last but certainly not least, Peter Mollinga, who has already been mentioned many times in disguise, as a member of several of the groups referred to above, and when I talk about 'our' stay and 'our' affiliation. Together we went to England and India. He has been important in many respects—intellectually and otherwise—and throughout the process—from making comments on the first draft research proposal many years back to suggestions related to the final version. For all this and much more, I want to thank him very much.

Although the book is shaped by and through my interactions with all these people, I am sure some of them do not agree with parts of it and prefer not to be associated too closely with it. They need not worry. As academic convention prescribes, I relieve them from any responsibility for the text.

June 1997

JOS MOOIJ

Contents

Figures and Tables

Abbreviations

AD	Assistant Director
ARD	Authorized Retail (ration) Dealer (in Kerala)
AWD	Authorized Wholesale (ration) Dealer (in Kerala)
CACP	Committee on Agricultural Costs and Prices
CSO	Central Statistical Organization
DC	Deputy Commissioner or District Collector
DD	Deputy Director
DSO	District Supply Officer (in Kerala)
EC	Essential Commodities
ECA	Essential Commodities Act, 1955
EGS	Employment Guarantee Scheme
FA	Food Assistant (the Deputy Director of the Food and Civil Supplies Department in Karnataka)
FCI	Food Corporation of India
FPS	Fair Price Shop
FPSO	Fair Price Shop Owner
GM	General Manager (of the KaFCSC or the KeSCSC)
GoI	Government of India
GoKa	Government of Karnataka
GoKe	Government of Kerala
IAS	Indian Administrative Service
IPS	Indian Police Service
KaFCSC	Karnataka Food and Civil Supplies Corporation
KAS	Karnataka Administrative Service
KeSCSC	Kerala State Civil Supplies Corporation
KRO	Kerala Rationing Order, 1966
LSD	Lok Sabha Debate

MD	Managing Director (of the KaFCSC or the KeSCSC)
MLA	Member of the Legislative Assembly (State Parliament)
MP	Member of Parliament (Lok Sabha)
NSS	National Sample Survey
NSSO	National Sample Survey Organization
PDS	Public Distribution System
PPA	Paddy Procurement Assistant
RMC	Regulated Marketing Court
RMO	Rice Mill Owner
TPDS	Targeted Public Distribution system
TSO	Taluk Supply Officer (in Kerala)

1

Introduction

In 1997, the Indian people celebrated the fiftieth anniversary of independent India. Fifty years earlier, in August 1947, the British withdrew from India, leaving the power to govern the country in Indian hands. Jawaharlal Nehru, addressing the Constituent Assembly, then had declared that the Independence just achieved meant the redemption of a pledge. But he also stated that this achievement 'is but a step, an opening of opportunity, to the great triumphs and achievements that await us... the ending of poverty and ignorance and disease and inequality of opportunity'.[1]

Undeniably, in the course of the fifty years that have passed since, an enormous number of activities have been undertaken to fulfil these ends. And indeed, in several fields considerable progress has been made. As Drèze and Sen (1995) remind us, an important achievement is the elimination of substantial famines. Other successes mentioned by these authors include the establishment of a multiparty democratic system, and economic and social development in many different fields. On the other hand, the tasks as identified by Nehru—the ending of poverty, ignorance, disease, and inequality of opportunity—are still far from accomplished. Despite huge efforts, large sums of money and the participation of many active civil servants, politicians and others, in the late 1990s hunger, illiteracy, and deprivation still persist on a large scale.[2]

This book is about one specific government intervention: the public distribution system (PDS). It is a welfare measure—as it involves distribution of subsidized foodgrains to the needy—but simultaneously it is also an instrument to influence the foodgrain market and a means to promote foodgrain production. It started in 1939 on a small scale in certain selected metropolitan centres, but gradually it expanded in terms of financial expenses and people covered. In the mid-1990s,

[1] Jawaharlal Nehru's speech at the Constituent Assembly, New Delhi, 14 August 1947. Quoted from Drèze and Sen (1995), p.1.

[2] See Drèze and Sen (1995) for an analysis of the way in which India has addressed the tasks as identified by Nehru.

the public distribution scheme costs Rs 50,000 million per year,[3] which is about 3 per cent of central government expenditure, and less than 1 per cent of the gross domestic product. In principle, it covers almost the whole Indian population. Nevertheless, despite this impressive programme, hunger and malnutrition are still endemic. In this book, I analyse how the public food distribution system functions in reality—who profits, who is excluded and why this is the case. It is a detailed analysis of the working of one of the most important welfare interventions in post-Independent India.

1.1 THE SUBJECT AND THE STRUCTURE OF THIS BOOK

Let me start with an example from my research diary, November 1991:

My research assistant and I got off the bus in a small village about 15 kilometres away from the district capital. We were doing some inventory work, visiting a few villages and exploring ideas about the public food distribution system. This whole area which we had chosen for our first case study was well covered by the distribution system. Every two or three villages had a fair price shop, and also in other respects the region was well developed; a few kilometres away from the village there was a canal, and there was a fair amount of rice and sugar-cane production. The village where we got off the bus was mainly inhabited by agricultural labourers, while the landowning farmers lived in a neighbouring village.

Immediately next to the bus stop there was a grocery shop, in front of which about eight people were chatting with each other. We joined this group, which consisted of men only. Now and then one or two passers-by stopped and listened to our discussion; after a while they continued on their journey. My research assistant explained that I was a researcher from abroad, and that I was interested in the public food distribution system. Not that I had any influence on this policy, he emphasized; as a researcher I was just curious and eager to know more about it. Could the villagers tell me anything about it? Immediately this question led to a lively discussion. 'Almost all of us have green cards', the men told me. (A green card allows a family to buy 10 kilos of foodgrains per month at a cheap rate.) 'You see, there was a survey some years back. We are all poor, so we got a green card. Only a few migrant families were away at the time of the survey, and someone else was in hospital. Till this day they don't have a green card, but just now the government did a re-survey, and within four-five months these families will have a green card too.'

[3] January 1995, Rs 100 were equal to £ 2.02. At the time of fieldwork (1 January 1992), Rs 100 equalled £ 2.08. This means Rs 50,000 million is about £ 1 billion.

'But the problem is', these villagers told me, 'the fair price shop is always closed. Only one day a month this shop is open. Politicians neglect our village. We don't have any political representatives; there are no volunteers, no social workers. All the funds go to the neighbouring village; they have a school; they have a canal. Also the fair price shop owner is from this other village. But in fact, he does not live there either. He lives in Akkipura town,[4] the district capital, where he has a grocery shop. He is a powerful person. He is from the ruling party and he is a member of the Mandal Panchayat, a local elected council. So, he usually stays in the district capital to do his political work and to run his shop there. Only now and then he comes here to open his fair price shop. Then we have to take a day off from work. We have to borrow some money and try to purchase foodgrains in his shop. We cannot wait for one day, as the next day the door will be closed again. It is an open secret that the fair price shop owner also sells part of these PDS foodgrains in his own shop in Akkipura town.'

'We ourselves have to go to his shop; we can't send our wives or our children. They would not get the ration. But this man ...'and they referred to the shop owner in front of whose shop we were talking, 'does not have to wait in queue. He just sends a slip, and then the foodgrains are set aside, and later he can come and collect them.' The shop owner confirmed this story. He also said that he could get more than the official quota, but did not want to disclose how much more.

Later that day we did some more interviewing about the relevance of PDS in the same village, as well as in the neighbouring village. The additional information more or less confirmed the ideas ventured in the first discussion. In one village people were complaining, while in the other, villagers were rather satisfied. We also interviewed a woman who had wanted to run a ration shop in this region, but who was bypassed by Mr Yogappa, the present fair price shop owner, perhaps because he bribed the officials. We visited Mr Yogappa in his house in Akkipura town, which was located in a new extension of the town. The area looked somewhat bare and empty, but the house was not bad. It was well-furnished with a table, chairs, beds and a television. There were several young children around, some of whom spoke good English. We were offered tea, and then Yogappa explained how he got his fair price shop. 'They advertised in the newspapers for agencies to run a fair price shop, and I applied. There was a policy to give licences to people from scheduled castes or tribes, or to unemployed graduates. I was an unemployed graduate, so I got the licence.'

Yogappa may have been formally unemployed, but he was certainly not a poor man. He told us that he owned 20 acres of irrigated land. Furthermore, he proudly said, he was very much involved in the Congress (I) party, for over

[4] All names of persons and places in this book are fictitious, except the names of the two States, Karnataka and Kerala. Also unimportant details of stories are sometimes changed in order to enhance anonymity.

fifteen years now. But he denied having a grocery shop in the town (which would have been illegal).

There is nothing special about this story, although the villagers may have exaggerated a bit. In fact, it is only one of the many accounts that I have collected in the course of my fieldwork.

The story illustrates a number of points. First, the foodgrain that is (or should be) distributed cannot be regarded solely in terms of its nutritional qualities, as a source of protein and calories. PDS foodgrain is also an economic commodity as well as a political commodity (a source of power). For villagers, many of them landless and un(der)employed, the subsidized foodgrain can be of vital interest to their survival. Even though the actual amount of subsidies that reach them is small, for poor families every additional calorie is welcome. For others, PDS foodgrains are a means to make profit. I was not able to confirm whether Yogappa, the fair price shop owner in the story above, indeed had a grocery shop in Akkipura town, but it is a fact that several fair price shop owners (or their close relatives) do have their own shops as well, where they illegally sell PDS commodities. Alternatively, they sell a part of the PDS commodities to private traders. The story further illustrates that Yogappa was not only able to increase his income, but being a fair price trader also enhanced his status as a Congress (I) politician. He was considered a politician who cared for 'his' village. To put it more generally, the commodities are an additional source of power and influence for those who control them. Food distribution produces and reproduces a relationship of power between those who are in command and those who are in need of foodgrains.

Second, the story illustrates that the public food distribution system is not implemented, enforced or imposed in a straightforward manner. Actual social relations structure the practices of implementation and the final effects. If we follow the course of foodgrains in the case just described, we can assume that only a part reaches the fair price shop in the village. Another part is sold in Akkipura town. The food distributed in the fair price shop goes to card holders in both villages, as well as to the local grocery shop owner, who perhaps sells this food to the same villagers at a higher price. Looking at the social relations, we observe Yogappa's relation with the food bureaucracy (he is locally influential; he bribed some officials?) and his connections with the world of politics (as an active member of Congress(I)). There is Yogappa's differential relation with the two villages. For one village he has probably done a number of things, acted as a 'social worker' as he said himself, while he has given much less attention to the other village. There is the observation that men have easier access to the fair price shop than women and that a local grocery shop owner—whose father happened to be a clerk in the court in Akkipura town—gets preferential treatment.

Phrased in a more general way, the story illustrates the social relations that influence access to and flows of food, that define powerlessness and strategic positions in the process of food distribution, relations that link the food bureaucracy, politicians, local elite, food producers, traders and consumers in specific configurations, and that shape the concrete form of public food distribution 'on the ground'. That is to say, while the PDS may be based on a well-thought-out plan and a rational policy, the actual interactions and effects are crucially influenced by existing social relations and may, hence, differ substantially from the plans on paper.

Related to this is a third point, the pluriformity of and within the Indian state.[5] Not only is there a difference between plans on paper and actual practices, there is also a large heterogeneity within state institutions as well as a great diversity of policy practices. Commitment on part of the government to find a reliable fair price shop owner coexists with accepting bribes from potential candidates. A genuine interest in bringing down the food insecurity of the poorest households in one village can go together with a neglect of the poor elsewhere. In more general terms, the story suggests that the state at issue is both a 'public interest' as well as a 'private interest' state (Mackintosh, 1992).

Despite evidence of the relevance of these three points—the same points can be concluded on the basis of many other everyday experiences with the PDS—they are usually neither visible nor reflected upon in academic work on the subject. In contrast, most studies on food policy in India are either a description of policies, quantities, prices, infrastructure, availability, etc. or an attempt to model and predict the effects of these interventions,[6] on prices and incomes. Both types of literature overlook the fact that food is not only an article

[5] The term 'State' (with capital) refers to the federal State, the constituent unit of the Indian nation. Without capital ('state'), the term refers to the state apparatus. See Section 2.2 for a further discussion of the concept.

[6] Examples of the first category are Acharya (1983), Bapna (1990), Bhatia (1991), Chopra (1988), Dandekar (1994), Pal, Bahl and Mruthyunjaya (1993), Tyagi (1990) and Venugopal (1992), while Binswanger and Quizon (1988), George (1979), De Janvry and Subbarao (1986) and Radhakrishna and Indrakant (1991) fall into the second category. In fact, De Janvry and Subbarao combine model-based calculations with a

to consume, but also an economic and political commodity, that real food policy is embedded in social relations and shaped by processes 'on the ground' rather than a logical result of official statements and intentions, and that the state implementing these policies is not a homogeneous bloc, but a multifarious entity.

Research questions

These points correspond to three questions, namely:

1. What are the effects of the food distribution policy, in terms of consumption, economic redistribution and power?
2. In and through which social processes is food distribution shaped historically and reproduced on a day-to-day basis?
3. What are the implications of the experiences with the Public Distribution System for a conceptualization of the Indian state?

The first two questions are particularly important for an understanding and evaluation of the PDS in all its dimensions. Although this study is one of many evaluations of the PDS it is of a different kind. While most other studies of the PDS use the official policy objectives—either explicitly or implicitly—as a kind of filter to select data for an evaluation, this study starts from day-to-day experiences with the PDS and interprets these not so much in terms of official policy intentions, but in terms of what the PDS does to consumption, economic redistribution and power. Chapters 4 to 7 contain detailed descriptions, interpretations and analyses of everyday experiences with the PDS, as they were observed by me or described by the actors involved. I describe day-to-day interactions between officials responsible for procurement and rice mill owners; recurrent problems that ration dealers are faced with; difficulties poor consumers have in accessing distributed food and their activities to improve this situation; day-to-day interactions between politicians and officials that determine the functioning of parastatal food corporations.

The interactions, negotiations and conflicts form the starting point of analysis. In this analysis I have especially higlighted the political dimension of the PDS, while the impact of the PDS on economic redistribution, and especially the impact on consumption, gets less

---

political-economic analysis. Harriss' work on food policy (1983, 1988, 1991) falls into neither of these two categories as she investigates concrete implementation processes at the local level.

emphasis. This is partly the unintended result of my research methodology (I did not undertake a food consumption survey) and partly due to a conscious decision to focus on those aspects that are most underreported in other studies.

The third question is particularly relevant in the present era, in which the dominant political discourse stresses the failure of states and state-led development efforts, and the virtues of the market.[7] This anti-state discourse has also pervaded the debate on the role and nature of the Indian state. It is argued that the public sector is too large and inefficient. Economic growth would be inhibited rather than stimulated by the state, and politics would be fundamentally corrupt, if not criminal. On the basis of a detailed analysis of the PDS, the book tries to evaluate this interpretation of the Indian state. Is this interpretation right, or is the reality more complex and consistent with a more positive interpretation of the Indian state?

This study is informed by several disciplinary traditions. As far as data collection is concerned, the study combined intensive fieldwork as practised by anthropologists with the more inventorial approach of a sociologist (see also Section 1.4). The final analysis, as presented in this book, is a mixture of narrative ethnography and political economy. The chapters that follow contain many detailed descriptions of practices and interactions, but also attempt to see the social relations of power and structural features of society constituting these practices. In addition, I have used insights developed in the public administration literature, sociology of law, policy studies and economics.

Such analysis with a strong emphasis on processes 'on the ground' is of necessity spatially and temporally specific. So, in contrast to most other work about the PDS in India, this book concentrates on a few selected areas. It is based on fieldwork in two States in south India, Karnataka and Kerala. And even within these States I have concentrated on some particular areas only. Nevertheless, despite the local specificities and difficulties of generalization, such insights gathered in a micro-study of the PDS have a wider relevance. They show the systematic nature of what others have called 'distortions' or 'bottlenecks', and hence, can offer a contribution to our understanding of food policy as it exists 'on the ground'.

[7] For critical reviews of this 'counter-revolution' or 'dominant consensus' in development thinking, see respectively Toye (1987) and Pedersen (1992).

Structure of the book

The first two chapters are introductory chapters. While the introductory chapter introduces the reader to the book (1.1), the PDS (1.2), the two research areas (1.3) and the research methodology (1.4), the second chapter contains a theoretical elaboration of food policy and the Indian state. The largest part of the chapter is a description of several theoretical perspectives on the Indian state. I distinguish four different perspectives, three of which are very critical of the state. Together they support the dominant view that there is something fundamentally wrong with the Indian state. These three currents of thought emphasize (a) the rent-seeking character of the Indian state (i.e. individual civil servants and politicians make use of their discretionary powers in order to enrich themselves and/or enhance their status and popularity), (b) the 'erosion' of the political system (the decay within the Congress party and the opportunism and corruption in politics generally), and (c) the idea that state professionals form a dominant proprietary class, which together with the other two classes (industrial capital and labour) determines economic developments in India. The fourth interpretation maintains the concept of the developmental state: a state capable of contributing to economic growth and social development. Apart from a description of these four perspectives, the chapter also contains a discussion of food policy: if these interpretations were correct, what then could we expect with regard to the functioning of the food distribution system?

The third chapter provides a historical interpretation of Indian food policy. The purpose of this chapter is to describe the most important features of the PDS in the different phases of its history. It analyses which social processes have led to its emergence and further developments, and which political functions the PDS has served in the course of time. The period between 1939 and 1965 is a starting period, in which the system expanded and acquired more objectives. Throughout this period, the programme was characterized by a marked 'urban bias' and its main function was to support industrial development. This changed in the subsequent phase: 1965–90. From 1965 onwards, a new price regime was introduced which aimed to support agricultural production and farmers' incomes. Distribution expanded enormously; in some States the rural areas were covered as well. With the declining importance of the Congress party and increasing political awareness of large parts of the population, food policy began to play a crucial role in attracting votes. In 1991, when the Indian government started to implement a structural adjustment programme, a new phase started. Soon after 1991 the programme landed in a crisis: issue prices were increased, the demand for subsidized food fell, procurement continued on a large scale and the costs of the programme increased.

Chapters 4 to 7 are all based on fieldwork in south India and contain detailed descriptions and analyses of experiences with the PDS, as they were observed by me or described to me. The fourth chapter analyses government procurement of rice for the PDS in Karnataka. (Since 1980 there has been no procurement in Kerala.) The chapter illustrates the fact that there is a struggle over rice. The government wants to purchase it, but traders and rice mill owners want to protect their profits. The chapter describes the various actors involved in procurement and their interactions. These interactions are partly of a conflictual nature (threat, coercion, bribery, fights in court), but there is also cooperation. The result of all these various types of interactions is that the government more or less succeeds in purchasing the target amount of foodgrains. A 'by-product' of procurement is the production and reproduction of a specific type of foodgrains market, a market in which social networks and relationships are crucial assets in competing with others.

The fifth chapter discusses food distribution in Karnataka and Kerala. I describe the various mechanisms that influence (often restrict) the relevance of the PDS for consumers. It is shown that the way in which food distribution takes place (no possibility to buy on credit, compulsory offtake of wheat when rice is purchased, limited opening of the shop) restricts its usefulness as far as the most vulnerable consumers are concerned. In addition, it is sometimes difficult for the consumers to obtain a ration card, a necessary condition in order to become a beneficiary. The chapter also explains how and why a part of the PDS foodgrains never reaches the card holders because it is black marketed. Despite these restrictions the system is not considered irrelevant by the least privileged people. Generally, they buy the subsidized foodgrains whenever they can. But the system suits the other less needy categories of people much better. In Karnataka the operation of the system has adapted itself to the local structure of patronage, and some traders can make considerable profits by illegal sale of the commodities. In Kerala illegal sale also takes place, but due to a much more assertive and politically mobilized population, food distribution generally works better than in Karnataka.

Chapters 6 and 7 examine the functioning of two major policy institutions: the food and/or civil supplies corporations and the most important law: the Essential Commodities Act (EC Act). The sixth chapter describes the working of the food corporations: parastatal organizations which buy and sell foodgrains, and so create a market parallel to privately organized trade. The purpose of this market intervention is to exercise a downward pressure on foodgrain prices and to discipline private trade. Three structural dilemmas which crucially influence the functioning of these corporations are discussed. These have to do with contradictions in objectives (selling cheap food without making losses), contradictions in relations with private traders (competition with private trade, but also cooperation with and dependence on private trade), and the difficulty of operating in a flexible way in a situation of strict regulation, frequent controls and political interference. Besides the official objectives, the corporations serve a number of other functions. They contribute to state legitimacy. State food and/or civil supplies corporations offer a possibility to State governments to show how important food security is. Furthermore, the corporations function as an additional arena and resource for politicians in charge to reproduce and reinforce their influence. Despite this use and misuse of the corporation, the prospects are not totally gloomy. Within both corporations there was much self-criticism about the operation of the corporations, and a will to improve their performance, if conditions allowed.

The seventh chapter analyses the role of the EC Act in the implementation of food policy. This law is the main statutory backing of the PDS. If traders or others do not comply with the stipulated regulations, they can be sued and penalized under the EC Act. The chapter discusses the law itself, and analyses the role of this law in various social practices. It is argued that the main function of the EC Act is that it can be used as a threat. The prospect of risking prosecution makes many traders comply with the law. Although the conviction rate is low, the humiliation that comes with prosecution has such a deterrent effect that compliance with the law is enforced to some extent.

In the eighth chapter I come back to the three main research questions. The effects of the PDS on consumption, economic redistribution and power are summarized, as well as the historical emergence and day-to-day reproduction of the programme. As far as the interpretation of the Indian state is concerned, it is concluded that the centre and the Karnataka and Kerala state governments are both rent seeking and developmental. Although corruption and political opportunism are very common phenomena, it is too simple to say that all civil servants and politicians are primarily intent on the maximization of individual profit, status and/or votes. For many of them professional life is more complex. They identify both with the developmental objectives of the state and with the rules and regulations characterizing a corrupt bureaucracy. Their day-to-day activities are a mixture of individual enrichment and working towards the developmental goals of the state. What this means is that the state is characterized by 'normative pluralism': there are different, formal as well as informal, normative systems within the same bureaucracy.

In addition, the last chapter also discusses the future of the public distribution programme. In order to resolve the present crisis situation, two proposals are put forward by policy makers: the introduction of targeting of the PDS, and replacement of the present PDS by a system of food stamps. The chapter discusses the advantages and disadvantages of both proposals. It is concluded that a systematic introduction of neither of these proposals is very likely, in particular because they threaten various types of vested interests. A solution to the present crisis must be not only cost-effective, but also politically viable. Furthermore, the necessity to involve consumers/clients in the organization of the PDS is stressed. In the short run this would enhance the accountability of the government, while in the long run it would stimulate political mobilization, which is a prerequisite of more radical redistributive policies in the future.

One final remark before the reader is introduced to the PDS in somewhat more detail. So far in this introduction, I have used the terms 'food policy' and 'PDS' more or less interchangeably. I realize that the terms have different meanings. PDS refers to a specific state intervention: the buying, storing and distribution activities of the state. This type of intervention came into being only in 1939 (see, e.g. Bapna, 1990; also Chapter 3 of this book). Food policy is a much wider term as it may, in principle, refer to all policies regarding the food system. Long before the emergence of the PDS, there was already a food policy, laid down for instance in the Famine Codes, formulated at the end of the nineteenth century (see Bhatia, 1991: 182–209). Also in the present period, there are government food policies that fall outside the scope of the PDS, such as legislation against food adulteration or programmes to stimulate oil seed production. This book is about the PDS, not about Indian food policy generally. Nevertheless, I do take an unconventionally broad perspective on the PDS, which has to do with the need to understand all the different factors influencing the way the PDS works out in reality. This means, for instance, that I also analyse the functioning of the Essential Commodities Act, a subject usually left out. Also, in the rest of this book, I often use the terms PDS and food policy interchangeably, referring to the PDS in the narrow sense *plus* all the supporting food policies, regulations and institutions.

1.2 PDS IN INDIA

A brief history and evaluation

In the mid-1990s, almost sixty years after its inception, the PDS is still an issue in public debate and policy. It is presented and interpreted in different ways by different actors—even sometimes by the same actors in different contexts—and contradictory policy measures are introduced. For instance, on the one hand, the system is presented as very costly and inefficient. Since 1991, when India took on board various structural adjustment reforms, advocates of these policies have stressed the enormous waste of money implied in the PDS. On the other hand, the PDS is presented as the safety net *par excellence* to help the needy through difficult periods (including one that results from structural adjustment). Since 1991, PDS prices for consumers have been increased several times in order to bring down government subsidies. On the other hand, some State politicians have introduced great expansions of the PDS and have allocated large sums for this purpose. These are only a few examples of the many contradictions that surround the present day PDS.[8] What are the characteristics of this institution that is now so controversial?

The public food distribution system in India dates from the Second World War. During and after the Bengal Famine in 1943, in which between 1.5 and 3 million people died, the need was felt by the colonial government to develop a comprehensive food policy for the country. Originally the policy was restricted in size and objective. Over the years the system expanded enormously, as well in area covered, in quantity of foodgrains handled as in costs involved (Bapna, 1990; Chopra, 1988; Bhatia, 1991). A major breakthrough came in 1964–5 with the establishment of two institutions: the Food Corporation of India [FCI] and the Agricultural Prices Commission [ACP] (now Commission on Agricultural Costs and Prices. The former is a large parastatal trading corporation responsible for procurement, storage,

[8] See Sections 3.3 and 8.3 for more systematic discussions of PDS in the 1990s.

transport and distribution of foodgrains. The latter advises the Indian government on pricing policy for agricultural commodities. Since the mid-1960s, the PDS serves several objectives simultaneously, namely (*a*) to cope with emergency situations, eg. droughts; (*b*) to distribute food at fair prices to vulnerable people; and (*c*) to guarantee remunerative prices to farmers (see Chapter 3). Over the years, these objectives have sometimes become mutually conflicting, as various observers have pointed out.[9]

In 1991–2 a total amount of 16.6 million tonnes of foodgrains was distributed. This is about 10 per cent of total production, and results in an average per capita distribution of approximately 20 kg per year. See Table 1 in Appendix 1 for the growth, and sometimes decline, of the PDS over the years. Apart from foodgrains, the system also includes sugar, kerosene, sometimes palmolein oil and occasionally even sarees and dhotis. As these commodities are much less important or essential—both from the perspective of PDS infrastructure and management, and from that of consumers—this book will focus mainly on foodgrains, that is rice and wheat.

Until the beginning of the 1960s, the PDS was largely based on imported foodgrains. There was hardly any internal procurement. With the advent of the Green Revolution and consequently increasing wheat, and later rice production in certain areas of the country, procurement within India became the most important means of acquiring food. Wheat procurement takes place almost exclusively in north India. In the 1980s only three States, that is Haryana, Punjab and Uttar Pradesh, supplied more than 98 per cent of the total government wheat stock. The procurement of rice is less unevenly spread over the country; a fair amount comes from Andhra Pradesh and Tamil Nadu, but here too the Punjab is by far the most important supplier. See Table 2 in Appendix 1 for State-wise procurement figures in the 1980s.

Apart from procurement, distribution is also rather unevenly spread over the country. This is shown in Table 3 of Appendix 1. The average distribution in the whole of India in 1986–7 was 18.1 kg per capita per year. In Kerala, per capita distribution came to three times this amount, while people in States such as Bihar, Haryana, Madhya Pradesh, Punjab and Uttar Pradesh received much less than the all-India average.

When evaluating the relevance of the PDS for consumers, two

[9] See, for instance, S.K. Das, 'Food Policy Yet to Make a Dent in Poverty', in *Times of India,* 8 July 1991, or Narendar Pani, 'Quiet Collapse of the PDS', *Economic Times*, 17 June 1994.

important points of success are mentioned in the literature. First, the PDS has effectively contributed to famine prevention. Despite the occurrence of severe droughts and floods, there has been no large-scale famine in India since Independence, which is a great achievement. Second, the PDS is said to have contributed to an increase in physical and economic access to food. Per capita foodgrain availability increased from less than 400g per day in 1951 to more than 450g in the 1980s. Furthermore, in the 1970s and 1980s food prices rose at a much slower rate than per capita incomes (Tyagi, 1990: 218; see also Bhalla, 1994: 150–4). Of course, this increased access cannot be attributed solely to food policy. According to Tyagi, it is a result of total development policy for the agricultural sector, in which food policy and the system of its management played a major catalytic role (1990: 48–86).

On the other hand, several weaknesses and failures of the system are noted. The first is the persistence of endemic hunger and malnutrition. Average access may have increased, but there is still large-scale undernutrition. Drèze and Sen (1989: 214–15) estimate that each year 3.9 million people die in India, over and above the 'normal mortality', due to causes related to endemic hunger and deprivation. Table 3 in Appendix 1 illustrates the unequal spread of PDS over the States and the fact that States with many poor people are also poorly covered by PDS. Moreover, also within relatively well-off States, the poorest people sometimes fall outside the scheme (e.g. Harriss, 1991 on Tamil Nadu).

A second failure relates to the exclusive concentration on rice and wheat, and the neglect of coarse grains, in the system. For this reason the PDS failed to protect the interests of the most vulnerable producers—who produce mainly coarse grains in the dry areas—and consumers—whose food intake consists in part of relatively cheap coarse grains (Tyagi, 1990: 220; also Bhalla, 1994: 156–60). A third weakness is the decreasing financial viability of the system. In the mid-1990s the system requires an annual subsidy of more than Rs 50,000 million. Moreover, due to various price increases, the price difference between the PDS and the open market has become marginal. Consequently the offtake has come down. Considering these problems it is not surprising that several observers in the 1990s claim that the PDS has landed in a severe crisis and faces an uncertain future.[10] In

[10] For instance, B.M. Bhatia, 'Failed System—PDS heading for Collapse?', *Times of India*, Aug. 1992, or Narendar Pani, 'Quiet Collapse of the PDS', *Economic Times*, 17 June 1994.

Section 3.3 this present crisis situation is described in more detail; in Section 8.4, I discuss the options for reform and their feasibility.

Organizational structure, dual market and interwoven markets

The organizational set-up of PDS is a mixture of Union and State tasks and responsibilities. The Government of India decides, in dialogue with the relevant States, how much foodgrain should be procured in each State. It also decides on procurement prices. This is done on the basis of advice from the Commission for Agricultural Costs and Prices [CACP], which calculates the costs of production and estimates a reasonable, remunerative price for the farmers.[11] In principle, these prices are the same for each State. There are different prices for different qualities, but there are no price differentials that relate to ecological and/or other production conditions. In the implementation of procurement policy, individual States make small adjustments—always upwards—to these recommended prices.

In contrast to the centrally administered prices, the mode of procurement is decided by the State governments. Procurement may take place through open market purchases, by market purchases in which the government exercises the right of pre-emption, by a levy on producers, traders or millers, by agents under a system of monopoly procurement, etc. In many States procurement is supported by a law specially made for this purpose. Usually the Food Corporation of India [FCI], a Union government institution, is the procurement agent. The FCI, however, cannot enforce procurement policy. The State Food and/or Civil Supplies Departments and special Police Task Forces are responsible for enforcing procurement policy. Dependent on the mode of procurement and the price difference between the open market price and procurement price, this enforcement is more or less troublesome. See Fig. 1.1 for a schematic outline.

The FCI has many large warehouses in different parts of the country where foodgrains are stored after procurement. Food may be transported from one FCI warehouse to another on the basis of distribution decisions made by the Government of India (GoI) in consultation with State governments. Apart from allocation to the States, the GoI also fixes the issue price, that is the selling price of the FCI.

[11] According to the Indian Constitution food is a Union, (i.e. national government) responsibility, while agriculture belongs to the realm of the States. Nevertheless, foodgrains price policy is largely a matter of the CACP, a Union organization.

As far as distribution within the States is concerned, the State government is, again, the policy-making institution. It can decide how to distribute the allocated food (to everybody, to targeted groups only, to concentrate on cities or on rural areas, etc.) and at what price.

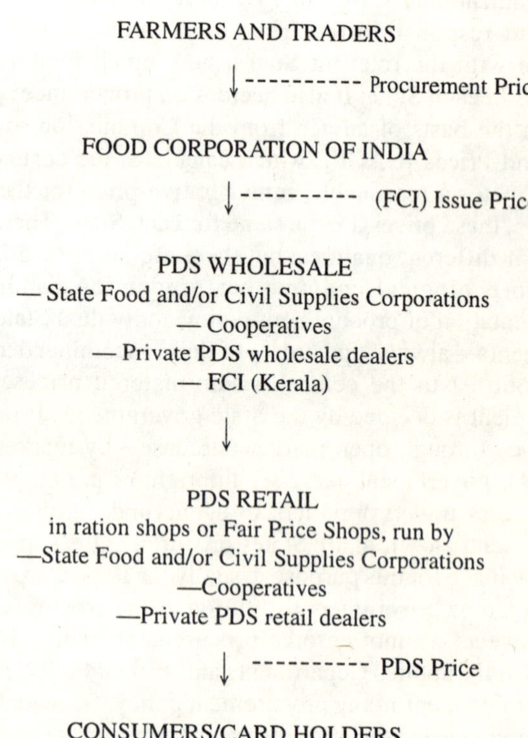

Fig. 1.1 A schematic outline of the PDS

Each State has its own distribution policy. The State department of Food and/or Civil Supplies monitors this distribution process. In many States parastatal trading corporations have been established which act as (PDS) wholesalers. They bring food from FCI warehouses to storage places near to the retail points, the so-called fair price shops. The retail sale of PDS commodities is undertaken either by these State corporations or by cooperative societies or by private fair price shop owners.

This is a schematic outline of flows of foodgrains and distribution of responsibilities. It is important to add that not all procured foodgrain is readily available for distribution. The GoI of India also maintains a buffer stock of 20–30 million tonnes, to be drawn upon only in times of severe scarcity. Furthermore, the above described scheme is (*a*) cross-cut by several GoI distribution programmes meant for selected categories of people (for instance food for work programmes), in which not the State governments but the central government formulates distribution policy, and (*b*) supplemented with additional State government programmes in the sense of (own, State-wise) procurement and distribution activities.

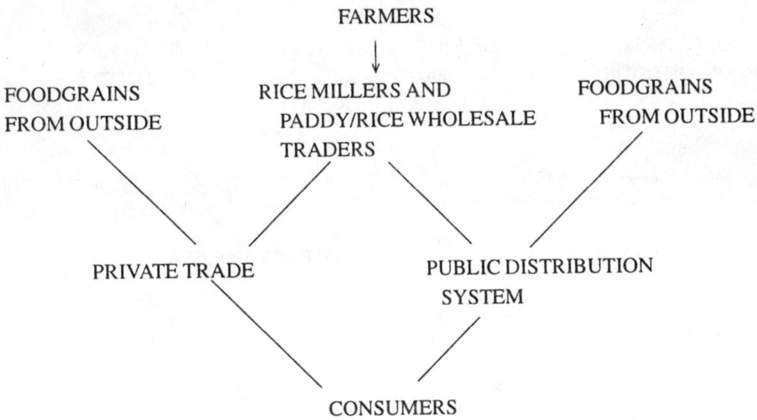

Fig. 1.2 A schematic view of the foodgrain market in south India: parallel markets

While Fig. 1.1 is a schematic outline of the PDS, to the neglect of the open market in foodgrains, Fig. 1.2 is a schematic view of the whole foodgrain market in south India. The figure clearly shows a dual marketing system. The PDS exists alongside the open market. The flow of foodgrains is split at the top of the figure. The largest part of the foodgrains is channelled to the open market, while about 10 per cent of rice and wheat goes to the PDS. Consumers purchase from both sources. The figure is meant to describe the situation in south India.[12] It focuses on rice production and procurement, as there is hardly any wheat production in south India. Both the open market and the PDS are partly supplied by foodgrain stocks from outside the State.

[12] In Kerala, there is no government procurement at all, so the connecting line between rice millers/paddy-rice traders and the PDS does not exist. All PDS foodgrain comes from outside the State.

This figure of a dual marketing system presents a highly idealized picture. In reality there are many cross-connections. The flow of foodgrains does not just split at the top, only to come together again at the bottom when consumers buy from both sources. At many more points within the chain there are exchanges and interconnections, as shown in Fig. 1.3 and discussed later in this book.

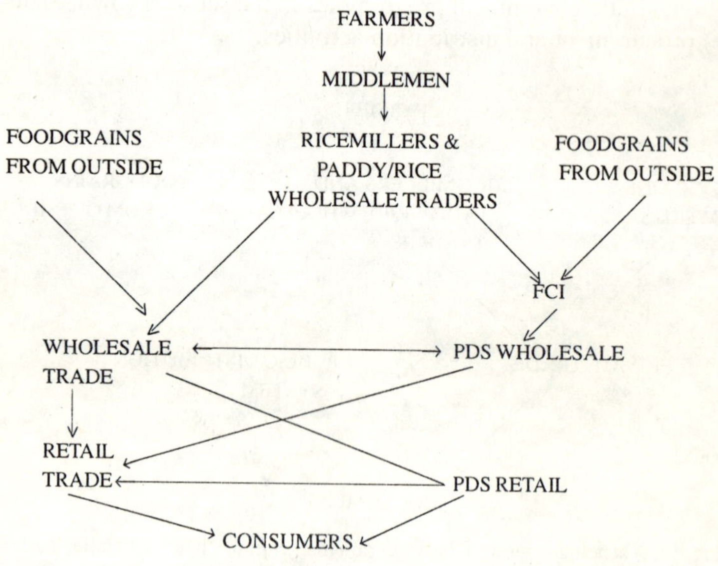

Fig. 1.3 An expanded view of the foodgrain market in south India: parallel markets: interwoven markets

PDS in context: poverty and markets

Although poverty estimates vary enormously,[13] it is clear that a very substantial part of the Indian population lives below the poverty line,

[13] Gupta (1994, Tables 2 and 3) provides poverty estimates obtained by two different measures. According to the CSO (Central Statistical Organization) method 20 per cent of the Indian population lived below the poverty line in 1992–3, while the NSSO (National Sample Survey Organization) method results in an estimation of 41 per cent in the same year. Also the establishment of trends over time is controversial. The editorial comment of the *Economic and Political Weekly* (27 January 1996, p. 183) tells us that '[i]n recent statements, finance minister Manmohan

which means that their income is not sufficient to buy enough food. About 80 per cent of these poor people live in rural areas (ILO-ARTEP, 1993). These poor people may be agricultural labourers, marginal producers, fishermen, village craftsmen, or persons employed in construction or local industries. In many cases, they are underemployed. Sometimes they are involved as small peasants in food production themselves, but forced to sell a high proportion of their output after the harvest to meet immediate cash requirements like outstanding debts. Later in the season, these peasants have to buy again on the market for their daily needs. This cycle of distress buying and selling usually under the compulsion of debts has been analysed as 'forced commercialization' (Bhaduri, 1985).

Extreme poverty and insufficient access to food coexist with self-sufficiency at the all-India level. With the exception of a few years of droughts and bad harvests, since 1976 India has produced enough foodgrains to feed its population. Of course, this does not imply that each region is self-sufficient. Some regions depend on large food imports, while others export foodgrains.

It is estimated that between 75 and 80 per cent of the foodgrains is marketed.[14] The remainder is exchanged outside the market or consumed by the producers themselves. Marketing is done by private agents and by the state (see Fig. 1.2 and 1.3). According to Clay et al. (1988: 23) private trade is of a polarized nature, with large mercantile firms on the one hand and petty traders handling insignificant quantities on the other. This means that despite the large number of traders, the food market is an oligopolistic market dominated by relatively few large trading firms.

The strategy of the Indian government to change these characteristics of the food market has been at least three-fold. The

---

Singh and other government spokespersons have highlighted the preliminary results of the Planning Commission exercise, based on National Sample Survey data, which reportedly show a decline in the proportion of people below the poverty line from 25.5 per cent in 1987–88 to 19 per cent in 1993–94. This is remarkable because, using the NSS data available up to now, many independent analysts had come to the conclusion that poverty had increased significantly during the early 1990s.' Also Drèze and Sen (1995: 211) state that '[p]reliminary results from the 48th round of the National Sample Survey suggest that the incidence of poverty in India in 1992–93 (in terms of the head-count ratio) was somewhat higher than at the end of the eighties'.

[14] According to Clay et al. (1988: 23) 70 per cent of foodgrains is handled by private traders. As approximately 10 per cent of the rice and wheat produced is handled by state trading agencies, my estimate is that between 75 and 80 per cent of all foodgrains is marketed through either private or public channels.

government has (*1*) taken measures to promote growth of production, through producer-friendly food price policy, technological inputs, subsidies to farmers etc.,(*2*) organized interventions in the food system: procurement, maintaining of a buffer stock and distribution of subsidized food, and (*3*) introduced regulation and control of private trade practices through so-called regulated markets and additional legal measures (e.g. the EC Act).

Despite the official commitment of the Indian state to organize an alternative to private trade and to curtail the power of private trading firms, it is also important to realize the fundamental dependence of the state on private trade. At the most general level, the state depends on the market for its resources. Sales tax is one of the most important sources of income. In 1989–90, sales tax contributed around 20 per cent of the total tax revenue of the Centre, State and Union Territories combined. The State governments are the collectors of sales tax. On average in 1989–90 more than one–third of the tax revenue of the States and Union Territories came from sales tax.[15] For the State governments, sales tax is by far the most important source of income. Looking at the Centre, States and Union Territories combined, sales tax comes next only to customs and excise duty, and is more important than corporation and income tax. This illustrates the overwhelming importance of sales tax for government revenue and, hence, the dependence of government finance on market transactions. The more trade, the better the state revenue position.[16]

But apart from this financial dependence, there are other ways in which the state is influenced by private trade. Harriss (1984b) even characterizes the Tamil Nadu State as a 'merchant state', not only because the state acts as merchant, but also because of the 'role of the mercantile sector in the unlinear and interactive process of formation and implementation of state policy' (ibid.: p. 315). Either through individual payments to political parties or through lobbies of traders' associations directed at the political or executive system, traders crucially shape what policy is and does.[17] In other studies, Harriss further describes the collective political activities of merchants in Tamil Nadu and in other parts of India and Bangladesh (Harriss, 1989;

[15] GoI (1991), Table 1.2, p. 5 and Table 3.1, p. 22.

[16] Some States have exempted foodgrain transactions from sales tax. This was not the case in Karnataka and Kerala at the time of fieldwork.

[17] This is a reference to Schaffer's apt formulation: Policy is what it Does (Schaffer, 1984). See also Harriss (1988).

Harriss-White, 1993). These writings clearly illustrate the many activities traders deploy *vis-à-vis* the state, and the fact that the state is not unaffected by these lobbies, manipulations, bribes and other interventions. The following chapters will provide several examples illustrating the influence of private traders on government policies.

1.3 RESEARCH AREAS: TWO STATES, KARNATAKA AND KERALA

This study deals with the PDS in two south Indian States: Karnataka and Kerala. Within these States I have collected relevant data regarding food distribution in (*a*) the State as a whole, and (*b*) particular locations and within particular locations. The reasons for the selection of these two States are discussed in the next section, in which other methodological questions are also taken up.

As I have outlined above, procurement and distribution policy are formulated at the level of the individual States. So consumers in different regions of the same States are faced with a similar set of distribution criteria, just as traders and/or producers in different regions have to deal with similar procurement arrangements. Information on these State-wise policies and institutions as well as prices and quantities is usually given at the beginning of each chapter. The fact that the PDS is at least partially organized by the individual State governments, justifies the decision to take States as a unit of analysis. At the same time, one has to realize that social relations, implementation practices and policy effects may differ widely in different areas of the same State. In this section, I will discuss the relevant characteristics of the two States and of the particular localities of fieldwork. In the rest of this book, some additional contextualization is presented whenever necessary.'

Karnataka: A short introduction

Karnataka is a south Indian State of 192,000 square km, with a population of 45 million people in 1991 (Bose, 1991). The capital is Bangalore, a large industrial city with just over 4 million inhabitants in 1991 (ibid. 1991). Bangalore is the fastest growing city in India (*Frontline*, 8 Apr. 1994), and one of the fastest growing in the eastern hemisphere. Yet it does not have some of the dreadful characteristics of large metropolises. There are slums and there is poverty, but compared to cities such as Bombay or Calcutta, urban deprivation is limited. Because of its friendly image, gardens and pleasant weather conditions, Bangalore has attracted well-to-do people from other parts of India and non-residential Indians to settle or retire. The city houses computer as well as electronics industries and a large service sector. The street panorama in the city centre is dominated by western-style shops, post-modern architecture and yuppie-like youngsters.

Apart from Bangalore, there are no other metropolitan cities in Karnataka. Mysore, the second largest town and the old capital, has approximately 650,000 inhabitants (ibid. 1991). The great majority of the population of Karnataka lives in villages. More than two-thirds of the population depends on agriculture for its livelihood, not necessarily as farmers but also as agricultural labourers, small traders, or persons otherwise occupied in rural occupations. There are a few large-scale irrigation systems and there are approximately 40,000 tanks. The agro-climatic zones vary greatly, from almost semi-arid in the north-east to tropical rain forest towards the western coast and in the southern parts of the State. Foodgrain production varies accordingly: from dry crops such as sorghum and millet in the dry zones, to rice in the irrigated and wet parts of the State. There is no wheat production in Karnataka. The State is almost self-sufficient in foodgrains. It contributes to the Central food pool, but only marginally. In fact, Karnataka has always received more from the Central pool than it has contributed to it.

In terms of general welfare indicators, Karnataka is an above average State within India. Life expectancy in 1988–91 was 62.7 (all-India average 59.1) (EPW Research Foundation, 1994), while the infant mortality rate was 74 per 1000 in 1988 (all-India average 94) (ibid. 1991). The literacy rate in 1991 for people above 7 years of age is 56 per cent (67 per cent for males; 44 per cent for females), while the all-India average is 52 per cent (ibid. 1991).

Karnataka's political and social history has not witnessed many extreme situations and/or periods (Manor, 1989). Since Independence, State politics have been dominated by the Congress (I) party, with one interruption between 1983 and 1989, and a second period from December 1994 onwards.

In the context of this study, three periods are worth highlighting in Karnataka's political history. The first is that of the Devraj Urs government, which lasted from 1972 to 1980. Urs' regime was important in at least three respects. First, Urs succeeded in creating a shift in the power base of the Karnataka state. Before 1972, the old dominant landed groups—particularly the Vokkaliga and the Lingayat subcastes, together 32 per cent of the population—dominated the Congress party and the state machinery. Although these groups remain important in Karnataka politics, Urs succeeded in undermining the incontestability of their dominance to some extent (Manor, 1984; Srinivas and Panini, 1984). Second, Urs introduced several welfare measures: a land reform, a small farmer programme, minimum wage legislation, caste reservations, etc. Although the redistributive effects of these measures may have been limited, as Kohli (1987) argues,[18] the ideological effects were substantive. According to Srinivas and Panini (1984: 690) Urs 'established the norm that the task of any elected government was to work for the betterment of the living conditions of the poor who constituted the majority'. A third consequence of Devraj Urs' regime was the expansion and systematization of corruption in Karnataka politics and administration. As a member of a non-dominant caste he had to satisfy many defection-prone members of the Assembly by giving them important positions or by literally buying their support. This meant that he had to raise money, which he did by amassing public funds, by collecting money from industrialists or contractors, and by introducing levies on jobs in the government or house sites in the city (Kohli, 1987; Srinivas and Panini, 1984). Moreover, the defeat of Congress (I) at the national level as well as in many States after the Emergency meant that a small number of States (Karnataka being one of these) had to bear the responsibility of co-financing the rebuilding and consolidation of party machinery in the rest of the country.

Urs, who had split from Congress (I) in 1979 and founded his own political party, was defeated in the 1979–80 elections, and died in 1982. Till 1983 a Congress (I) government ruled the State. Then a second important period in Karnataka's political history started with the election in 1983. For the first time, a non-Congress government was elected, of which the Janata politician Ramakrishna Hegde would become leader. This government firmly put 'basic needs' on the political agenda and widened the scope of public food distribution (see Chapter 3). Furthermore, it made serious work of democratization processes by introducing legislation for decentralization of tasks and responsibilities to the district or village council (see Chandrashekar, 1984; Slater and Watson, 1989).

[18] But not everybody would agree with this, as Kohli himself acknowledges. Manor (1978: 793), for instance, writes that Urs' land reform law is 'unusually practicable'.

In 1988, Chief Minister Hedge resigned. His successor did not remain in power for long, and eventually the Government of India intervened and imposed so-called President's Rule, which lasted till the 1989 elections brought a Congress (I) government to power again. After a change in leadership in October 1990, S. Bangarappa became Chief Minister. His rule would last till October 1992, when he was dismissed by the Congress (I) High Command. Bangarappa's era is the third period worth mentioning here. It was during his government that the fieldwork for this book was carried out. Bangarappa came from the *Idiga* (toddy-tappers) community, a backward subcaste with a number of members who had become very rich in the liquor trade. In the course of the twenty-five months that he was in power, his regime got a very bad reputation, especially due to his style of government and corruption. Internal dissension within the Congress (I) in Karnataka was considerable. It must have cost Bangarappa a fortune to win over as many legislators as he could. The money was partly collected by the administration. The system of payments for transfers within the bureaucracy (see Wade, 1985; de Zwart, 1992) flourished during these years. Even lower and middle cadre clerks had to pay for routine transfers. The number of transfers increased rapidly. All this was at the expense of bureaucratic efficiency. Unfortunately there is not much positive to add about his government. (See also Pinto, 1992.) In 1992, Bangarappa was finally forced to resign, and his government was replaced by another Congress (I) government. In December 1994, the Karnataka electorate decided that it was time for a change, and voted *en masse* for Janata Dal, the successor of the Janata Party that had ruled from 1983 to 1988. In these elections, access to food played an important role, as the Janata Dal promised to revitalize the cheap food programme it had introduced earlier.

Fieldwork in Karnataka was concentrated in two locations: Bangalore and one district; let us call it Akkipura. Akkipura is a relatively well-developed district; the soil is fertile and there are several irrigation schemes. It is one of the major rice producing areas in the State. Other crops grown are sugar cane, areca nut, coconut and dry crops such as cotton. Agriculture is to a large extent commercialized. It is hard to produce figures about marketed surpluses, but my definite impression is that the lion's share of all rice—and the other major crops are cash crops anyway—is sold; only a relatively small part is kept for home consumption. (See Vijverberg, 1994 for a description of rice production and trade in one village in Akkipura district.)

The rice market in Akkipura district is dominated by rice mill owners. These rice mill owners, who are often traders as well, occupy a very strategic position in the food chain. They buy paddy from farmers, dry, dehusk and hull the paddy in their mills, and sell rice to other wholesale traders and/or retail rice merchants. In Akkipura district, almost all paddy processing is done in modern industrial mills with a capacity of 1.5 to 3 tonnes of rice per hour. This means that relatively few rice mill owners take a position among a large number of paddy producers, a large number of rice retail dealers and an even larger number of rice consumers. Apart from this strategic position, many rice mill owners are also wealthy and influential in other respects. The value of the land, building and machinery of a modern rice mill is about Rs 1.5–10 million[19] and the investment—in rice and paddy—required to run a mill is high. Many of the rice mill owners cum traders are well-connected in political circles, are big property owners and/or belong to the dominant caste.

Apart from the rice mill owners cum traders, the position of the poorest producers and consumers in the food chain is also important in the context of this study. I do not have much information on this in Akkipura district, except for Vijverberg's case study on poverty and food strategies in one particular village. Her study suggests that both marginal rice producers and the poorest consumers (often the same people) are tied up in various interlinked market arrangements. Poor producers take production credit or consumption loans from moneylenders (often paddy traders) or from other known persons. Because they are marginal farmers, they cannot get loans from a credit society or a bank. The consequence of taking a loan from a paddy merchant is that the debtor is obliged to sell his paddy to this merchant only. The price that cultivators get in such an interlinked situation is usually lower than the price paid to free cultivators (Vijverberg, 1994: 56–61). Also poor consumers are tied up in market interlinkages or similar arrangements. They purchase food on credit from small local grocery shops, but pay a higher price (ibid. 73–4). Of course, these credit-rice interlinkages are not a universal phenomena. It is especially the poorest households who are caught in such situations, in which exploitation can be pushed beyond 'conventional limits [that exist] in any one single market' (Bharadwaj, 1985: 13), and in which bargaining with the local elite is doubly difficult.

[19] See n. 3 above for the value of the Indian rupee.

Kerala: a short introduction

Kerala is one of the smallest States in India. It is only 36,900 square kms. In 1991 it had approximately 29 million inhabitants (Bose, 1991), which makes it one of the most densely populated States. The land is a small strip in the south-west corner of India, running from the sea inwards to the slopes of the Western Ghats. Thiruvananthapuram, or Trivandrum, located at the far southern end, is the capital of the State. It is a relaxed place which looks more like a rural town than a State capital, as it stretches over a large area and has pieces of farmland and many trees in between houses and office buildings. Kochi or Cochin, a few hundred kilometres to the north, is a much more cosmopolitan city with an industrial area—including a free trade zone—and a large harbour. Kochi also has more inhabitants than Thiruvananthapuram (1.1 million versus 825,000 in 1991) (Bose, 1991). Government activities and services are spread between these two cities. The majority of them are located in Thiruvananthapuram, but the Kerala High Court and the Kerala State Civil Supplies Corporation (KeSCSC) for instance, are both in Kochi.

The population of Kerala lives mostly in between the various towns and villages. Settlement patterns in Kerala are strikingly different from those elsewhere in India (Hill, 1986). While in Karnataka, for instance, rural people live in villages, that is clusters of huts and houses with agricultural fields in between, Keralites live everywhere, more or less dispersed. Most houses or huts have a small garden around with a few coconut trees and some other vegetation. Furthermore there is paddy production in certain areas and tea, coffee, rubber, cashew or other plantations elsewhere. Coconut is undoubtedly the most important crop. In 1988–9 coconuts covered 28 per cent of the cultivated area, surpassing rice (19 per cent) and rubber (11 per cent).[20]

The State has a long history of maritime trade. As early as the sixteenth century Kerala's economy was largely geared to cash crop production, while the State was deficient in rice (Mencher, 1978: 349). The British started plantation agriculture in this fertile land. Since the mid-1970s rice production has been declining, both in terms of area covered and in terms of annual yield (Radhkrishanan, Thomas and Jessy Thomas, 1994: 160–5). This is a despite the fact that there is abundant water in Kerala: the two monsoon periods (June-September

[20] Calculated on the basis of figures in *Economic Review 1990* (Government of Kerala).

and October-November) give an annual rainfall of more than 2500 mm on average. Rice is the major staple food—tapioca is also eaten, especially by the poor—but now, at the end of the twentieth century, most of it has to be imported from other parts of India.

In the context of this study, there are four interrelated features of Kerala's economy and society that need special emphasis. The first concerns Kerala's outstanding record in health and welfare. This is remarkable, as economic development in Kerala is stagnating (Krishnan, 1989) and per capita income is lower than in most other Indian States.[21] Life expectancy in 1988–91 was 70.8 years (all-India average 59.1) (EPW Research Foundation, 1994) and infant mortality rate was 28 per 1000 in 1988 (against an all-India average of 94) (Bose, 1991). This makes Kerala comparable to countries such as Malaysia and the Republic of Korea in this respect. The literacy rate of people above 7 years of age is 91 per cent (the all-India average is 52 per cent). Not only is male literacy high (94 per cent), but also the female literacy rate (87 per cent) is much higher than in any other Indian State (ibid., 1991).[22]

The second feature worth emphasizing here is Kerala's food deficiency. It is estimated that rice production within Kerala covers approximately 30 per cent of its requirement.[23] The remainder is imported from other parts of India. The 30 per cent locally produced rice hardly enters the market. Most rice production is on very small plots meant for self-consumption only. This means that the rice market

[21] This statement is, however, somewhat misleading. A large number of Keralites are employed in the Gulf countries, and send (part of) their money back home. If this income were taken into account, the per capita income might be higher by about 15 to 30 per cent (Thomas Isaac and Mohana Kumar, 1991; Krishnan, 1994).

[22] These characteristics of Kerala have attracted much scholarly and policy-oriented attention, both from within and from outside Kerala. Some of these authors even speak of a 'Kerala model'. While others reject the idea of a special Kerala model as both the sustainability and the replicability of the model are doubtful, (e.g. Tharakan, 1994), the fact that Kerala has performed very well in terms of health, welfare and literacy is beyond doubt. There are several factors mentioned as explanatory elements by these various authors, such as high density and good accessibility of services due to high population density and the specific settlement pattern, matrilineal culture, enlightened rulers in the princely States before Independence, and political awareness, public action and a capable state. See, e.g. Caldwell (1986); Centre for Development Studies (1977); Drèze and Sen (1989); Franke and Chasin (1992); Tharakan and Thomas (1995); Jeffrey (1992); Kannan et al., (1991); Nag (1989); Ramachandran (1995).

[23] Official data regarding foodgrain imports (and exports) from other states in India are not available. I have assumed a per capita consumption of 330 g (NSS Report No. 370/2, 44th Round 1988–9; GoI). Total production of rice at the end of the 1980s was just over one million tonnes per year.

in Kerala handles almost entirely imported rice, imported either by the government or by private traders. This makes Kerala very dependent on non-Kerala agencies. The food situation in the State depends on outside markets; prices within the State may fluctuate according to the whims of traders elsewhere; increasing railway charges in the rest of India immediately influence foodgrain prices; and if the Government of India decides to reduce foodgrain allotment to Kerala or to increase FCI issue prices, Kerala's food situation is immediately affected.

The result of this food deficiency and dependency on markets elsewhere is that food issues have come to occupy a prominent place in the political consciousness of people in Kerala (see Sathyamurthy, 1985). Rising food prices are a possible motive for demonstrations or agitations, and political parties attempt to win over voters by expressing grave concern with food prices and by promising more interventions on this front.

The third important feature is the radical reform movements in Kerala politics. This started with religious movements in the nineteenth and the beginning of the twentieth centuries. (See, e.g. Alexander, 1989; Mathew, 1989; Panikkar, 1989). In the 1930s these religious reform movements were complemented by a radical leftist movement, as gradually class-based organizations started to emerge. These were, for instance, a Tillers Association in Malabar and an agricultural labour union in Travancore. After Independence, the communists became the major force behind peasant mobilizations (Oommen, 1985: 81). There were several important agitations, among them a land grab movement in 1970 and an excess-land struggle in 1972. As a result of these agitations, the Kerala Land Reform Act of 1969 was relatively successfully implemented. Tenancy was abolished, but the implementation of a land ceiling failed (as virtually everywhere in India). Most agricultural labourers got, however, at least 10 cents[24] of land around their hutment, which provided them with some basic security as they could no longer be evicted from their homes by landlords.

Leftist political parties have not only organized agitations and mobilizations from the sidelines; several times in Kerala's history they have been elected to power, and formed governments: from 1957 to 1959, from 1967 to 1969, from 1980 to 1981 and from 1987 to 1991. In between these periods there were Congress (I)-led coalition

[24] One cent is one-hundredth of an acre.

governments or periods of President's Rule. The two political blocks are more or less equal in strength. This means political rivalry is a permanent feature of Kerala politics, while in many other States in India political rivalry exists only at election time. The positive effect of this situation—two blocks that keep a check on each other—is that it contributes to political accountability, which is relatively high. The ruling party cannot afford to neglect the citizens/voters; there is always a competing political party eager and able to take over the torch of government.

A fourth important characteristic of the situation in Kerala is the income brought in by migrant workers. While the Kerala economy suffers from stagnation, many Keralites have migrated to other areas in India or abroad—notably to Gulf countries. The result is that large financial remittances come into Kerala which are mainly used for consumption. These remittances vary between 15 and 22 per cent of the state domestic product (Krishnan, 1994: 8). It is estimated that on average about 16 per cent of total consumption in Kerala might be due to remittances (Krishnan, 1994: 7). If this income were included in the per capita income, Kerala would no longer be seen as one of the poorer States in India.

Fieldwork in Kerala was concentrated in three locations: Thiruvananthapuram, Kochi and a district I gave the name of Madhyapura. In Thiruvananthapuram and Kochi I interviewed mainly government officials, managers from the KeSCSC, representatives of traders' organizations, advocates and others.

The case studies in the chapters that follow come from Madhyapura, where I studied social practices around the implementation of food distribution. Madhyapura is a district that runs from the coast, to the low hills and valleys eastwards, and finally to the forested hills on the Western Ghats. The most important food crops are paddy, sugar cane, and tapioca. Rice is the staple food. Sesame, coconut and rubber are the major cash crops. There are several industries located in the district, such as coir and cashew nut processing. In general, the industrial sector is in decline; factories close down or move to Tamil Nadu. Unemployment or underemployment is high, as everywhere in Kerala. There is sizable migration to Gulf countries. Political consciousness is well developed in the district.

Despite the lack of economic growth, the visitor does not get the impression of extreme poverty and deprivation in Madhyapura. Generally, the houses and huts in the rural areas look rather well maintained, and the people not too destitute, as compared, for instance, to the village(r)s in Karnataka. An exception to this generalization are the tribal people, who live in the most backward forest areas of the district.

1.4 RESEARCH METHODOLOGY[25]

Though fieldwork took place in different localities in two different States, this book is not a systematic comparison of Karnataka and Kerala. These two States differ in so many respects—political history, foodgrain production, foodgrain allocation from the Centre, population density, health services and welfare provision—that it was impossible to make a systematic comparative study. Nevertheless, comparison was an important tool during fieldwork as well as during the stage of analysis. Different locations prompt different questions. The researcher is reminded not to take too much for granted; things that look self-evident prove to be different elsewhere. This helps one to think through the conditions for certain events to take place, or for a certain status quo to exist. In this latter sense, the fieldwork and this book have profited from a comparative approach.

Why did I select Karnataka and Kerala? Generally, the political climate in south India seems to be more receptive and suited to the implementation of food distribution policy than that in north India. Kerala, of course, is the most striking illustration here, but the other south Indian States have also made considerable efforts in the field of food distribution. The governments of Andhra Pradesh and Karnataka have introduced large distribution schemes for the rural poor in the 1980s (Olsen, 1989; Radhakrishna and Indrakant, 1991), while the Tamil Nadu government runs 'what is arguably the biggest nutritional feeding programme of its kind in the world' (Kumar and Stewart, 1992: 277). Although such programmes are not altogether absent in other parts of India, south Indian States have a better record in this respect. In order to study the social construction of food policy, south Indian States thus provide interesting examples. Nevertheless, among the southern States there are big differences in the role food (distribution) has come to play in social and political relations. I selected Kerala because of its food deficiency and the pressure from

[25] A detailed discussion of this subject (titled: *The Black Box of the State: Studying the Politics of Food Distribution Policy*) was presented at the Grain Group seminar 'Analytical and Field Methods in the Study of Agricultural Markets', held at Oxford, December 1991 and will be published by Macmillan.

below on the government to increase access to cheap food. Karnataka was selected because it would give an opportunity to study the connection between food policy and populist politics.[26]

Within each of these two States I selected one district, in which I carried out most of the fieldwork. The major criteria for selecting these districts, Akkipura and Madhyapura, were (*a*) of practical nature—the areas were reachable by train—and (*b*) related to the food economy. To be more precise, in Karnataka I wanted to study distribution *and* procurement, so there should be rice production in the area. In Kerala, where there is no procurement, I selected an area with not much rice production, so that distribution would matter to the people. Within the selected districts I chose one *taluk* close to the capital and one less accessible *taluk*.[27]

The selection of taluks only played a role in the collection of data about distribution practices (Chapter 5). For this my research assistant and I, but my assistant did the lion's share of this work, visited eight villages in each of the two selected *taluks*. Within these villages, we interviewed the ration dealers and a number of randomly selected card/ holders. Although these interviews were useful, it was clear to me that there were many things that would never be revealed in such 'representative' study. I therefore did additional interviews with purposefully selected persons: private rice and wheat merchants, government officials known for their commitment, local politicians, representatives from traders organizations, etc. These informants were not selected because they belonged to the selected *taluks* but

[26] By populist politics, I mean the tendency of governments, politicians and political parties to address the citizens as if no internal differentiation exists. Populist policies are meant for a wide public: with slogans appealing to, and programmes meant to accommodate, as many people as possible. One of the objectives of populist politics is often to gain popularity among a large part of the population in order to broaden the social base of the government, politician or political party. Originally, the term populism stems from the rural development literature. It is a label used by some Marxists to refer to others—the (neo) populists—who argue that rural transformation can and should be based on small-scale family farms. This label was first used in the controversy between 'neo-narodniks' or 'neo-populists' and their Bolshevik critics around the turn of the century in Russia. While the first school was convinced of the efficiency of peasant family labour farms, the latter believed that differentiation of such producers into distinct classes was not only a reality in the Russian countryside but also a necessity in order to achieve economic development. In the contemporary literature on rural development, the controversy still persists. See Harris (1982: 37–43) for a short introduction; Lipton (1977) is a prototype of a contemporary populist, while Byres (1979; 1988) is a forceful Marxist critique.

[27] A *taluk* is an administrative unit below the district level.

because of their specific knowledgeability and willingness to talk. They could tell me things I was interested in and that were not disclosed so far.

As far as data gathering for other subjects was concerned (the Essential Commodities Act, State trading corporations, rice procurement), the *taluk* locality played an even smaller role. I selected my informants mainly on the basis of two criteria. The first was the specific expertise of the informants. I consciously searched for respondents with a certain experience, who had been involved in certain conflicts, who had a certain opinion, who had certain connections. Whenever I realized there were lacunae in my data, I tried to find informants who could help fill these gaps. Also when I had formed preliminary ideas or interim conclusions, I tried to find informants whose case would throw new light on the issue. The second criterion was a good introduction. Especially when the subject is sensitive, it is important that interviewees are willing to talk, that they trust the researcher. This is indeed facilitated by a good introduction. So I was not only investigating social relations, I was also led by social relations and social networks myself. For instance my Indian supervisor introduced me to a colleague at the university, who suggested I visit his classmate in Akkipura, who then introduced me to one of his close friends, who then arranged several interviews for me. Of course, I tried to diversify my strategies for selecting informants. I did so by operating in several networks myself, by exploring as many entry points as possible. This led to some surprise meetings with unexpectedly useful informants. I also tried to be flexible enough to explore new routes when new ideas were brought up or new suggestions were made by my informants. Although I was dependent on introductions and suggestions, the research process was not arbitrary or of an ad hoc nature. The logic was brought in by myself. Because I often consciously searched for specific suggestions, introductions and informants, the course taken and phenomena investigated were decided by me.[28]

[28] Fieldwork lasted approximately one and a half years. Apart from interviews I also collected a great deal of other material: statistics, policy documents, court cases, newspaper clippings, secondary data, pamphlets, minutes of meetings, government orders, letters, memoranda, State budgets, inquiry reports, departmental annual reports, and so on. Going through this book, the reader will note that different types of material dominate in different chapters, though all in all the interviews conducted by myself have been the most important source of information and insight. The reader will also

My research work in Akkipura district was greatly facilitated by a friend *cum* key informant. He himself was very knowledgeable about the rice trade and rice procurement, and was eager to talk about it. He introduced me to many of his friends who were traders and/or rice mill owners. He conducted a lot of interviews with me, suggested interesting cases and also collected some information independently.

During the entire fieldwork period, I was assisted by a research assistant who acted as an interpreter during the interviews, and who also did much independent research work. I myself had managed to learn some Kannada—the language of Karnataka—but I could not dream of doing interviews in Kannada myself, let alone in Malayalam—the language in Kerala. My research assistant mastered both languages. Working with an interpreter has its drawbacks. It takes time; it creates confusion; there is an extra mediator who colours questions and answers. Fortunately, many informants spoke English, so that I could also do many interviews on my own.

All in all, I conducted approximately 400 interviews with different kind of informants. This excludes all the semi-structured and structured interviews done by my research assistant. I have written reports soon after each interview on the basis of notes made during the interview. These reports do not only contain first person accounts; more often they report what the informant has said, has not said, other observations as well as my interpretation.

The quotations presented in this book are, hence, not literal quotations, but restatements of the stories, arguments and perspectives of the informants. I have tried to remain as close to the original wording, meaning and intention as I could on the basis of my reports, but for the sake of the presentation I have also sometimes summarized or edited the argument. In my representations, I always refer to ration dealers, government officials, rice mill owners, politicians, etc. as 'he', rather than as '(s)he', because many of them are male.

By way of conclusion

It is not easy to classify the fieldwork methodology. Perhaps the best way is to describe it as a combination of the intensive method of the anthropologist and the more inventorial approach of a sociologist who

note that some data are missing. Some of the tables are not fully filled up (especially in Chapter 6). A completely empty space in a Table means that I lacked the data; '—' means that there was no activity.

is interested in 'big structures, large processes and huge comparisons' (Tilly, 1984). Both the field method described in this section and the anthropological methodology, (e.g. Hammersley and Atkinson, 1983; Long, 1989) are very much actor oriented: there is much interest in the experiences and interpretation of the respondent. However, where an anthropologist is interested in the whole lifeworld of the other, I had a very specific, restricted topic in mind, which, moreover, brought me to many different settings, different locations. Sometimes I had breakfast with an advocate, met one or two rice mill owners in the morning, visited government offices in the afternoon, while the next day I travelled 30 km to do some interviews together with my research assistant in a small village. In short, the variety of settings and the area covered were much wider than in most anthropological research. In addition, I depended almost wholly on verbal accounts, whereas for an anthropologist, observation and informal chatting are equally important. For me this was impossible, not only because I did not master the language sufficiently, but also because the number of localities to be observed was virtually endless, while many of the activities I was interested in could be easily suspended whenever my presence was felt to be a problem.

The similarity of my field method with other more inventorial forms of sociological research is that both are pragmatic. There is an immediate feedback of the gathered insights into the research process. Flexibility is built in, and there is no dogmatism regarding the best or only way to proceed. Different methodologies are combined; it all depends on what you want to know and the possibilities you have. However, as compared to sociologists who are interested in large-scale processes, I was more interested in details and case studies. There were many informants whom I met several times during a period of one year. I tried to collect and compare information from various sources about one and the same person or event and I regularly met my informants in different settings. This enabled me to develop a better understanding of the various actor-perspectives, the complexities of most interactions and social relations, and the development of events over time.

This research methodology, that is the combination of anthropological in-depth research with a sociological inventorial approach, may have a wider relevance than only to the research project under review in this book. It seems especially relevant (*a*) when the research theme requires fieldwork in many different locations, (*b*) when the research project includes the investigation of sensitive issues and activities that occur only occasionally and can be easily postponed, and (*c*) when the research population is reasonably capable of expressing itself discursively in a manner understandable to the researcher.

The methodology has several drawbacks. The researcher remains very dependent upon the cooperation of the research population and its willingness to explain things to an outsider. In the present study, I was lucky enough to meet a considerable number of informants who seemed to enjoy talking to an outsider. In part, I owe this to the fact that I was introduced to them by the right persons in the right way. Furthermore, it was clear that many informants from outside the government bureaucracy were annoyed with corruption and other problems they encountered when dealing with officials. Being a foreigner as well as a woman, I was obviously not involved. Although several informants will certainly not have told me everything, others took the opportunity to ventilate some of their grievances to me.

Another drawback, or rather a limitation, is that this methodology does not allow for conclusions in terms of numbers, averages or percentages. As in all intensive research, this methodology helps to understand why things happen as they happen, the mechanisms generating changes or reproducing a certain *status quo*, all in the specific space-time situation that is investigated. Whether or to what extent the discerned reasons or causes are 'representative', 'average', generalizable, or do exist at all elsewhere is a question that cannot be addressed with the help of this fieldwork methodology. But what can be said is that it is *likely* that similar mechanisms will produce similar events elsewhere when a number of specific and known conditions are fulfilled.[29] So research based on this methodology yields not only causal explanations of the production of the limited number of processes or events that are studied, but also hypotheses of what might happen elsewhere in similar or dissimilar circumstances. It is for this reason that insights generated in specific contexts, as presented in this book, despite their limitations, can nevertheless be of great interest and relevance outside the immediate geographical and historical boundaries that defined the fieldwork situation.

[29] See Sayer (1984) about strengths and limitations of intensive research.

2

Food Policy, State and Politics in India

Some theoretical considerations

Government's work is God's work
(Inscription on the *Vidhan* Soudha, the Assembly Building in Bangalore. Original in Kannada)

2.1 FOOD AND FOOD POLICY

Food, as Harriss-White writes, is not an article exactly like any other. It is special in many respects:

> It is the foundation, along with water, of our survival. It is both a basic need and a basic pleasure. As Audrey Richards explains: 'nutrition is more fundamental than sex. In the life of an individual it is the primary recurrent want while in the wider sphere of society it determines... the nature of social groups and the form their activities take'.[1] Food is a carefully chosen and classified means of social communication and the object of a richly expressive and varied aesthetic. Its production and distribution is a provider of work and livelihoods and the source of legitimacy to governments. It is an important building block of international relations. It is thus also a subject of conflict within the household, between social groups, between nations. Food excludes. It is a source of disease and discontent. Its production is one reason for environmental transformation and sometimes for its degradation and destruction. Food may be a cause of dependence and subordination. It is a tool of war. By examining the role played by food we come to understand much that is basic to human society as a whole (Harriss-White, 1995: 1).

For an understanding of food distribution policy in India, not all dimensions of food are equally important. In the rest of this book I shall pay no attention to, for example, the cultural embeddedness of food or the aesthetics of food preparation and presentation. Not that

[1] Cited in S. Mintz (1985) *Sweetness and Power*, Viking Penguin, New York (p.4).

these dimensions are irrelevant, but my prime concern is with others. In a study about food distribution policy at least three dimensions of food deserve attention, that is food as a nutritional commodity, as an economic commodity and as a political commodity. Let me briefly elaborate on these.

It is trivial point indeed that food is a nutritional commodity. People starve when their energy and protein intake is not sufficient over a period of time. In India, unfortunately, undernutrition is not at all a rare phenomenon. According to recent studies roughly between 200 and 400 million people do not have enough income to feed themselves properly.[2]

Apart from a nutritional commodity, food is also an economic commodity. Or, in Marxist terms, food has not only a use value but also an exchange value. As Marx (1954: 43–4) put it originally:

> A commodity is, in the first place, an object outside us, a thing that by its properties satisfies human wants of some sort or another. ... The utility of a thing makes it a use value. ... Use-values become a reality only by use or consumption: they also constitute the substance of all wealth. ... In the form of society we are about to consider, [i.e. capitalism], they are, in addition, the material depositories of exchange value.

The historical process by which exchange value comes to assume an increasingly important role in economies is called 'commoditization' (Bernstein, 1979; Long et al., 1986). It is an integral part of capitalist development, and it has taken place in various forms in almost all economies worldwide.

Also the organization of production, exchange and consumption of food in India is shaped in and through capitalist commodity relations. This means not only that capitalist relations have 'penetrated' agricultural production, but also that food is a source of profit in exchange. Traders, brokers, commission agents and/or other intermediaries in trade are less concerned with the nutritional content and function of food for human well-being than with its price. For them, food is primarily a source of profit, to be purchased as cheaply as possible and sold for a much higher price.[3] The result of this profit orientation can be speculation, impoverishment of the producers,

[2] Gupta (1994) on poverty in India. Gupta's poverty estimates are ultimately based on nutritional norms. See also note 14 of Chapter 1.

[3] '[For the owners of commodities who go to the market, the] commodity possesses ... no immediate use-value. Otherwise, he would not bring it to the market. It has use-value for others; but for himself its only direct use-value is that of being a depository

artificial scarcity, inadequate access to food by some who lack sufficient purchasing power, and famines even when food is available in the market (Sen, 1981).[4]

And lastly, food is also a political commodity. Because it is so essential for human survival food is a means of power. Those who have command over food can exercise power or influence political relations. Those whose access to food is insufficient and/or insecure are vulnerable and easy objects of control and domination exercised by others who control food. Food is the stake in many a political struggle: between nations, between governments and subjects, between traders, producers and consumers, within households, etc.[5] For those in command of food, it is a powerful resource that can be used to influence, manipulate or enforce one's will on others. For those less fortunate, food is not a resource in political struggles but an end in itself. This characterizes the fundamental inequality: the means of some are the ends for others.

Related to these three dimensions of food, public food distribution can be analysed along three different lines. Food distribution affects the distribution of calories, of economic benefits and of power. Food is purchased from some and distributed to others, which means a redistribution of calories. Simultaneously, this redistribution of calories is an intervention in the food market. It affects prices, as well as the structure of the market. Some market agents fare well under a regime of administered prices and forced purchase by the state, but for others such a regime means a decline of their incomes. Power relations are also affected. Food distribution policy creates new categories of people with command over food: government employees, warehouse managers, ration dealers. These people acquire a resource which they

---

of exchange-value, and, consequently a means of exchange.' (Marx, 1954: 89). For Marx, the exchange value of a commodity is a quantity determined by the labour time that was necessary for the production of the commodity. Labour time is not the prime interest of the traders. What matters to them is the absolute difference between purchasing and handling costs on the one hand and selling costs on the other.

[4] This observation is not meant as a moral judgement as, for instance, the Indian government makes when it refers to traders as 'hoarders [and] black-marketeers [who] are playing hell with the lives of millions of people' (preamble to the 1974 amendment of the Essential Commodities Act), or 'persons indulging in antisocial activities like hoarding and blackmarketeering and the evil of vicious inflationary prices' (Amendment of the EC Act, 1981). Instead, I want to stress that this profit motive is an inherent feature of a capitalist economy, in which making money, rather than the fulfilment of human needs, has become a driving economic force.

[5] See various essays in Bernstein et al. (1990).

can use to influence or manipulate others. When food distribution reaches the poorest and most vulnerable people, it also adds to *their* bargaining position. A more secure food situation makes vulnerable people slightly more powerful, or less powerless, in their interactions and negotiations with more powerful agents such as landlords or moneylenders.

Accordingly, any government that devises and implements food policies has or may have an official or hidden agenda in these three different fields: to increase consumption and eliminate malnutrition, to affect prices, incomes and the market structure, and to support particular categories of people or political projects. The PDS in India has objectives of these three kinds. The first two are usually uncontroversial and stated publicly. It is widely known and accepted that food distribution policy is an intervention in consumption and profits. Not many people would contest the legitimacy of this undertaking. That the PDS is also a political intervention, that specific categories of people are supported or excluded, that food distribution is used to support particular political projects or to undermine others, is proclaimed less. But, as I hope to show in Chapter 3, it is also true. Food policy in India is strategically employed by the Central and State governments to support particular political and economic projects. In the course of history the projects have changed, but the general point—food policy as a tool in politics—has remained valid.

Despite its importance, most investigations and evaluations of food distribution policy in India have neglected this political dimension. Almost all studies[6] evaluate food policies in terms of the first two dimensions: distributed/consumed quantities and the effect on prices (but, generally, not on profits and the market structure). Sometimes the political background of a particular food programme is briefly mentioned, (e.g. Venugopal, 1992: 169) but this dimension is seldom analysed with the same depth and rigour as the other two.

The most notable exception to this general neglect is the work of Harriss.[7] She analyses the effect of food policies on the (economic) power of traders and vice versa. Her work illustrates the fact that food policy is an inherently political phenomenon: policies are shaped in political processes, and through policies particular categories of people are supported rather than others. The landless labourers who should be the prime beneficiaries of public distribution do not benefit very

[6] See note 7, Chapter 1, for references.

[7] See, for instance, Harriss (1984, 1988) and Harriss-White (1993)

much. Rather, in their place, categories of people within the state, as well as private merchants profit from the policies (Harriss, 1984). Harriss also analyses political mobilization of traders, and the effects this has on government food policies. Through lobbies and other activities merchants often succeed in increasing their power. Although many policies were designed to reduce the opportunities for them to make money, in reality traders are often supported rather than inhibited in any way.

The present book focuses on the politics of food distribution, but in contrast to Harriss the emphasis is less on traders and market structures and more on the state, particular state institutions and their dealings with other actors. This book evaluates how food distribution policy in India emerged, how it is shaped in day-to-day practices and what its effects are. Although all three dimensions—calories, economic redistribution and power—receive some attention, the main emphasis is on the last one: food as a resource and food policy as an instrument to influence the distribution of this resource.

The political relationship between food policy and power is two-sided. Food policies are shaped in and through political processes. Because food is so precious, necessary for survival and useful for profits and power, there are many stakeholders who indulge in political activities with the objective of influencing the food policies (on paper), as well as the real practices of food distribution. On the other hand, once food policy exists, it may affect political relations and balances of power. This may be intended (food policies can be used to support particular groups or political projects) but it may also be that shifts in power relations are unintended and perhaps not even wanted by those initiating the policies.

The Indian state is crucial in these processes. This is true for two reasons. The state is a central agent: it formulates and pursues food policies, and puts them into practice more or less effectively depending on the available resources and the responses of those affected. In addition, state institutions and regulations provide the political environment in which struggles over food and food policy are contested. The form of the state itself influences political mobilization, political capacities and demands of various sectors in society.[8]

The remaining part of this chapter is a theoretical exploration of the relationship between the Indian state and politics and food distribution

[8] See Skocpol (1985)

policy. Depending on our interpretation of the Indian state and politics, we might develop different expectations about the way food distribution policy is used by the state, the categories of people and political projects that are supported by it, and the way food distribution policy works out. Section 2.3, hence, contains a discussion on the Indian state and politics. This in not barren terrain. In fact, a lot has been written about the Indian state. It is not my intention, neither is it within my capacity, to review this whole body of literature. Rather I present some of the most leading recent interpretations of the Indian state and politics.[9] After this discussion I come back to the politics of food distribution policy in Section 2.4. What would follow from these interpretations of the Indian state for state food distribution policy? If these interpretations are correct, what then can we expect with regard to the functioning of the public distribution system? But before embarking on a discussion of the various interpretations regarding the concrete historical Indian state, it is first necessary to define the concept on a more abstract theoretical level. What actually is meant by 'the state'?

2.2 CONCEPTS: STATE AND POLITICS

In this book, the term 'state' is used in several ways. In some contexts the term refers to federal States, the constituent units of the Indian federation. In such instances I use a capital 'S'. In other contexts, 'state' refers to the state apparatus. In those cases I mean a set of political, administrative and coercive institutions and organizations, headed and, more or less, well coordinated, by an executive authority—the government. Almost all states are involved in defining and enforcing binding decisions on the inhabitants of their territory, which generally happens in the name of the common interest or general will.

This definition of 'state', as well as the following elaboration of the concept is based on both Jessop' study (1990: 341) and Skocpol (1979: 29–30).[10] Although it seems strange to combine insights from these two authors, I think it is defensible. Jessop is part of the Marxist tradition of state theorists. Jessop's study (1984) is an elaborate treatment and critique of perhaps all important Marxist state theorists so far,

[9] Some of the earlier literature includes Bettelheim (1968,), Hanson (1966), Kurian (1975), Morris-Jones (1971), Myrdal (1968) and Weiner (1967).

[10] Jessop (1990: 341) suggests defining the state as follows. 'The core of the state apparatus comprises a distinct ensemble of institutions and organizations whose socially accepted function is to define and enforce collectively binding decisions on the members of a society in the name of their common interest or general will.' According to Skocpol

plus an attempt to develop guidelines for constructing an adequate theory of the state. Jessop (1990) contains a number of essays on issues related to state theory, again based primarily on the Marxist body of thinking. Skocpol, on the other hand, should be placed within the Weberian tradition, as she puts state institutions up front. Skocpol dissociates herself explicitly from Marxist and neo-Marxist theory. In her opinion:

> ... virtually all neo-marxist writers on the state have retained deeply embedded society-centred assumptions, not allowing themselves to doubt that, at base, states are inherently shaped by classes or class struggles and function to preserve and expand modes of production. Many possible forms of autonomous state action are thus ruled out by definitional fiat. Furthermore, neo-marxist theorists have often sought to generalize—often in extremely abstract ways—about features or functions shared by *all* states within a mode of production, a phase of capitalist accumulation, or a position in the world capitalist system. This makes it difficult to assign causal weight to variations in state structures and activities across nations and short time periods, thereby undercutting the usefulness of some neo-marxist schemes for comparative research (Skocpol, 1985: 5).

Skocpol obviously puts up a straw man here for the sake of her argument: defending a state-centred instead of society-centred approach. The Marxist body of thought is, however, richer and more diverse than she suggests, and does not preclude state-centred interpretations. As Jessop (1984 *passim*; 1990: 86–93) shows, there are many different Marxist interpretations of the state. There are Marxist authors who maintain that the state is an instrument of the dominant class or that in the end all state action is determined by the logic of capital, but there are others who argue that politicians and officials may develop their own interests or that states in capitalism do not necessarily always act as capitalist states. In fact, Jessop also classifies his own approach as state-theoretical (rather than as capital- or class-theoretical, or society-centred in Skocpol's terms).

Jessop's main critique of Skocpol and other state-centred theorists is that these authors draw a dichotomy between state and society, suggesting that 'both exist as independent entities which are fully constituted, internally coherent and mutually exclusive and that one always unilaterally determines the other' (Jessop, 1990: 287). Also Jessop does not do full justice to Skocpol's ideas. Notwithstanding

---

(1979: 29) the state is 'a set of administrative, policing, and military organizations headed, and more or less well coordinated by, an executive authority.'

Skocpol's slogan 'to bring the state back in' she explicitly asserts and analyses the state's 'intrinsically dual anchorage in class-divided socio-economic structures and an international system of states' (Skocpol, 1979: 32). So I hold that the differences between these two state theorists are less significant than they themselves claim.

What I added explicitly to the definition is the term 'political'. This is not a real addition to the ideas of Jessop and Skocpol. Indeed, both authors regard the state as intrinsically political. But in order to avoid any misunderstanding I included the term in the definition. This means that the state consists of political, administrative and enforcing institutions (Lipton, 1991: 93).

This explicit reference to 'political institutions' is not meant to take politics apart and to separate it from administrative or coercive institutions. By 'political institutions' I refer to for example, politically elected bodies like the parliament or the *zilla parishads*, the Indian district councils. In such contexts, the term 'political' is used in the narrow sense, linked directly to specific state institutions. In this book, however, 'politics' or 'political' often has a broader meaning than only this: politics is also a universal part of society. As Held (1991: 5) states, the broad interpretation of 'politics' or 'political' holds that politics is about power: that is about the capacity of social agents, agencies and institutions to maintain and transform their social and physical environment. Accordingly, politics is not restricted to a specific set of state institutions, but exists in all state institutions, as well as other spheres of life.[11]

This definition of the state implies that the state is not merely an instrument of class rule or an effect. It is a set of institutions that matters, that may itself have a significant effect on other social institutions, relations and practices. Skocpol distinguishes two ways in which the state may affect social change and politics:

On the one hand, states may be viewed as organizations through which official

[11] Schaffer's work on bureaucracies illustrates that non-political (i.e. administrative /bureaucratic) institutions are also inherently political (e.g. Schaffer, 1984: 157-163). Schaffer refers to this phenomenon as 'bureaucratics': what goes on inside bureaucratic organizations is not separate from what goes on outside them. Power relations are translated into institutional procedures, and institutional procedures keep things going: some in power and offices in being. More concretely and related to India, Potter explores the relationship between (senior) public administrators and politics. In his account, these administrators do all kinds of political work. As one civil servant remarked, 'Politics, let there be no mistake, is the senior civil servant's breath and staff of life, whether he perceives it or not in the tasks he performs' (quoted in Potter, 1986: 229).

collectivities may pursue distinctive goals, realizing them more or less effectively given the available resources in relation to social settings. On the other hand, states may be viewed more macroscopically as configurations of organizations and action that influence the meanings and methods of politics for all groups and classes in society(1985: 28).

In other words, states as actors with certain capacities, and states as arenas or political 'ambiences' that have an impact on 'the formation of groups and the political capacities, ideas and demands of various sectors of society' (ibid.: 21).

This insight that the state itself may have a central role in social change, politics, and policy making is not only an article of faith or an abstract methodological principle. In the Indian case, it is also an obvious empirical reality. Alavi, as Pedersen (1992) points out, was one of the first political scientists who drew attention to the relative autonomy of state apparatuses in many post-colonial societies.[12] According to Alavi (1972, 1982), these societies had inherited an overdeveloped state which was often manned by people who had become socially and culturally somewhat distinct from other categories of people. Moreover, the particular class configurations of these societies, with several dominant propertied classes with partly conflicting interests, made it possible for this overdeveloped state to wield considerable power over other sections of society. The post-colonial Indian state is a clear example of what Alavi calls an overdeveloped state. The Indian Administrative Service (IAS), the powerful successor of the colonial Indian Civil Service, is often referred to as 'the steel frame' of society. The experiences with economic planning show that the Indian state has, at times, been able to operate as a relatively independent powerful force.

By conceiving of the state as a *set* of institutions, it is implied that there is no necessity that the state be a homogeneous *bloc*. The various institutions may differ in intentions, approach or practices; they may even conflict with one another. Most states are, indeed, heterogeneous and fragmented. This is also true of the Indian state, in which several lines of cleavages exist (Lipton, 1991: 99–100). First of all, the Indian state consists of several layers. In addition to the political centre in Delhi there are federal States, district administration and even lower

[12] For the debate about the 'relative autonomy' of the state, see Laclau (1975), Miliband (1973), Poulantzas (1973, 1976). Alavi (1982) is a welcome contribution to this literature. In contrast to the other authors his aim is not to defend or define a general theoretical principle, but to explain autonomy as a concrete empirical phenomenon.

forms of government. Each layer has it own responsibilities and jurisdiction. Food, for instance, is a responsibility of the central state, while agriculture belongs to the realm of the federal States. But there are other potential lines of cleavages as well: between various departments, between the legislative, executive and judicial power, between the official policies and sets of rules on the one hand and the informal agreements and institutionalized practices on the other. In short, there are many contradictions, differences of interests and possibilities for conflicts and fights over state power.

Often it is not easy to draw a rigid boundary around the state. As Jessop (1990: 342) states: '[a]bove, around and below the core of the state are found institutions and organizations whose relation to the core ensemble is uncertain. States never achieve full closure or complete separation from society....' This means the precise boundaries of the state are usually difficult to ascertain, and often contested. To be more concrete, it is sometimes an empirical question whether or to what extent a particular person or institution is part of the state. Members of the State Legislative Assemblies (MLAs), for instance, should be considered as part of the state because they are members of a key political institution. Often they have access to state resources and are able to distribute some of these to the inhabitants of their constituencies. On the other hand, politicians who have been MLAs but were voted out at the last election despite the fact that they have large followings, are formally excluded from the legislative procedure and state resources. Nevertheless, they may still be very close to the centres of state power, from which they may still draw political prestige and perhaps also material resources occasionally. In such cases, it is difficult to draw a line between state and non-state, unless we recognize that there are various dimensions to the issue. According to the normative borderline constructions these ex-MLAs do not belong to the state. However, in terms of real practices and actual social relations between the state and others, these politicians are, to a greater or lesser extent, part of the state.

As mentioned in the definition, states usually claim to act in the name of the common interest or the general will. They claim to represent the citizens and to do what is best for society at large. This claim is their major source of legitimacy, and states actively try to present this claim as truth. Legitimacy, for most states, is crucial. As Weber, Gramsci and other state theorists argued, states rule not only by force, but also by consent or compliance.

Often both the general claim that it is the function of states to act in the name of the common interest or general will, as well as the particular claim of a specific set of rulers that they act accordingly, is indeed to a greater or lesser extent accepted by the citizens, but this is not necessarily so. State legitimacy is never a given. It is always contested (or established) in and through politically relevant discourses (Jessop, 1990: 341–2) in which the function of the state, the general will and common interest are defined, and in which the actual state performance is interpreted.

Although the outcome of these discursive struggles may be that, temporarily, the rulers are accepted as legitimate holders of state power who serve the general interest, any state always remains the state of some more so than that of others. There is no common interest that encapsulates all particular interests. Nevertheless, as Jessop (1990: 341) asserts, 'the claims about the general will or common interests are a key feature of the state system and distinguish it from straightforward political domination or violent oppression.'

2.3 PERSPECTIVES ON THE INDIAN STATE AND POLITICS

Since the 1980s, the Indian state has been under serious attack. While in the first decades after Independence the state was seen as the main vehicle of economic growth and development, the dominant consensus (Pedersen, 1992) in the 1980s and 1990s is very critical of the state. It is held that the public sector has expanded too much and has become inefficient. Economic growth is blocked rather than promoted by the state. The general public has become very critical of the provision of state services. A recent study of public services in Bangalore revealed that the level of public satisfaction with the performance of public agencies is low. Services are considered unreliable, waiting times are long, and 'speed money' is often required (Paul, 1993). Newspapers frequently report alleged cases of corruption. Politics has become a dirty word. It is associated with favouritism or, worse, criminal gangs. In short, the overall political climate in India is characterized by a pervasive anti-state discourse.[13]

[13] India is not exceptional in this respect. In the 1980s and 1990s development theory and policy have generally been dominated by the neo-liberal paradigm, which holds that the state is a less appropriate instrument to achieve economic growth and development than the market. The proposed strategy is, hence, to 'roll back' the state's dominant position in the economy (Toye, 1987).

Theoretically, this dominant consensus is supported by at least three currents of thought.[14] The first type of critique of the Indian state is voiced mainly by neoclassical political economists who are concerned with the role of the state in economic growth. They argue that the Indian state has developed into a rent-seeking state, with all the attendant disadvantages. The second critique of the state is expressed particularly by political scientists, whose main concern is not so much economic growth, but the nature of the Indian political system and democracy. In their view the political system is suffering from serious 'erosion'. The third type of criticism focuses on the bureaucracy. It holds that the professionals in the public sector have developed into a dominant proprietary class or a 'third actor'. Each of these three currents of thought has its own authors, body of literature, and debate. There is little overlap between the various debates, especially between the first and the second current of thought. Economists hardly refer to the insights developed by political scientists, and vice versa.[15] So the striking thing is that despite a dominant consensus and despite a rich literature, *the* debate about the nature of the Indian state does not exist. The literature is too fragmented to bring it all under one heading.

Apart from the three currents of thought falling within the dominant consensus, there is a fourth body of literature that remains somewhat outside. Here I am referring to the (mainly) political economists who are concerned with the nature of Indian planning and/or other development efforts. Exponents of this literature are not uncritical of the Indian state, but the general position is one in defence of some sort of state intervention rather than uncompromised withdrawal and reliance on the price mechanism.

In the discussion on the four approaches that follows I will briefly summarize the main issues and observed problems that triggered the

[14] Pedersen (1992) also distinguishes three currents in the state-critical literature: the neo-liberals, the Marxists and those who claim that the state bureaucracies are not rational enough (in the Weberian sense). This is a general categorization, not specifically related to India. With regard to India, this classification does not hold. Political scientists who are concerned with democracy and the political system are excluded from this classification. Moreover, in India the Marxist position cannot be simply regarded as one of the state-critical strands. Both the second and the third currents of thought mentioned in the text include some Marxists (e.g. Vanaik, 1990 and Bardhan, 1984 respectively). There are also Marxists who do not fall within the dominant consensus, but who defend the state in one way or another, (e.g. in Byres, 1994).

[15] An exception is Joshi and Little (1994). In their analysis of macroeconomic polity in India, these authors combine insights from the first two strands of literature. Another exception is Bardhan (1984).

analysis, the explanations and/or insights developed and the strategies proposed to solve the main problems. The overview presented here is not exhaustive, but the most important spokesmen and points of view are included.

The rent-seeking state

The main concern of neoclassical political economists is economic growth and stagnation, and as far as the state is concerned, the role of the state herein. In contrast to earlier neoclassical theory, in which the state was treated as a black box, this new branch of neoclassical economics tries to open this black box (Evans, 1989). To be more specific, it decided to apply the standard tools of neoclassical economics to the analysis of the state (Srinivasan, 1985).

The application of the theorem of individual optimization to the study of the state implies that the state is conceived of as the sum of all individual government officials and politicians (methodological individualism) and that all these people in public office are seen as rational optimizers. They need votes and public support and they try to maximize their income. They distribute resources such as subsidies, jobs, loans, food, contracts, etc. to their supporters, in exchange for support. Or they appropriate monopoly rents arising from trading in government licences and other scarce rights and facilities they are in charge of.

Poor government performance is easily explained from this perspective. Like all other people government officials respond to incentives and disincentives. It is unlikely that they undertake policies that would meet broad resistance or that would weaken their power base. Instead, they 'make deals that keep them in power and maintain the revenue, votes, or whatever underlies their power' (Levi, 1988: 201). In short, incumbents of public posts cannot be expected to do anything that is not (also) in their own interest.

Krueger (1974) was among the first who applied this model to India. Her interest was in the allocation of government licences for imports. When licences are quantitatively restricted while considerable profits (rents) can be made, competition, i.e. competitive rent-seeking, is likely to occur. Sometimes this competition is legal, but in other instances rent-seeking takes illegal forms, such as bribery, corruption, smuggling and black marketeering. In Krueger's model, there is competition not only for licences but also for government jobs. Since government officials themselves receive part of the rents, competition for jobs is also a form of competitive rent-seeking.

This perspective has been further developed theoretically, (e.g. Bhagwati, 1982; Buchanan, Tollison and Tullock, 1980; Colander, 1984; Scott and Lal, 1990; Srinivasan, 1985), as well as applied to the Indian situation (Bhagwati, 1993; Joshi and Little, 1994; Lal, 1988; Roy, 1984).[16] Bhagwati, for instance, argues that the system of controls on industry and trade has contributed to rent-seeking activities:

[The cost of controls over production and investment were considerable.] These costs have now been extensively analysed. The stifling of private initiative, the diversion of resources into unproductive rent-seeking activities stimulated by the controls, and costly bottle-necks reflecting artificial rigidities are only illustrative of the unnecessary economic costs imposed by this control-infested system. But the mounting evidence of the system's corrosive influence on the moral ethos and the integrity of political and public life, as corruption was inevitably spawned by politicians and (largely lower-level) bureaucrats tempted to exploit the control system to their advantage cannot be dismissed from the final accounting of what this regime cost India (Bhagwati, 1993: 56).

In addition to these neoclassical economists, the work of Robert Wade deserves some attention in this section, (e.g. Wade, 1982; 1985). Although Wade is not a neoclassical economist, he is interested in similar phenomena: various types of rent-seeking and the effects on state performance. Both civil servants and politicians are regarded as individual optimizers. Officers aim to 'maximize revenue and minimize complaints' (Wade, 1985: 470). Politicians are to a large extent independent entrepreneurs (Wade, 1985: 480) who have to find their own funds and buy their own support.

[16] Another economist who is sometimes grouped, (e.g. by Toye, 1988) under the heading of rent-seeking theory is Jha (1980). In Jha's account, the Indian state is dominated by the so-called intermediate class, consisting of market-oriented peasant proprietors, small manufacturers, traders and other self-employed groups. This class has benefited enormously from the economic system of controls and protection and, hence, does its best to perpetuate and reinforce it. And with success. According to Jha the Indian state can be charaterized as an 'intermediate regime'. The consequence of such a regime is that funds 'have been diverted from large into small industry, from high to low priority industries, and from industry as a whole to trade' (Jha, 1980: 94). Hence, economic stagnation. This economic system has also corrupted the body of politics. A part of the money earned by the intermediate class has been illegally donated to the political parties, which 'boosted the prospects of the Jana Sangh and similar *petit bourgeois* parties in the 1960s, as well as forcing the Congress Party into more populist attitudes and more dubious electoral practices' (Toye, 1988: 107).

Wade's work is very interesting since it is based on intensive fieldwork. As a result Wade is able to develop a very rich account of the processes within the state. His study of the irrigation bureaucracy in south India reveals how officials raise vast amounts of illegal revenue from the distribution of water and contracts. A part of that revenue is distributed to superior officers and politicians. The mechanism of this redistribution is the transfer system. Almost all officials are liable to be transferred from one post to another. Some posts are desirable because of good amenities and avenues for money collection. Other posts are undesirable. There is competition for desirable posts. People are willing to pay large sums for them, sometimes up to forty times their annual salary (Wade, 1985: 475). Politicians are always in dire need of money, because they need to buy party tickets to be candidates in the next election or otherwise to satisfy their political supporters. So money extraction from contractors or via transfers is essential for them in order to maintain their power base. This corruption-transfer system is, according to Wade, one of the important reasons 'why the Indian state is not better at development' (1985) .

The political conclusion of the neoclassical political economists is often a state-minimalist one: to free the economy of the regulatory system that has so many disadvantages. This is clearly summarized in Colander (1984: 5), who argues that there are two central ideas in this literature: 'rent-seeking occurs primarily through the political process and, second, ... the best way to limit rent-seeking is to limit government' (quoted in Lipton, 1991: 107). Krueger (1974) refrains from any political conclusion. Wade's (1985) suggestions do not go beyond the transfer system and increasing social control of the bureaucracy. But even when a 'rolling back' argument is not made explicitly by the authors, this conclusion can be drawn often by default. In as far as the regulatory system is seen as a problem (this is less so in Wade then in Krueger and the other economists), liberalization and deregulation are the logical answers.

On the other hand, the perspective hardly allows any possibility for decontrol to take place. If self-interest is the main driving force of those in charge of the state and if these people benefit from regulations and controls, there is a deadlock situation. This is indeed acknowledged by some of the rent-seeking theorists. Roy (1984: 67), for instance, points out that:

> ... even a limited liberal agenda (for India) would appear doomed to be still-born. Incumbent politicians, government officials and the public-sector unions

in general would vigorously oppose any reduction in government intervention in the economy for fear of losing the rents and sinecures of the status quo (Quoted in Toye, 1988: 104).

This is not the place to develop an extensive critique of this perspective on the state (see e.g. Bagchi, 1993; Evans, 1992; Lipton, 1991; Pedersen, 1992; Toye, 1987), but two points are worth mentioning. The first relates to the starting assumption of individual optimization and methodological individualism. These are dubious starting points. As Evans (1989: 5) writes:

> ... even the most primitive activity of the state—coercion—requires an apparatus that acts corporatively rather than as a collection of individuals. A protection racket whose trigger-men cut individual deals at the first opportunity does not last very long, and the larger the coercive apparatus involved, the more difficult the problem. Without the existence of a powerful motivational logic to constrain individual behavior in the direction of consistency with collective aims, the state would be unable to perform even its minimal role as an enforcer of contracts. Even the minimal state requires that incumbents redefine individual aims in ways that motivate them to pursue corporate goals.

The second point is that the approach neglects the fact that state intervention is often positively (cor)related to economic growth (Ram, 1986; Wade, 1990). More generally, the approach is better at explaining state failure than state success. From the rent-seeking perspective, it remains mysterious why some states are indeed 'developmental' (Evans, 1992), why sometimes state regulation is successful, or why some states, such as the Indian, have adopted deregulation and liberalization policies when these would weaken the power base of the state incumbents. These things happen. In fact, they are not uncommon, but neoclassical political economics does not offer much help for understanding them.

Erosion of the political system

The second perspective on the Indian state focuses on the nature of Indian democracy and the political system. Much of this literature makes reference to the 'dominant party system', a concept and interpretation developed by the Indian political scientist Rajni Kothari. A 'dominant party system' is a multiparty system with free elections, that is dominated by one political party (Kothari, 1964). In India, this dominant party system or Congress system lasted till 1967 when the Congress party lost power in several States (Manor, 1988).

An essential feature of a 'dominant party system' is that there are various political parties but these play dissimilar roles. During the first fifteen-twenty years after Indian Independence, the chances of opposition parties winning elections were minor. Yet they had some influence because they functioned as pressure groups. By addressing themselves to like-minded groups within the dominant party, opposition between political parties became opposition within the Congress party. This opposition could be effective because the Congress party was flexible enough to respond to these pressures. According to Kothari:

> ... there was a marked tendency towards accommodation by agglomerating various groups and sub-groups into a loose and amorphous organisational structure.... The result was a fragmented and amorphous structure of authority that bred even more fragmented and amorphous Opposition, which were often hard to distinguish from the coalition in power (Kothari, 1988: 26).

The political leaders of the Congress party were committed to democracy and the party organization functioned efficiently, not only in the sense of balancing the various interests, but also as a system of political patronage (Manor, 1988).

This Congress system began to break down in the second half of the 1960s. Not only did the role of opposition parties change after they had succeeded to power in several States, but also the Congress party as an organization began to collapse. Most importantly, intra-party democracy diminished. Decision-making became increasingly centralized, and institutions within Congress began to erode. Indira Gandhi, who had come to power in 1966, her sons and various local leaders, became the personifications of the party and political power.

This institutional decay not only involved the Congress party, but it also affected the other political parties, although the more cadre- and ideology-based Communist parties and the Bharatiya Janata Party (BJP) less than others.

Over the years, the craft of politics has changed. The new generation of politicians who entered into politics in the decades after Independence are in a different mould from the ones who occupied public positions in the first years of independent India. While the latter were often respected because of their participation in the freedom movement, the younger generation is 'chosen because of their primordial ties or their access to the increasing amounts of money needed to fight elections' (Wood, 1984: 12). Politicians have become 'political "contractors" who [are] willing to go to any length to dragoon votes, systematically replacing discursive techniques with money and subtle forms of coercion' (Kaviraj, 1986: 1699).

Political ideology has become less and less important. Since the 1970s elections are single issue referenda, in which the electorate is asked to decide about rhetorical questions, such as whether one wishes to see poverty removed (Kaviraj, 1986: 1702). Political leaders and parties have begun to indulge in populist politics. They make large promises, present themselves as representatives of the poor, and claim that the fate of the deprived and destitute lies safely in their personal hands and in those of the party they represent. In short, their legitimacy as politicians is no longer based on years of self-sacrifice in the nationalist movement or real commitment to democratic values, but they try to establish a new kind of legitimacy that is based on grotesque claims and promises, and that stands or falls with the leader's charisma. Some of these leaders, especially in the southern States, have had previous careers as film stars, where they often played the role of benefactors or semi-gods. In fact, as Dirks (1994) notes, the line between cinema and politics, 'reel and real', has become rather blurred, with politicians playing heroes in movies and staging equally dramatic events in reality.

The result is a serious crisis of governance. According to Manor (1988: 87), the Congress-I organization (but this is true for other political parties as well) was in the first half of the 1980s:

> ... insubstantial, highly corrupt in many regions, wracked with factions that engaged in severe conflicts, unrepresentative of the broad array of social groups for which it claimed to speak, and very inefficient at delivering goods and services to them and at arranging bargains between them. It was very short of idealists, intellectuals, and, most essentially, honest, skilled managers. Those it possessed were often excluded from positions of influence.

While there is considerable consensus among political scientists about the 'dominant party system' and its breakdown, the causes of this erosion are interpreted in different fashions. From a Marxist perspective, Vanaik puts considerable emphasis on the rise of the agrarian bourgeoisie. In the 1950s, when the *Panchayati Raj* system was established and when local bureaucracies were growing, the rural rich had sufficient opportunities to expand their capacities and increase their access to resources. However, by the mid-1960s these avenues were exhausted and this class began to look for alternative structures, pressure groups and political parties (Vanaik, 1990: 83). In a number of States this resulted in violence in the countryside, the rise of opposition parties and defeat of the Congress party. Frankel (1978) also stresses the relevance of agricultural commercialization and the consequent undermining of traditional social relations in the countryside as explanation for political decline, de-institutionalization and instability. The political mobilization of other sections of society, based on caste identities, religious faith, regional background or mother tongue, is another factor mentioned by several political scientists (see contributions in Frankel and Rao, 1990; Kohli, 1988). In part this mobilization is a result of the democratic process itself. Political awakening occurred among large masses of India's voters. According to Manor, voters:

> ... became more assertive and competitive, and their appetites for resources from politicians grew. Interest groups crystallized and came increasingly into conflict, so that it became harder to operate a political machine that could cater to every organized interest, as Congress had very nearly done in the Nehru years. India became increasingly democratic and increasingly difficult to govern (1988: 72).

Yet another type of explanation refers to the characteristics of the political leadership, in particular the centralization of power by Indira Gandhi, and the fact that many policies were ill-adapted 'to India's economic resources, to the basic needs of its people, to its social order, and to the political values of its educated classes' (Brass, 1990: 246).

The solutions proposed by political scientists often stress the necessity of strengthening the relative weight of civil society *vis-à-vis* the state. On the one hand, this means that political mobilization should operate through grassroots movements, voluntary non-governmental organizations, etc. These non-party formations would be able to redefine the content of politics and allow people who do not have access to the conventional political arena to participate in political struggles (Kothari, 1988). On the other hand, shifting the balance between state and civil society implies decentralization of power from the Centre to the States, districts and villages (Brass, 1990; Kothari, 1988). It would also mean reducing state action, withdrawing state intervention from spheres of life where it is not essential. In this respect, the vision comes close to the ideal of the neoclassical political economists. Other political scientists seem to hope that a major cleansing operation will emerge from within the political parties themselves (e.g. Manor, 1988), or stress the structural constraints on political mobilization of the lower classes (Kohli, 1980). None of the political scientists discussed here is overly optimistic. It is generally acknowledged that, in the words of Brass (1990: 336), 'a grave systemic crisis is in progress'.

State professionals as proprietary or political class

The most influential exposition of the idea of state professionals—bureaucrats and technocrats—as a proprietary class was made by the economist Pranab Bardhan. His Radhakrishnan Memorial Lectures, later published as a book (Bardhan, 1984), is a short and wide-ranging piece of work. Bardhan's main concern, as the title of the book indicates, is the political economy of development in India. His book is often referred to, and his ideas about the Indian state and bureaucracy have been influential.[17]

According to Bardhan there are three dominant proprietary classes in India. The recognition of the first two classes, industrial capitalists and rich landowners, is uncontroversial. They have been regarded as the two dominant classes by many political economists before (e.g. Mitra, 1977). But to distinguish a third dominant class was a more novel and original idea. This third class consists of professionals within the state, both civilian and military, including white collar workers in the public sector. The political leadership is not included. In Bardhan's view, there are two reasons to conceive of this category of workers as a class. They share a common resource, 'human capital in the form of education, skills and technical expertise' (Bardhan, 1988: 51). And second, this class holds the state in its possession. The state is used as its private property; it is its material base.[18]

This analysis of three dominant proprietary classes, which form a dominant coalition together, enables a further exploration and understanding of the political economy of India's development, since, according to Bardhan, the conflicts between these dominant classes

[17] In fact, the remark made earlier on the fragmentation of the debate about the nature of the Indian state is less true for Bardhan. His ideas are based, in fact they incorporate, several of the insights of the other three currents of thought. And his work is also taken seriously by people from different schools of thought, (e.g. Brass, 1990; Chakravarty, 1985; Kaviraj, 1986; Vanaik, 1990).

[18] Somewhat in the same vein, Ashok Rudra (1989) has tried to make a case for considering the 'intelligentsia' as a ruling class. In Rudra's account, the intelligentsia is not a proprietary class, as there is no property base, but it is a ruling class, with interests distinct from those of the labouring class. Rudra's third class is broader than Bardhan's, as it also includes politicians, journalists, white collar workers in the organized private sector, doctors, lawyers, engineers, etc. For a discussion, see also Bardhan, 1989 and Béteille, 1989.

'have serious repercussions on the fortunes of economic growth and of the democratic polity' (1988: 54). Bardhan discusses two such conflicts. The first type of conflict is the rural-urban divide. It is a conflict between the agrarian bourgeoisie on the one hand and the industrial and professional classes on the other, and it centres on the issues of prices and the terms of trade between the agricultural and industrial sectors. The second type of conflict is fought between the professional class and the other two classes—in particular the industrial bourgeoisie. Here the issue is the creation and appropriation of bureaucratic rents, arising from foreign exchange regulation, industrial licensing, credit and input rationing, administered prices, etc.

The effect of these conflicts on economic growth is negative. There is a 'proliferation of subsidies and grants to placate [all the three proprietary classes]' (ibid. 1988: 61), as well as a huge government salary bill. As a result less surplus is available for public capital formation and raising productivity. The effects of these conflicts on the political process are rather contradictory. On the one hand, India owes its parliamentary democracy partly to the heterogeneity of the dominant classes. Because all the three classes are sufficiently strong to exert pressures and pulls in different directions, they are served by a democratic framework in which there is a channel for them to voice their demands and in which they are called to order when they overstep the mark (see also Bardhan, 1988). On the other hand, Bardhan notes a crisis of political legitimacy. The lower classes, which are excluded from the important arenas of decision making and which do not share in the benefits of economic growth, are increasingly dissatisfied with this situation.

A somewhat similar perspective is Rudolph and Rudolph's (1987) interpretation of the state as 'third actor'. Third, because private capital and organized labour are usually identified as the two main actors, at least by Marxists writing about the western world. According to Rudolph and Rudolph (1987: 397–8), the Indian state:

> ... not only benefited from historically determined high stateness, legal sovereignty, and cultural orientations (the state as father and mother and as chief patron) but also benefited from its sectoral resources, what in Indian terms is referred to as the economy's 'commanding heights'.
>
> The state could be a third actor in the organized economy partly because its sectoral resources (the state sector) made it in considerable measure self-determining. The possibility of a self-determining state opened up another possibility, the 'state for itself' and raised yet another question: under what conditions and for what reasons would the state, in claiming to be the means for solving problems and achieving goals, itself become the problem?

The state as 'third actor' created, as the Rudolphs assert, a political class, consisting of public sector employees and managers, petty and high-level officials, professionals and elected politicians. These categories of people form a class as they share the ownership or control of state property, resources and authority (ibid.: 1987: 62).[19]

Both Bardhan (1984) and Rudolph and Rudolph (1987) do not elaborate on how the perceived problems (such as retarded economic growth and the state as self-serving interest group) could possibly be overcome. Despite their critique both are ambivalent about the role of the state. Rudolph and Rudolph expect the state to remain a third actor, which is not a wholly positive description. On the other hand, they credit the Indian state with contributing to 'pluralist politics'. Bardhan is critical of the state in so far as he describes the rent-seeking characteristics of the third class, but he also acknowledges the positive contribution of the Indian state to economic growth. So the implication of the analyses of these authors is certainly not an anti-state pro-market strategy, but what it is remains unclear.[20]

[19] While both Bardhan and the Rudolphs acknowledge the class-like character of the state, their interpretation differs as far as other agents are concerned. In Bardhan's view there are two other dominant proprietary classes. The Rudolphs, on the other hand, defend the irrelevance of class in Indian politics and economy, (e.g. Rudolph and Rudolph, 1987: 19–35). The key to understanding Indian politics, in their view, is pluralism of interest groups, such as those based on caste, religious and language communities, and regional nationalisms (1987: 396). The marginality of class is apparent, according to the Rudolphs, from the fact that centrism is such a characteristic feature of Indian politics. Neither organized labour nor industrial capital have been capable of challenging the centrist ideology and politics.

The Rudolphs' critique of the concept of class, and Marxism generally, is not very convincing. They criticize a simple class model (industrial bourgeoisie versus labour class), while almost all Marxists writing about India have argued that the Indian class structure is more complicated: at the minimum the agricultural bourgeoisie should be included. The Rudolphs' type of argument is basically empiricist: classes are not clearly visible as such and, hence, not important. (Why the state is referred to as the 'third actor' when the other two would hardly exist is also puzzling.) Moreover, the Rudolphs do not succeed in formulating an alternative to class. The 'demand groups' they pay most attention to are the industrial workers and the agricultural 'bullock capitalists'. Both are essentially described in terms of relations of production. So although the Rudolphs claim that social formations based on caste, religion, language and region are more important than class for the way people define their own interests, they do not give much weight to these formations when they discuss 'demand groups'. See also Byres (1988) for a critique and Rudolph and Rudolph (1988) for a defence.

[20] In 1991, Bardhan argued along the same lines as, e.g. Kothari, against the all-pervasiveness of the state and in favour of decentralized autonomous development.

The nature of development planning

The last perspective on the Indian state discussed here is concerned primarily with development planning: what has been its origins, what are the problems, strengths and weaknesses. Because the state is the central actor in planned economic development, this body of literature reviews and evaluates implicitly or explicitly the characteristics, capacities, activities and motivations of the state. Although much of the literature is fairly critical of the achievements of planning, the general thrust of the argument is not anti-state or anti-planning.

The real challenge, it is stated, it to make planning more effective (e.g. Chakravarty, 1987). Further, even when planning and state intervention are inefficient in economic terms, they may well be socially or politically efficient in the sense that they reduce economic inequality and social conflict (Baru, 1994: 532).

After Independence,[21] there was a general feeling among the political elite that planning was the best way to overcome structural constraints to development and to transform Indian society into a modern one. The idea was that India was a poor and technologically backward country as compared to Europe and North America. The economy had been stagnant over the period 1900–50. Nevertheless, India was seen as:

> ... possessing natural resources and human skills capable of ensuring that within a space of perhaps twenty five years it could develop and diversify its economic structure in the same way as the West had achieved since the mid-nineteenth century. The main barrier to be overcome was the lack of capital stock both in quantity and quality; so the development process would require the formation of adequate savings for rapid growth of investment. ... the driving force in this process of forced savings and accelerated growth had to be the newly independent Indian state, through the instrumentality of a freely elected government representing the interests of all citizens (Mozoomdar, 1994: 74–5).

The National Planning Committee, established in 1950 by the Congress Party of India, subscribed to a '*profoundly interventionist economic philosophy*' (Chakravarty, 1987: 9).

This strong faith in planning and state intervention is located by several authors in the legacy of colonialism: de-industrialization and drain of surplus from India to Britain:

> The Indian economy as an open market for British manufacturers and a source

[21] 'Planning for planning' (Chatterjee, 1994) had started already before Indian Independence. In 1938, the Congress Ministries formed a National Planning Committee with Nehru as Chairman.

of unilateral transfers suffered structural deformation, of which mass pauperisation and unemployment, and falling consumption per head of basic staples, were blatant manifestations. We inherited an unemployment problem of unprecedented dimensions (Patnaik, 1994: 271).

Against this background it was realized that 'the unrestricted operation of market forces and openness of the economy in an ex-colonial country, given a world still dominated by predatory international capital, would only perpetuate industrial backwardness' (U. Patnaik, quoted by Baru, 1994: 530). Economic planning and state intervention became crucial elements of post-colonial development.

It is not within the purview of this short review to discuss the various interpretations of the successes and failures of Indian planning (see Chakravarty, 1987; and contributions in Byres,1994). But what is worth noting is that most evaluations compare 'plans on paper' with implementation, 'planning in theory' with 'planning in practice', plan formulations with plan outcomes, (e.g. Chakravarty, 1987; Mozoomdar, 1994). In effect, this means the official claims of the state form the starting point of the analysis. The plans on paper define the research question: to what extent have the planning goals been achieved. In short, the perspective of the researcher is that of the state.

What this implies for the conceptualization of the Indian state is that the self-image of the state, i.e. of the planners, is taken over by the researchers. Despite the critique and the evaluation of planning failures, the idea of the developmental state is upheld: a state that fosters long-term developmental perspectives. Perhaps not always, perhaps not in the most efficient way, perhaps with some diversions, but yet, on balance, the state is held capable of promoting economic growth, reducing inequality and working towards other developmental goals (see Evans, 1992; White, 1988 about developmental states).

In addition to the political economists referred to so far who are concerned with *economic* planning, there are others whose main object of study is *social* policy and the role of the Indian state in *social* development. Examples are Drèze and Sen (1995) and Mundle (1994). These authors too combine a critical evaluation of the Indian state with some faith in the possibility (and conviction of the necessity) of the developmental state. The state should withdraw, it is argued by these authors, from the economic sphere, but expand its activities in the social sphere.

So what is characteristic about this fourth approach is that, despite the critique, it is argued that the state has an important role to play, if not in economic, then certainly in social development.

2.4 FOOD POLICY AND POLITICS

So here are four different approaches to the Indian state, focusing sometimes on somewhat different aspects of the state or interpreting the same phenomena in different fashions. They all give tools and ideas for an understanding of state activities: how and why policies emerge, and how they work out in reality. Each perspective gives rise to a specific set of expectations concerning the evolution, process of implementation and spread of benefits as a result of state policies. The focus of this book is food distribution policy. I have earlier discussed the special character of food. Food is essential for human survival. It is also an economic and a political commodity. We may, hence, assume that food distribution policy matters, that it is not just a marginal arbitrary appendix to overall state activities and policies. What food policy is and does, is in one way or another related to the nature of the state generally. Thus given the above descriptions of the Indian state and political process, what can we expect of food distribution policy? Why does it exist (in the form it has) and how does it work out?

From a rent-seeking perspective the policy and practice of food distribution is to be understood as a result of the individual interests of those involved. The purpose is to maximize status, influence, popularity or income of those who devise or implement food distribution. Redistributive objectives and anti-trader ideologies, which suggest that the state has a corporate goal that exceeds and may even contradict the private interests of the individuals working within the state, function as a cover or cover up for the self-interest of those in charge of food distribution, and bear no necessary relationship to actual policy practices.

Food distribution, we can hypothesize, can serve various purposes. It can be used to buy political support. Politicians may try to enhance their popularity by distributing food or introducing price regimes favourable to constituents they want to woo. Moreover, food subsidies create an opportunity to earn an extra, rental, income. It is likely that this opportunity will be used by all who are in a position to do so. Hence we can expect competition to be there for the posts from which food is distributed: wholesale and retail dealers, positions within the Food and/or Civil Supplies department or corporation.

It is to be expected that those who profit from food distribution policies do their best to perpetuate and consolidate the system. Their interest is not only to enlarge it, but also to render it ineffective (in terms of the official objectives). This is so because as soon as food security increases, the marginal utility of each quantity of food, in terms of rent, power and influence that could be derived from it, diminishes.

The second perspective, focusing on the institutional erosion of politics, gives rise to a slightly different set of expectations. Reasoning from this perspective we could hypothesize that the political relevance or function of food distribution changed when the dominant party system broke down, and when the deinstitutionalization of Indian politics took hold. Food distribution has always had a political function, one can hypothesize but while this function had to do with strategic long-term political projects during the first phase, arbitrariness and opportunism dominate the political use of food distribution in the period afterwards. We would expect food programmes to be easily promised by opportunistic politicians who want to enlarge their support base. Sometimes these promises will be fulfilled, but not necessarily so.

In contrast to the first perspective, this second perspective draws attention to the role played by non-state agents. In line with Vanaik's and Frankel's contention that the rise of the rural bourgeoisie contributed to the breakdown of Congress supremacy, one can expect that rich farmers will have tried to influence food distribution policy to their advantage. Wheat and rice farmers in particular have an immediate interest in procurement prices. We could expect a shift in food price policy in the second half of the 1960s when the agrarian bourgeoisie became a dominant political force. In addition the perspective highlights the awakening of the electorate. The notion that parties and political leaders should perform, that they should do something for and respond to the people they claim to represent, became stronger. When voters become more assertive and demanding, we may expect that they also demand food at reasonable prices. We can also expect that politicians who make large promises without any follow-up will not succeed in getting away with it. Continuation of office requires performance. So when large promises are made, they either have to be fulfilled to some extent, or a change of government is likely.

As compared to the second approach, the third one gives even more weight to activities of non-state actors to explain state policies and practices. Reasoning from this perspective, we would expect PDS to be the result of a compromise between the major contending categories of people in society. In Bardhan's view these would be the three dominant proprietary classes: industrial and rural bourgeoisie and state professionals. All these three classes have an interest in food distribution policy. Industrial capitalists have an interest in price stabilization and a low level of food prices, as this would forestall labour unrest and demands for higher wages. The interest of agrarian capitalists is the procurement price, which not only determines their income when they sell their produce directly to the government, but also affects the general level of off-farm prices. For state professionals the volume of food is of prime importance. The more food they distribute, the better, because command over food gives them influence and power. Similarly the more rules and regulations, the better, because this enhances their discretionary powers.

The Rudolphs' theory gives rise to almost the same expectation, except for the industrial capitalists' part. We can expect that two demand groups will try to force their will upon food distribution policy: agrarian producers fighting for remunerative prices and industrial labour demanding low consumer prices.[22] In addition to these demand groups there is the 'third actor', the relatively autonomous and self-interested state, whose main interest is to keep and expand its resources, in this case food and discretionary powers.

It is obvious that the interests of the various classes or demand groups in food distribution not only differ, but also conflict. Hence we can expect that difficulties in combining the various interests will arise. If all the demands have to be fulfilled to some extent, PDS will be an expensive undertaking, as the treasury will have to fill the gap between high procurement prices and low consumer prices.

As far as day-to-day implementation practices are concerned, the third perspective gives rise to similar expectations as the first. Implementation is dominated by self-interested civil servants. Those who are in a position to earn a rental income through the distribution of food, licences, permits, etc. will probably not renounce this possibility.

While self-interest and political opportunism are the overarching driving forces behind the emergence of state policies if we are to

[22] The Rudolphs discern a third demand group: students. As the demands of this group are mainly concerned with university politics and employment possibilities, it is unlikely that this demand group would affect the development of food distribution policy.

believe the first three approaches, the last approach puts more emphasis on long-term economic development efforts and strategies to solve poverty and inequality. Food distribution policy, we can hypothesize, is part of an overall attempt of the state to develop the Indian economy. It is a constituent building block of a wider, more encompassing, developmental plan. At the same time, it has its own objectives and rationale: to improve food security at the macro-and micro-levels.

State policies and practices, according to this perspective, are not the sum of individual attempts to optimize private interests. Rather, the state acts as a corporate unity. To a certain extent, individuals working within the state make their private interests subordinate to the proclaimed developmental activities of the state. In the day-to-day practices of implementation of food distribution, state employees are, to a certain extent, faithful to the official claims and objectives, and try to realize them. Hence it is possible that food distribution policy works reasonably well. The main obstructions, if any, may well come from categories of people outside the state. It is, of course, also possible that the state itself fails, but according to this perspective there is no *a priori* reason to assume that this will happen: that food is diverted to the black market by those in charge, or that various rules and regulations are primarily used to make a rental income. The state could well be developmental.

The rest of this book is an empirical investigation of this white line relationship between food policy, the state and politics in India. The concepts and perspectives discussed in this chapter (rent-seeking, erosion of the political process, state as class and developmental state) function as spotlights or heuristic devices in the following chapters. It is not my intention to systematically test the various hypotheses and expectations presented here, but the accounts and interpretations that follow do corroborate some expectations and falsify others. In the concluding chapter, I come back to the characterization of the Indian state. I will argue that no simple characterization holds, as there is diversity in normative structures, as well as in practices. Or more concretely and in terms of the theories outlined here, the Indian state is both rent-seeking and developmental.

3

The Public Distribution System
A historical interpretation

> The methods of counteracting the effects of famine are: distribute to the public, on concessional terms, seeds and food from the royal stores; undertake food-for-work programmes such as building forts or irrigation works; share out the royal food stocks; commandeer for public distribution private stocks of food; seek the help of friendly kings; shift the affected population to a different region; encourage [temporary] migration to another country; move the entire population [with the King and Court] to a region or country with abundant harvest or near the sea, lakes or rivers; supplement the harvest with additional cultivation of grain, vegetables, roots and fruits, by fishing and by hunting deer, cattle, birds and wild animals.
> (4.3.17–20 from Kautilya's *Arthashastra*, original in Sanskrit, written between 320 BC and AD 150; Edited, rearranged and translated by L.N. Rangarajan, Penguin Books, 1992)

As argued in the previous chapter, food is not only a nutritional, but also an economic and a political commodity. One of the implications of this statement is that governments that develop food policies can have official or hidden agendas in all these three fields: to eliminate malnutrition, to contribute to economic re-distribution and to support particular categories of people or political projects. The present chapter is a historical interpretation of the PDS. The aim is *(a)* to describe the most important features of the PDS in the various phases of its history, *(b)* to analyse the social processes that led to the emergence and subsequent development of distribution policy, and *(c)* to describe the various functions the PDS has served in the course of its history. Section 3.1 describes the emergence of the PDS between 1939 and 1965. Section 3.2 describes the period between 1965 and 1990, while Section 3.3 discusses the most recent period after 1991. In Section 3.4 are summarized the most important trends. Although this chapter focuses primarily on India as a whole, the situations in Karnataka and Kerala are highlighted in Section 3.2, not only because the rest of this book is about these two States, but also in order to illustrate some important trends that took place in this period at the level of individual States.[1]

3.1 THE EMERGENCE OF PDS, 1939–1965

The public food distribution system in India did not emerge at a stroke. It evolved over a long period lasting approximately twenty-five years: from 1939 to 1965. In the course of this quarter of a century, several times the system was virtually abolished and then revived a few years later. The year 1939 marks the start of the rationing system; the British government in India introduced foodgrain rationing, first in Bombay and later in other cities. The year 1965 marks the establishment of the Food Corporation of India and the Agricultural Prices Committee (later renamed Commission for Agricultural Costs and Prices). By that date the PDS stood on a firm footing.

The war and aftermath

Before 1939 there was no experience in India of government food rationing, nor of other forms of food control. Since the adoption of a *laissez-faire* policy in 1861, the Government of India had refrained from interference with trade and prices of foodgrains (Bhatia, 1991: 331). The Famine Codes, published in 1883 by provincial governments with the aim of laying down procedures to be followed in case of famine, did not deal with issues related to market intervention. They mainly discussed famine relief measures in the form of employment generation (Bhatia, 1991: 184–9). Thus as far as India is concerned, the idea of rationing was a novel one. In Europe, however, experiences in World War I had made clear the importance of an efficient rationing system. In Holland, preparations in case a second world war should break out, began as early as 1934 (Trienekens, 1987). Also in Britain the government started early preparations, with good results (Fenelon, 1952). So it is probable that rationing in India was partly based on the European model of how to cope with food crises in emergency situations.[2]

[1] For descriptions of the history of food policy at the all-India level, this chapter relies heavily on Bhatia (1991), Chopra (1988) and Dandekar (1994).

[2] However, it is important to emphasize that there were also substantial differences between rationing in India and in Europe. One crucial difference was the restriction of rationing in India to urban centres, while in Britain, in principle, food policy included the whole population.

And a food crisis there certainly was. On the eve of World War II, India's food situation was very delicate. During the forty years preceding the War, annual per capita food production had steadily declined from 254 kg (annual average in the decade from 1906–7 to 1915–16) to 181 kg (annual average in the 1936–7 to 1945–6 decade) (Bhatia, 1991: 315). Imports, especially rice imports from Burma, made up for the difference between domestic production and effective demand. The average level of consumption was very low. When the War started, scarcity soon became an important fact. The demand for foodgrains for the armed forces increased, prices rose due to speculation and hoarding, and after the fall of Burma in April 1942 imports from Burma stopped. The worst affected area was Bengal, where food entitlement failures caused a famine killing between 1.5 and 3 million people in 1943 (Sen, 1981: 52–85).[3] Also other parts of India were affected, though to a lesser extent.

There are two crucial periods in the emergence of public food distribution in India: the first between 1940 and 1943, the second between 1957 and 1965. After the outbreak of World War II, the Government of India's initial worry, as far as food matters were concerned was related to prices, especially wheat prices. Between 1939 and 1942, a number of Price Control Conferences took place. The first scheme for centralized purchase of foodgrains was discussed by the sixth Price Control Conference in September 1942. By that time, it had become very difficult to secure enough food in the deficit areas. The war had caused serious dislocations of foodgrains. During this conference the basic principles of a public distribution system were laid down: a central government organization that would make its purchases in surplus provinces, allocation of the supplies to deficit provinces, and distribution through fair price shops and cooperative societies in industrial areas and big cities. In December 1942, a separate Food Department was set up. In 1943 this department formulated an All-India Basic Plan that gave further shape to the developing food

[3] The Bengal famine of 1943 has been the subject of much scholarly research (e.g. Greenough, 1982; Sen, 1981). The interpretation of this famine in terms of a failure of (exchange) entitlements, rather than a decline in food availability, was put forward by Sen (1981). Put simply, the argument is that the Bengal famine was not a reflection of an overall shortage of foodgrains in Bengal. Instead, Sen shows that the whole of Bengal's population was not affected in the same way, but that specific categories of people suffered from starvation due to failing entitlement. For critiques and discussions of Sen's theory of famines, see e.g. Bowbrick (1986), Nolan (1993), Patnaik (1991) and de Waal (1990), and for replies see, e.g. Sen (1986, 1993).

policy. The Basic Plan included issues such as procurement, contracts for purchasing agents, distribution of supplies received under the scheme, inspection, storage, finance and district administration (Chopra, 1988: 33), all meant to keep down prices. Price stabilization, we can conclude, was the principal objective of food the emerging distribution policy.[4]

Inflation was high during these years and pushed up grain prices. The food situation was deteriorating not only in Bengal, but also in other places such as Bombay and Travancore-Cochin. The Foodgrains Policy Committee in 1943 recommended the introduction of rationing in urban centres with more than 100,000 inhabitants, a minimum ration of 1lb of cereals (about 1600 kcal.) per capita per day even if imports would be needed, and the establishment of a proper procurement machinery.

To give an example of rationing in this period: Calcutta, the major city in Bengal, was reasonably protected by subsidized distribution schemes when the famine of 1942–3 claimed a death toll of between 1.5 and 3 million people. To quote Sen:

> The official policy was based on the firm conviction that 'the maintenance of essential food supplies to the industrial area of Calcutta must be ranked on a very high priority among their [the government's] war time obligations', and as early as August 1942 the Bengal government had explained to the Bengal Chamber of Commerce that as far as Calcutta was concerned the government promised to do "all in their power to create conditions under which essential supplies may be obtainable in adequate quantities at reasonable prices" (Famine Inquiry Commission, GoI, 1945: 30).... [Several schemes were set up.] These schemes guaranteed freedom from starvation to more than a million employees and their dependents. In addition, 'controlled shops' were started in Calcutta in August and September 1942, supplemented in 1943 by a scheme of 'approved markets' by which government stocks were made available to selected private shops for sale to the public. The government helped to feed Calcutta.... Calcutta saw the famine mainly in the form of masses of rural destitutes, who trekked from the districts into the city.... [R]elief offered to them was quite inadequate... (1981: 56–7).

[4] In addition to food distribution, the Government of India also took steps to increase foodgrain production. Between 1942 and 1951, several measures were introduced as part of the Grow More Food Campaign. Among other things, these measures involved minor irrigation works, distribution of fertilizer and seeds, and land reclamation. All in all, the results of this campaign lagged behind the expectations (Chopra, 1988: 67–75).

Thus food distribution was exclusively focused on the urban centre and urban residents. The colonial government failed to take necessary action in rural Bengal. It is telling that 'the famine was even never "declared" as a famine, which would have brought in an obligation to organize work programmes or relief operations specified by the "Famine Code"' (Sen, 1981: 79).[5] The British Raj was obviously much more concerned with the military, civil defence works and strategic industries located in Calcutta than with agricultural labourers, fishermen, transport workers and others who were among the most affected groups.

After the end of the War these policies of distribution and procurement were continued for some time. The food situation was still seen as precarious by the government; production was insufficient, Grow More Food efforts were not successful and food scarcity was far from imaginary. The situation became only more difficult after Independence and Partition. Independent India got 82 per cent of the total population of the subcontinent, 75 per cent of the cereal production, and 69 per cent of the irrigated area (Chopra, 1988: 61). The second Foodgrains Policy Committee, appointed in 1947, recommended increasing domestic production within the shortest possible time, gradually reducing dependency on imports, gradually abolishing commitments towards consumers and creating a buffer stock. However, before the Government of India could accept or reject these recommendations, the influence of Mahatma Gandhi had overridden all others. He argued forcefully in favour of decontrol and convinced the policy makers as well.[6] In December 1947, a policy of decontrol was announced. This policy was shortlived; in September 1948 the government reintroduced a food policy based on control over prices, procurement and distribution of major foodgrains (Chopra, 1988: 61–7).

Doubts regarding the necessity and desirability of food controls persisted. In 1952–4 decontrol was again introduced, though this time in a less hasty manner. Movement restrictions were relaxed,

[5] Drèze and Sen (1989: 212, n 30) recount that it was a deliberate decision of the government not to invoke the Famine Code, in order to 'avoid the obligation to undertake the relief measures mandated by the ... Code'.

[6] Controls, according to Gandhi, 'give rise to fraud, suppression of truth, intensification of the black market and to artificial scarcity. Above all it [they] unmans the people and deprives them of initiative; it undoes the teachings of self help, they have been learning for generations, makes them spoonfed' (quoted in Chopra, 1988: 67).

procurement was virtually stopped, and by the end of 1954 rationing was very much reduced (see Table 1 in Appendix 1). This was a period of optimism. Agricultural production in India was high in these years. Imports of foodgrains fell from 4.7 million tonnes in 1951 to 0.8 million tonnes in 1954. It was thought that India was nearing self-sufficiency and that government intervention and control could slowly be broken down (Chopra, 1988: 84–106). But in 1955, food problems arose again. The weather was poor and the earlier low foodgrain prices had had an adverse effect on production. In 1957, the demand for foodgrains was outstripping supply. Distortions of the free market became increasingly evident. In 1957, the Government of India again reversed food policy and reintroduced controls (ibid:103–4).

From 1957 onwards: anchoring of PDS

The second crucial period in the history of the PDS was between 1957 and 1965, when a clear-cut policy took shape. The Foodgrains Enquiry Committee 1957 observed that in retrospect 'the total dismantling of controls appears to have been a hasty step, particularly inasmuch as Government failed to take the opportunity to build up buffer stocks as prices fell' (Ashok Mehta Committee Report, 1957: 50). The Committee stated that complete free trade was undesirable, since it tended to increase price fluctuations. Similarly full control, in the sense of complete rationing and procurement, seemed undesirable as the government responsibility would become too large to carry (ibid.: 75). Accordingly, the Committee argued in favour of controls of a flexible indirect nature, although, in the long run, socialization of wholesale trade was recommended (ibid.: 86). In the short term it suggested opening more fair price shops—where food is sold to consumers at a 'fair price'—and continuing zonal policy. The idea behind this latter policy was to create more or less self-sufficient zones. Deficit areas and surplus areas were brought together within zones, and the transport of foodgrains in or out of these zones was controlled. The purpose of this zonal policy was to stabilize prices within each zone.

An increasingly important objective of food policy became distribution to the 'poorer sections' of the population. While sales from fair price shops should normally be made on a 'no profit no loss' basis (ibid.: 97), an exception was made for people in distress for whom even the normal fair price would be too high. This second objective of PDS—that is to help the weaker sections of society—would gain prominence in the years to come.

The expansion of the PDS in the period 1957–65, both in terms of food distributed and number of shops, was greatly facilitated by large-scale imports under US Public Law-480 (PL-480) conditions. India imported cheap wheat from the USA, partly as a gift and partly to be paid for in local currency. These rupees were put into a fund that could be utilized for development purposes. For the USA, PL-480 was a way to dispose of its wheat surplus and to support US domestic farm prices. At the same time PL-480 was important in US foreign policy (see also Friedmann, 1982), providing a powerful means to impose the US will on India. Several times, the apparent charity was used as leverage upon the Indian state (Bhatia, 1991: 353–9; Byres and Crow, 1983: 27). Grain was withheld till the last minute, and India, desperate for food imports, accepted harsh conditions. Byres and Crow mention that:

> ... among other things, India agreed to the following: that for seven years the government should no longer have control over the pricing and distribution of fertilizers by private fertilizer firms; that the Indian government should drop its demand for fifty-one per cent ownership of joint ventures in the fertilizer field; that greater latitude be allowed to American private firms operating in India; that India should stop trading with North Vietnam. Apart from this, India's devaluation of the rupee by 36.5 per cent on 6 June 1966 was strongly influenced by American pressure (1983: 27 n 1).

In the period 1958–66, India imported nearly 50 million tonnes of foodgrains, most of it under PL-480 conditions. In the peak year 1966, India imported more than 10 million tonnes, which was about 14 per cent of the total amount of foodgrains available in the country. It is doubtful that India needed this large amount of foreign cereals, and it may even be argued that these massive imports were counter-productive. The crisis in domestic production that became clear in 1964–6 may well have been partly induced by the glut of cheap foodgrains in the Indian market (Bhatia, 1991: 350).

Due to these imports, foodgrains were relatively cheap in this period. According to Mundle (1981: 135–66), there was a specific price regime during these years in which the equilibrium price itself was reduced to a lower level due to extra, imported supplies. The result of this policy was that 'the government successfully blocked a potential shift of the terms of trade in favour of agriculture during this period' (Mundle, 1991: 149).

That the Indian government was eager to keep prices down and to favour industry over agriculture is not surprising. It is in keeping with the general development strategy of that period. The Second and Third Plans (1955–65) specially emphasized the building of a modern industrial sector. In these Plans food policy was predominantly regarded as a means to contain price rises and inflation. The Second Plan, for instance, argues for imports and market control, as 'high or rising prices of primary necessities are apt to create serious difficulties... [that could disturb the entire plan]' (GoI, 1956: 39). In this period, the PDS supported the industrial labour class, the industrial capitalist class, and the urban-based politically important middle classes. With the help of cheap food and the expansion of a distribution system the Government of India succeeded, as Chakravarty says, 'in maintaining a low rate of price increase (around 2.5 per cent per annum), which helped to maintain a sort of social equilibrium in the urban areas' (1987: 22).

The Foodgrains Prices Committee, set up in 1964, marks the next crucial step in the establishment of the public distribution system. The Committee recommended the setting up of the Food Corporation of India 'which will enable the government to undertake trading operations through which it can influence the market prices' (Report of the Jha Committee on Foodgrains Prices for 1964–5, quoted in Chopra, 1988: 320). Furthermore, the Foodgrains Prices Committee welcomed the constitution of an Agricultural Prices Committee to advise the Government of India 'on a continuous basis, on agricultural price policy and price structure in the context of the need to raise agricultural production' (Jha Committee Report quoted in Chopra, 1988: 214). Minimum support prices would be recommended by the Committee.

In this period, food policy in India acquired its third objective: to guarantee reasonable prices to the farmers and thereby act as an incentive to increase production. In Mundle's terms, a new price regime emerged, in which the equilibrium prices were considered too low by the government. The objective of food policy now became to raise the level of the equilibrium price itself. '[While] earlier the thrust of policy was towards preventing agricultural prices from rising, [now] the emphasis was on establishing price levels which would act as an incentive to domestic production' (Mundle, 1981: 153; see also Bharadwaj, 1994).[7] PDS supplies changed from imported to domestic foodgrains, while procurement prices were fixed at an attractive level.

[7] Agricultural price policy was not the only measure introduced to increase domestic production. Soon after 1965 the Green Revolution—with new seeds, fertilizer, irrigation and credit—took off from 1967–8.

This shift in foodgrain price policy had a lot to do with the desire to become self-sufficient in foodgrains. In view of the political conditions that accompanied US wheat, and India's desire to protect its national sovereignty, it is not surprising that stepping up domestic production was put high on the agenda.[8] Simultaneously, this policy shift was strongly stimulated by the United States. In the 1960s, advisors of the Ford Foundation were very critical of India's food and agricultural policy. Together with American experts they argued that the food problem could be solved through the application of modern technology, supported by large investments in modern inputs and price incentives to farmers. According to Frankel (1978: 275), foreign experts enjoyed a 'maximum influence on the thinking of the agriculture minister' in these years. At the same time, the political power of farmers themselves had also gained considerable momentum. By the 1960s, agricultural lobbies had started to influence politics in several States.[9] The introduction of a much more conscious producer price policy was a move to accommodate this increasingly powerful class of wealthy agriculturalists (cf. Mitra, 1977; Varshney, 1993).

In sum, the important features of the development of the PDS in India during the first quarter of a century have been the following. Up to 1957 there was no long-term food strategy. The PDS was virtually abolished twice to be re-established a few years later. From 1957, a consistent price and import regime was introduced with the objective of keeping foodgrain prices down. This policy changed in 1964–5.

[8] As early as in 1951, Nehru had argued in a broadcast: 'We have sought help from abroad ... and we shall continue to do so under pressure of necessity, but the conviction is growing upon me more forcefully than ever how dangerous it is for us to depend for this primary necessity of life on foreign countries. We can never function, with the freedom that we desire, if we are always dependent in this matter on others. It is only when we obtain self-sufficiency in food that we can progress and develop ourselves. Otherwise there is the continuous pressure of circumstances, there is trouble and misery, and there is sometimes shame and humiliation' (quoted in Bhatia, 1991: 345–6).

[9] Not only in the separate States but also at the level of the Union state, farmers became increasingly dominant in politics. 'While the ratio of representation of agricultural to business and industrial interests was 2:1 in favour of the agriculturalists in the first Lok Sabha in 1951, it increased steadily to 3:1 in the second (1957), 4:1 in 1976 as the Green Revolution was gaining momentum, 5:1 in 1971, and 9:1 in 1977 under the Janata government. It returned to 4:1 in 1980 as the Congress Party boosted the representation of business and industry under the influence of the late Sanjay Gandhi .... [T]he large farmers' interests gained control of the Agricultural Prices Commission to the exclusion of representation of consumers' interests' (De Janvry and Subbarao, 1986: 96). See also Varshney (1993) on the increasing importance of rural interests in the Indian polity.

Imports gradually stopped; the government started to fix minimum prices in order to support domestic agriculture (Mundle, 1981: 135–80).

Simultaneously in this process, the objectives of food policy widened. Initially, food policy was seen primarily as a means to tackle food emergency situations through price stabilization. After 1957, the idea of providing food at reasonable prices to the poor began to take hold. From 1964–5 onwards, protection of farmers' income and thereby stimulating agricultural production became a third policy objective.

In these first twenty-six years of the history of the PDS, food distribution was strategically employed by the government in a number of political and economic projects. First, in the War period, food was distributed in important urban centres such as Calcutta, where strategic industries, the central and provincial governments, and defence works were located. For the masses of rural destitutes hardly anything was done. Second, in the 1957–65 period, food distribution, which was concentrated entirely in urban centres, contributed to economic growth and political stability. It was part of a low-wage policy meant to support industrial growth, if necessary at the expense of agriculture. In this way, government food policy corresponded with the demands of the industrial sector, as it functioned as an indirect subsidy and forestalled industrial/urban unrest. Third, with the rise of political activism of capitalist farmers, the interests of this class were also incorporated in government food policy, and a more producer friendly price regime took shape.

In addition to these three ways in which the Indian government used food (distribution) as a political resource, the historical review also illustrates that food served as a political commodity for the United States. In several instances, the United States withheld shiploads of foodgrains in order to lend additional weight to their political demands. Food obviously served as a resource, perhaps even as a weapon, in political negotiations between India and the US.

3.2 FOOD POLICY 1965–1990: CONSOLIDATION AND THE EMERGENCE OF SPECIAL PROGRAMMES

During the next quarter of a century the public food distribution system gradually expanded. The total amount of foodgrains handled by the

FCI increased from 10 million tonnes per annum in 1965 to more than 18 million tonnes per annum at the end of the 1980s. In the same period the number of ration shops tripled. By the end of the 1980s, there were more than 350,000 ration outlets. The system also became more and more costly. In 1965, there was hardly any subsidy involved, while twenty-five years later the subsidy given by the Central government fluctuated around 25,000–28,000 million rupees (See Appendix 1, Table 1).

Apart from this quantitative enlargement, the system also expanded in qualitative ways. In the 1970s and 1980s, the PDS ruralized considerably. At the end of the 1980s, approximately 75 per cent of the ration shops were located in rural areas (GoI, *Economic Survey 1991–92*: 53). More than 70 per cent of PDS rice and more than 55 per cent of PDS wheat was sold in rural areas (NSS, 42nd round 1986–7).[10] Moreover, the number of special schemes through which food is distributed increased over the years. Examples are the Food for Work programme and Noon-Meal schemes. These schemes have introduced an element of targeting within public distribution policy. While the PDS is basically a universal programme, these special schemes aim to guarantee that part of the foodgrains reach the most needy people.

It is difficult to estimate the percentage of PDS foodgrains allocated to these special schemes, as most of them are organized at the level of individual States. My guess is that the percentage would be fairly high. The centrally organized Integrated Tribal Development Project (ITDP) distributed 1.88 million tonnes in 1990–1 (GoI, *Economic Survey 1991–92*: 54), which is about 10 per cent of the total PDS. Also special programmes organized in the States consume a substantial part of PDS foodgrains. The Green Card Scheme in Karnataka, meant for the rural poor, took 42 per cent of total PDS foodgrains in 1990–1.[11]

In the first chapter, I have summarized the major successes and failures of the PDS, but I will briefly recapitulate them here. (See also Bhalla, 1994; Tyagi, 1990.) There have been no large-scale famines in independent India, despite the occurrence of severe droughts. Moreover, physical and economic access to food has increased. On the other hand, the PDS has not eradicated persistent hunger and malnutrition. Furthermore, the system did not succeed in assuring reasonable prices to coarse grain producers. The system has

[10] But it may be that 'rural area' also includes local towns. The NSS reports do not clearly define the terms 'urban' and 'rural'.

[11] *Annual Report 1990-91*, Food and Civil Supplies Department, Government of Karnataka.

concentrated on rice and wheat, and hence on the relatively well-off farmers. Thus, Tyagi concludes, 'the food policy has not succeeded in protecting the interests of the most vulnerable sections of the population whether amongst the consumers or amongst the producers' (1990: 220).[12] In addition, in the mid-1990s, the PDS suffers from financial unsustainability combined with decreasing interest on the part of consumers. I will come back to this latter point in Section 3.3.

Food policy at the Central level remained more or less constant during this period while State governments took several initiatives. Therefore, in order to study the social construction of food policy between 1965 and 1990 in more detail, it is necessary to shift our focus now to the level of individual States. Karnataka and Kerala are taken as two examples.

Food policy in Karnataka: the Green Card Scheme

Until the 1980s food policy did not play an important role in Karnataka politics.[13] As in most parts of India, food distribution concentrated on towns. This changed, however, in 1985 with the Green Card Scheme.

In the 1983 elections, Congress (I) was defeated for the first time in Karnataka, and a Janata minority government was formed with Ramakrishna Hegde as Chief Minister. In 1985, a new election was held, and this time Janata got the majority of votes. Hegde would eventually stay in power till 1988. A short time before the 1985 election, the Janata government announced the introduction of a new food scheme in Karnataka, later known as the Green Card Scheme.

[12] It would require too much space here to discuss in detail to what extent foodgrain price policy and government procurement has supported the wheat and rice growing farmers. Mitra (1977) asserts that farmers have benefited considerably from these policies. Others like Kahlon and Tyagi (1980) have argued that the terms of trade have developed against agriculture. De Janvry and Subbarao (1986) review the debate and criticize the instruments used by both Mitra and Kahlon and Tyagi to calculate the relative profitability of the agricultural and non-agricultural sectors. They argue that government price policy 'did not cause any damage to producer incentives during the post-Green Revolution period' (De Janvry and Subbarao, 1986: 27). In the absence of land reform, there is a small class of large farmers 'that is able not only to influence policy to stimulate agricultural growth but also to monopolize and retain the benefits of growth for itself' (ibid.: 98). The North Indian farmers in Punjab and Haryana are especially advantaged, as 'the current practice of the [APC] to fix a uniform price for the country as a whole, on the basis of the costs of production in a high-cost state, resulted in the high-productivity regions enjoying substantial differential rents' (ibid.: 27).

[13] That is in consumer politics. For farmers, food procurement had become an

The scheme was to supply cheap food to the poorest consumers in rural areas. With the new scheme food distribution expanded. New fair price shops opened in rural areas and the total amount of foodgrains distributed through the PDS increased from 754,000 tonnes in 1984 to 1,165,000 tonnes in 1986.[14]

The criterion for acquiring a green card was an annual family income less than Rs 3500. In particular, the scheme was supposed to cover landless agricultural/rural labourers, village artisans, small and marginal farmers and recipients of government pensions. To avoid having virtually the whole population included in the scheme, it was decided that not more than 40 per cent of households could get a green card. Each district was allotted a maximum number of beneficiaries. Households that were not eligible for a green card could get another type of ration card. At the end of 1986, 3.1 million families were covered by the Scheme out of a total of 8 million card holding households.[15]

The Green Card Scheme involved the introduction of a differential price system for PDS foodgrains. Families holding a green card could buy rice in 1985 for Rs 2 per kg, and wheat or coarse grains for Rs 1.25–1.50 per kg. Other households holding ration cards would pay up to Re 0.75 more per kg in the fair price shop. The price difference was paid as a subsidy by the Government of Karnataka. Green card holders were entitled to a maximum of 10 kg of foodgrains per card (household) per month. Furthermore, sarees and dhotis were occasionally distributed. The amount of foodgrains allotted to other card holders varied according to stock availability.

There were several political developments within Karnataka that

---

important issue by 1980. In that period, procurement was organized through a farmers' levy: paddy cultivators had to surrender a part of their produce (as levy) to the government. There was much resistance on the part of farmers to this policy, and in some cases it led to violent confrontations. As one farmer leader told me: 'The police and the revenue inspector used to visit us in the night. It was gun-point procurement, which exists nowhere else in the world. What they did was very humiliating. It was as in a movie. They came like a gang of dacoits, and they left our houses after they had seized what they wanted.' This levy policy was one of the reasons for the farmers' agitations in 1980 (and even before 1980, as I was told by farmers' leaders), which would lead to the emergence of the farmers' movement, the Karnataka Rajya Ryota Sangha (see Nadkarni, 1987: 82–135, and on farmers' levy especially: 123–4).

[14] This increase proved to be only temporary, with 1986 as the peak year; afterwards the amount gradually came down again to approximately 800,000 tonnes.

[15] *Annual Report 1986–87*, Food and Civil Supplies Department, Government of Karnataka.

led to the implementation of the Green Card Scheme. Hegde's government was the first non-Congress government within Karnataka. This put him under great pressure to prove that it was worthwhile voting for Janata, especially after Indira Gandhi was murdered in 1984 and the subsequent landslide victory of Congress (I) at the central level. In Andhra Pradesh, the rice at Rs 2 per kg scheme, which resembled the Green Card Scheme but was larger, had proved to be very effective in this respect. N.T. Rama Rao, the Chief Minister who had introduced the scheme, had acquired massive popularity. In early 1985, shortly before the election in Karnataka, various observers predicted that Hegde would lose. It is against this background that he announced the Green Card Scheme. Hegde won the election and Janata got a comfortable majority in the Karnataka assembly.

Apart from those direct political pressures, there was a tendency to assign 'minimum needs' a high place on the political agenda anyway. One of the members of the Economic Planning Council, which was Hegde's think-tank, told me in an interview:

> In the EPC we discussed policy priorities. For a long time priority was given to infrastructural developments, such as power, irrigation and also industry. Our idea was that we should change our priorities in accordance with minimum needs problems. So we proposed that more money should be spent on food, drinking water, clothing, health, rural roads, housing sites etc. We had quite an argument with the Finance Department. They told us there was no money for a Minimum Needs Programme. Our main counter-argument was the 'equity' argument. We asked them: 'how much does the cost-of-living allowance cost yearly?' That was something like 98 crores (Rs 980 million), if I remember correctly. Our initial estimation of the welfare programme was that it would cost 88 crores (Rs 880 million). So we told them: 'if there is a case for cost-of-living allowance, then there is an even stronger case for a Minimum Needs Programme'.

The Minimum Needs Programme was not solely an idea of benevolent planners. It was also a result of political pressure and demands. The regime of Devraj Urs in the 1970s had made serious progress with land reform, caste reservations and other social policies (see also Section 1.3). The result of these policies was that groups that had always been excluded became represented and politically involved. Urs also redirected a substantial portion of the political spoils towards poorer groups (Manor, 1989: 349). The idea that any elected government should work for the poor took root during his regime.

The government of Urs' successor, Gundu Rao (1980–3), failed completely by this criterion, and in 1983 the Karnataka electorate decided that it was time for a radical change. For the first time, it voted out Congress (I). As a result it was up to the new Janata government to build further upon Urs' legacy. The Minimum Needs Programme was one of the efforts made in this respect.

Governments after that of Hegde also felt they had to do something visible for the poor. The 1989 elections brought a new Congress (I) government, headed from 1990 onwards by Chief Minister S. Bangarappa. Although his policies were far less radical than those of Urs, he also claimed to work for the poor, and distributed favours to lower caste members. During his government the green card was replaced by a tricolour card, with a photograph of Indira Gandhi on it, which illustrates how social policies have become tied up with efforts to engineer a personal leadership cultus.

Food policy in Kerala: food riots, food rights

Unlike Karnataka, food issues used to play a big role in Kerala politics. The year 1964 was a crucial starting point in this respect. Rationing existed before that date, but it was in 1964 that fair price shops became available to large numbers of people in Kerala (Franke and Chasin, 1992: 29). In this year there was a food shortage in the whole of India, but the problem was particularly acute in Kerala. Kerala produced mainly cash crops while it was deficient in foodgrains. The decision to extend the rationing system in Kerala was taken at the Central level, at a conference of Chief Ministers of all States. It was agreed that 'the quantity of rice required for issue under the scheme would be made available to the State from the respective Central Storage Depots and that it would not be generally necessary for the State Government to procure any quota direct from other States'.[16] In short, the Centre would take responsibility for food supplies in Kerala.

Since then, food distribution continued to be important, not only in the relationship between the Centre and Kerala, but also in politics within Kerala.[17] In March 1965 elections were held in Kerala, but these did not lead to the formation of a government. Instead, Kerala was brought under President's Rule. Despite the recent commitment, the Centre did little to relieve worsening food conditions in Kerala. Food rationing was temporarily stopped. Throughout these years up to the 1967 election, political forces that were opposed to the

[16] From the Administration Report 1964-5, quoted in Government of Kerala, (1989: 10).

[17] The following two paragraphs draw heavily on Sathyamurthy (1985: 230–40).

government (in particular leftist parties) concentrated their attention on the food question. In January 1966, a general strike took place as a protest against the Central government's policy of withholding PDS food from Kerala.[18] Although the Congress party paid lip service to these mass demands, it never joined in the agitation. On the other hand, for the opposition parties 'the experience of organising joint struggles against food policy of the Indian Government served as a prelude to the formation of an anti-Congress coalition to fight the 1967 elections on a common programme [which concentrated on food and land reforms]' (Sathyamurthy, 1985: 230–1).

This coalition won the election in 1967, and for the second time a Communist-led ministry was formed in Kerala. By that time 'the majority of the people had already been under half ration regimen for well over 8 months. The new ministry's first act consisted of approaches to the centre for food allotment in order to sustain the normal rationing system in the State' (Sathyamurthy, 1985: 237). As one of my informants recounts:

> Food was a very important issue at that time. I was a high school boy, but I remember the scene vividly. The Chief Minister E.M.S. Namboodiripad went to Delhi, and after he came back with the airplane, he went straight to a mass meeting to report about his mission.

Soon the Central government's tactic of withholding food from Kerala led to the desired result: the active cadres of the Marxist Communist party (CPI-M) resumed agitation, even though the party was in power. Although this led to conflicts between the CPI-M and its coalition parties, this twin strategy of agitation *cum* administration proved to be highly effective in the realization of fairly radical legislation—in particular land reform. With regard to food, it meant that rationing remained high on the political agenda, and that the activities of the Food Minister were closely watched by politicians from opposition parties, the general public and the press.

Although food lost its top ranking on the political agenda in the following decades, it has remained important. Periodically, the Central government reduced allotment to Kerala and regularly marches and manifestations were organized in Kerala in protest against reduction or against rising prices. The issue is also important during elections

[18] It was in this year, under President's Rule, that the Kerala Rationing Order was enacted. This order comes under the Essential Commodities Act. It lays down procedures concerning selection of ration dealers, issuing of cards, inspection of ration shops etc. (See also Chapter 7)

when both Congress (I) and the leftist parties promise to keep a check on price rises and to expand the PDS. In particular the *Maveli* system serves these populist purposes very well.[19] Since 1980, the number of *Maveli* stores has increased continuously, despite problems with financial viability and provision of the stores. Opening new stores is definitely one of the strategies through which politicians aim to win political support.[20]

Populism and popular protests

In short, in the period 1965–90, the PDS expanded enormously. The amount of food dealt with by the FCI multiplied, as well as the subsidies involved. Also the number of people covered by rationing programmes increased. The expansion of the system—in particular the implementation of special schemes for the rural poor—means that the original urban bias has been somewhat modified over the years. However, easy generalizations are not possible in this respect, due to large variations between States and the effect of foodgrain price policy on farmers' incomes and, hence, on intersectoral relations.[21]

The descriptions of food policy in Karnataka and Kerala illustrate the changing function of food policy in economic development and politics. While food distribution was seen primarily as a supplementary arrangement meant to support industrial development in the period up to 1965, it got more prominence and became an end in itself in the next phase. In Karnataka, the expansion of the PDS was never a

[19] In 1980, the left coalition government introduced so-called *Maveli* stores and markets, run by the Kerala State Civil Supplies Corporation. The stocks in these stores—including rice, sugar, pulses and periodically also vegetables—were supplied by the Kerala State Civil Supplies Corporation. The system thus operated—and still operates—independently from the centrally provisioned PDS. See Chapter 6 on the Kerala State Civil Supplies Corporation and the *Maveli* initiative.

[20] This is illustrated in the following fragment of a newpaper report: 'At his first press conference after taking charge as Minister, Mr Mustafa, said ... the Government had already begun initiating steps to [roll back prices]. Of immediate concern to Keralites, he would assure them that the prices of essential commodities would not be allowed to rise from the present figures during the coming ONAM festival and that efforts would be made to bring down the current prices. ... Referring to the plans to expand the public distribution system, the Minister said at present there were 390 Maveli Stores through which the Civil Supplies Corporation distributed essential commodities. Their number would be raised so that every Assembly segment [140 in total] would have a minimum of three Maveli Stores. ... It was also proposed to set up [Maveli] supermarkets in all [14] district headquarters.' (*The Hindu*, 6 July 1991).

[21] This latter aspect especially is often neglected in statements about a presumed

political issue as such, but the overall political climate, as well as the immediate threat of losing the 1985 election were instrumental in the expansion of the system. Food became an issue on the political agenda. Also in Kerala electoral considerations have prompted politicians to promise and/or organize expansions of the food distibution schemes. This connection between food and populist politics is not exceptional; it exists in other States as well, such as Andhra Pradesh and Tamil Nadu.

Often conscious efforts are made by leading politicians to link the special food schemes to their own personality and parent-like care. The government generally, or the Chief Minister personally, is presented as a benefactor who gives a helping hand to the poor. Elsewhere, I have analysed the dominant food policy discourse in this period as a 'donative discourse' because of the emphasis on charity and generosity of the government.[22] The Noon Meal Scheme in Tamil Nadu, launched by Chief Minister M.G. Ramachandran, was originally called the Chief minister's Nutritious Noon Meal Programme; later it was renamed as 'Puratchi Thalaivar (Revolutionary Leader) MGR Nutritious Meal Programme'. Sometimes kinship terminology and religious symbolism are evoked in this discourse. In the 1980s, the Andhra Pradesh Chief Minister N.T. Rama Rao was called *anna* (elder

---

urban bias of the PDS. Recently two pairs of researchers have investigated the issue on the basis of NSS data (42nd round) on utilization of the PDS in 1986–7. Dev and Suryanarayana conclude that 'there is no single criterion by which one can unambiguously state whether the PDS is urban biased or not. The nature of bias varies between commodities depending upon the criterion used. However, since rice and sugar account for more than 60 per cent of total value of PDS purchases, one can safely say that the PDS is in general rural biased at the all-India level. But at the regional level, the picture varies' (1991: 2361–2). The criteria used in this study were (*a*) per capita quantities purchased from the PDS, (*b*) per capita consumption from the PDS, (*c*) the relative dependence on the PDS, and (*d*), the extent to which the PDS meets the needs of those who depend on the market for their food provisioning. A second pair of researchers, Howes and Jha, used different measures of urban bias, namely (*a*) per capita quantities consumed, (*b*) per capita subsidy implied in purchase of rationed goods, and (*c*) accessibility of the PDS. Their conclusion is that 'an overall urban bias is present in half of the 18 states.... Three states ... show a rural bias. The other six [including Karnataka and Kerala] show mixed results' (1992: 1072). Both pairs of researchers have worked with a narrow conception of urban bias as only the rationing side of the PDS is included. The effects of government procurement and foodgrain price policy on farmers' incomes—and hence on intersectoral relations—are left out.

[22] Mooij (1995). See also Schaffer (1984) and Wood (1985: 358–9) about donative versions of reality.

brother) in relation to his role in the rice at Rs 2 per kg scheme, while the previous Tamil Nadu Chief Minister Jayalalitha was referred to as *amma* (mother or mother goddess) by her subordinates.[23] N.T.Rama Rao, M.G. Ramachandran, and Jayalalitha, are all, or were, popular film stars. In some films, N.T. Rama Rao played a god or a saintly figure who championed the cause of the poor.

Despite this donative discourse, several decades of food distribution have produced not only grateful clients, but also demanding, claiming citizens. Over the years, the idea that citizens have a right to decent living, and government's duty to contribute to this, has gained importance (cf. Breman, 1993). Food at fair prices takes a prominent place in this idea. This expectation is most developed in Kerala where broadly supported struggles and agitations around food have been organized for more than thirty years. A large part of Kerala's population is knowledgeable about the State's claim that the Central government had committed itself to provide Kerala with sufficient food. In turn, the Kerala government is held accountable when food price rises or allotment and distribution falls short. In other States also, a similar idea of having a right to food distribution is developing. This becomes clear, for instance, each time that targeting of the PDS to the most needy people is proposed. Often, as soon as such a proposal is launched, those sections of the population which would be excluded protest vigorously and, usually, succeed in securing the continuation of supply.

3.3 FOOD POLICY AFTER 1991: CHANGES UNDER ECONOMIC ADJUSTMENT

The next phase of food distribution started in 1991, when India adopted a structural adjustment programme. The direct cause of this economic reorientation was an acute balance-of-payments crisis. There were also longer-term economic problems that led to this shift in economic policy, related to the inefficiency of public sector units and underperformance of the private sector. The structural adjustment programme the Indian government took on board consisted of

[23] The Indian bi-weekly *Frontline* (1993: Vol. 10, No. 14, p. 108) quotes one of the staff members of a noon meal centre. 'When Indira Kumari [Social Welfare Minister] visits a [noon meal] centre, her first question is "Where is the picture of Amma [Mother: Chief Minister J. Jayalalitha]?" But the Government does not supply us with these pictures. If we don't display Jayalalitha's picture, we are immediately given marching orders. Therefore, I bought a photograph.'

measures such as convertibility and devaluation of the Indian rupee, trade liberalization, facilitating foreign investments, deregulation of the industrial and financial sectors, and containment of government subsidies.[24]

The effect of this economic reorientation on food distribution has been twofold. On the one hand, there is a tendency to stress the need for reduction, or at least rationalization, of government expenditure (Bhagwati and Srinivasan, 1993; Pursell and Gulati, 1993). In the mid-1990s, government subsidy was approximately Rs 50,000 million per year, and it was argued that this is too much. It is important to note here that the rise of the subsidy bill in the 1990's may seem considerable (Appendix 7 table 1), but that this only so at current prices. At constant prices, or as percentage of GNP, the rise of the food subsidy is much less dramatic. Periods of a rising subsidy have alternated with periods of a reduction (Swaminathan, 1996). Nevertheless, popular phrases in the 1990s are 'streamlining of the PDS', 'pruning of the PDS', 'revamping the system', 'making the PDS viable' and 'subsidy burden'. They all stress the lack of financial means to sustain the system. Targeting is depicted as the solution, as it would combine the provisioning of food to the most needy people with a reduction of government expenditure.

On the other hand, the safety net aspects of the PDS came again to the forefront. It is generally acknowledged that the new economic policy hit the weakest sections of the population hardest. In 1993, the Government of India wrote that:

> structural reform ... involves social costs and it is important to ensure that these costs do not fall heavily on those least able to bear them. ... Government has recognised the need to create a social safety net for this purpose.
>
> - A National Renewal Fund has been set up to fund schemes for compensation, retraining and redeployment of workers affected by the restructuring....
> - The Public Distribution System has been strengthened and expanded in 1700 specially identified blocks.
> - Expenditure on the social sectors ... has been substantially stepped up in the Budget 1993–94... (GoI, 1993: 19–20).

In the 1990s, the PDS is regarded as a crucial component of the social safety net, meant to alleviate problems of poverty, partially induced or aggravated by structural adjustment.

[24] See, e.g. Basu (1993), Cassen and Joshi (1995), Patnaik and Chandrashekar (1995).

When we look at actual practices, we can observe a number of different policy changes. The new economic climate has certainly been conducive to several increases in PDS prices since 1991. Between 1991 and 1994, the issue prices of PDS foodgrains—that is the selling price of the Food Corporation of India—have gone up by more than 40 per cent. The result is that the price difference between PDS foodgrains and open market foodgrains has become small. Consequently, the off-take of PDS foodgrains has come down.[25]

This increase in issue prices has not resulted in a reduction of overall food subsidy. On the contrary, food subsidy has nearly doubled in the 1991–4 period. This is due to a simultaneous increase in procurement prices. Between 1990–1 and 1994–5, procurement prices increased by 60 per cent in the case of rice and 66 per cent in the case of wheat (*EPW* editorial, 10 June 1995). Thus, in effect, the subsidy became more a producers' subsidy than a consumers' subsidy.[26]

A paradoxical situation has emerged in that both procurement and distribution prices more or less equal open market prices. PDS off-take has come down. Procurement, though, was very high. Consequently, the buffer stock has tripled in 3 years (more than 37 million tonnes in June 1995, as compared to 12.2 million tonnes in April 1992) (Hanumantha Rao and Nayyar, 1994: Table 3; *EPW* editorial, 16 March 1996). The maintenance of this buffer stock added to the food subsidy bill. In January 1996, the stocks were reduced again to 25 million tonnes, but not because of increasing PDS off-take but because of open market sales and exports (*EPW* editorial, 16 March 1996).

Targeting—in the sense of excluding particular groups—has not been introduced. Although advisory committees have regularly recommended its introduction, it has never been implemented. The trend towards targeting without excluding other groups altogether continues. At the Central level, there was the 'revamping the PDS' effort: the reallocation of PDS foodgrains to 1700 selected blocks, without any formal decision to exclude the other 3400 blocks henceforward. From 1997 onwards, there is a differential pricing system: poor households get PDS foodgrains at a lower price than

[25] 'During 1993, against an allocation of 90.53 lakh (9.053 million) tonnes of wheat, the offtake was only 47.39 (4.739) tonnes and against an allocation of 121 lakh (12.1 million) tonnes of rice, the offtake was a mere 80.46 lakh (8.046 million) tonnes' (Gargi Parsai, in *The Hindu*,6 Feb. 1994).

[26] See also Varshney (1993: n 21).

households not classified as poor. At the level of the individual States, there are similar schemes. This type of targeting can never contribute to a reduction of the system. It only means the PDS expands and becomes more expensive.

Thus what we witness in the 1990s is a Janus-faced policy. On the one hand, issue prices have been increased in an effort to curtail food subsidies and to reduce the system. On the other hand, new expensive schemes are created to serve the poor. Contradictory as it is, this Janus-faced policy enables the government to pursue various strategies and serve various interests simultaneously. First, the interests of farmers and/or traders who profit from procurement. In the mid-1990s, farmers' movements are still an important political phenomenon to be reckoned with (Brass, 1995; Varshney, 1993). Capitalist agriculturalists have formed powerful lobbies and they are represented in almost all political parties. No political party can afford to neglect these interests. Moreover, with a Prime Minister from the south and increasing representation of southern interests in the Central state, it is no longer mainly the wheat lobby from north India that is able to exercise pressure on foodgrain price policy, but increasingly also southern rice producers. Second, food policy remains one of the ways in which politicians and political parties try to establish the legitimacy of their claim to state power. Despite the economic ideology of the 1990s that stresses the virtues of the market and the failure of planning, it is still through government programmes and distribution schemes that politicians try to woo voters, who generally tend to prefer—and vote for—direct material benefits rather than economic policies with potentially positive long-term effects but with a possible detrimental short-term impact on employment and prices. Although the special programmes are initiated both at the Central and State levels, so far it is primarily the regional and non-Congress (I) political parties (Telugu Desam in Andhra Pradesh, Janata Dal in Karnataka) that have been able to make political capital out of them. Third, apart from its role in political legitimacy at the national level, food policy is also part of a project to establish political legitimacy in the international arena, in which aid agencies and UN organizations and summits stress the need of social policies and a social safety net,[27] while international banking institutions put more emphasis on a reduction of government spending.

[27] For example, the Social Summit held in Copenhagen, 1995.

3.4 CONCLUSION: THE VARIOUS FUNCTIONS OF FOOD POLICY

Very briefly, the general point I hope to have established in this review of the emergence and evolution of the PDS, is that food policy is an inherently political phenomenon. First, particular policies are shaped in and through political processes. Specific political-economic relationships influence the direction in which the PDS develops. Second, food policy is strategically employed by the (Union and State) government in political and economic projects. In the course of time, the content of the various projects changed, as I pointed out in this chapter, but the general point remains true. Third, once it exists, food policy feeds back into political processes. One of the obvious results of an exposure to subsidized food is that the beneficiaries develop the idea that they have a right to cheap food, and that the government has an obligation to provide it. The result is that, as a Director of the Karnataka Food and Civil Supplies Department explained: 'Once a programme exists, it is very difficult to cut it down. That is a most unpleasant decision to take for any government.'

The first type of consistent food policy emerged in 1957. It was based on large-scale imports and food aid, and it aimed to bring down the prices of foodgrains by releasing large quantities at low prices. As Dandekar (1994: 219) stated, this food policy 'was politically acceptable and it did not cost anything financially to the government'. The economic function of food policy in these years was to support planned economic development. Economic development and policy was mainly directed at industrial development, and food policy contributed to low food prices especially in urban areas.

From 1965 onwards, food policy entered a second phase. The idea was no longer to bring down the foodgrain price level, but to support foodgrain production through an increase in the equilibrium price level (Mundle, 1981). This shift coincided with a general trend in economic policy to give more emphasis to agricultural development. The Green Revolution took off in the second half of the 1960s, boosting first wheat and later also rice production, mainly, but not exclusively, in north India. Gradually, India became self-sufficient in foodgrains. As a result of the Green Revolution, a new class of capitalist farmers emerged who gained considerable political power in the course of time (Mitra, 1977). Not only did they become influential in almost all political parties, they also succeeded in penetrating into various policy institutions, for instance, the CACP.[28]

From the 1980s onwards, food became an issue in populist politics. Cheap food was among the promises with which politicians or political parties tried to win the favour of the electorate. The political-economic background that gave rise to this development is intensified political competition. Opposition parties emerged and became influential in many States. Moreover, increasing political awakening and emancipation of large parts of the population made it necessary for politicians and political parties to formulate policies that appealed to these voters.

A third phase started in 1991, when the Indian government introduced various macroeconomic reform measures. The PDS became part of a safety net, but at the same time an attempt was made to prune the system and reduce the subsidy. In Chapter 8, I will discuss the present and the future of the PDS in more detail. But let us first have a closer look at the way in which the system operates on a day-to-day basis in two south Indian States.

[28] The CACP is the successor of the Agricultural Prices Committee that was established in 1965. The CACP, as Varshney (1993: 183) recounts, was initially envisioned as a purely technical body consisting of economists, statisticians and agricultural administrators. However, 'a governmental decision in the mid 1970s gave the CACP a "farmers' representative" appointed from among the politicians, and another decision in 1984 split the Commission into three technical members and three farmers' representatives'.

4

Rice Procurement in Karnataka About 'the levy' and power

Where there is jaggery, there are ants

(Kannada expression)

In contrast to the rest of this book, the present chapter deals with Karnataka only. There has been no rice procurement in Kerala any more since 1980. Before that year there was a producer levy: depending on the size of the holding and productivity of the land, each paddy producer had to sell a certain quantity of paddy to the procuring authority. In the period 1965–74, on average 101,000 tonnes of paddy were procured yearly, which came to between 3 and 4 per cent of total production in Kerala (Panikulangara, 1976). After the mid-1970s, the area and production of rice began to decline, as did procurement. By the end of the 1970s, it was next to nothing compared to procurement in other parts of India, and by 1980 it was stopped altogether.

Karnataka is also a marginal supplier of foodgrains to the Central food pool. The annual procurement of rice is between 100 and 150 thousand tonnes,[1] amounting to approximately 1 per cent of the total Indian procurement. Although comparatively speaking, this is a small amount, within Karnataka itself procurement is a significant phenomenon, especially in the rice-producing areas in which most procurement takes place. Akkipura is one of those districts.

Let me begin here by presenting a small impression—based on my research diary—which illustrates the importance of procurement for certain people in Akkipura, and also gives an idea of the social relations and activities involved.

Procurement season in 1991–2. It was August when I visited Akkipura district for the first time. It was still raining now and then, and I was impressed by the glorious green of the paddy fields, especially in combination with the darker shades of areca nut and coconut trees. When I started my interviews about

[1] In Karnataka rice is procured, rather than paddy. Paddy is unhusked rice, which first needs processing before it can be consumed as rice.

government procurement, most people told me that there was nothing to see at the moment. Government officials were not bothered about procurement, and also rice mill owners were relaxed. The warehouses were virtually empty, and FCI officials were reading newspapers in their offices or passing their time in a teashop close by. They had ample time for an interview, but advised me also to come back after a few months.

Things changed indeed in the course of the year. It was as easy to meet officials in their offices in August, as it was difficult in December or January. I had no problem in finding rice mill owners or traders to interview—they could usually be contacted in their rice mill—but their stories changed over time. In August and September some of them explained me about their difficulties with levy procurement, the harassment by officials they had to endure, and the court cases they or their family members had been involved in. But at that very moment it was quiet, a kind of lull before the storm.

In October, the new levy policy was announced. The district targets were decided and the procurement price was fixed. In October–November it was harvest time, and rice milling activity really took off in November and December. In December and January procurement was in full swing. During these months government officials paid regular visits to the rice mills. Many interviews with rice mill owners started with an occasional remark that the District Collector or some lower official had just visited the mill. A couple of times the Director of the Food and Civil Supplies Department came over from Bangalore to visit some rice mills. Invariably the purpose of these visits was to pressurize the rice mill owners to surrender levy rice to the government. Sometimes these visits meant an outright threat. For instance Shekar, a small rice mill owner who does only custom milling and who is not officially obliged to sell levy-rice, told me that the *Tahsildar* had just visited him before I came for an interview:

He came at 10.30, and he stayed in my office for more than two hours, just to harass me. So far I have not given any levy. He told me that there is a meeting tomorrow about levy with all the rice mill owners of this *taluk*. He said that when I come to this meeting tomorrow I should have 5 vouchers with me showing that I have given 5 loads. I told him that is impossible. 'Why should I listen to all those objections. I don't want to hear these things.' That is what he told me. He threatened to close the mill and to seize all the paddy. But this is not my paddy; it is the farmers' paddy. 'That is none of my business', he said, 'You have to see how you repay the farmers.' When he left he took away my stockbook and also all the slips from the village accountants saying that this is indeed farmers' paddy and that, hence, no levy needs to be paid. He has not even given me an endorsement letter that he has taken all those things.

In February–March, things changed again. By now the rice mill owners complained severely about the paddy prices and the losses they incurred on each load of levy. Some of them told me about the officials' increasing greed for money. Furthermore, due to a shortage of irrigation water in the area, the paddy harvest in the second season was expected to be small. Traders and rice mill owners began to feel that serious injustice was being done to them. Their association called for a meeting, and they decided to send a delegation to the State capital to convince the Food Minister and the top officials that the situation was untenable. Together they collected a few lakhs (hundreds of thousands) of rupees to help in this negotiation, and then some representatives went off. Several meetings and dinner parties followed; the end result was no official change in policy, but policy implementation was put on ice. This situation continued till the end of the season. Procurement had virtually stopped in the district. The officials kept quiet, and the rice mill owners waited for better times to come.

This short description summarizes procurement policy in a nutshell. Although I have left out many details and events during the year, some of which will be elaborated upon later in this chapter, the story illustrates several points. One is that policy implementation is a matter of negotiation and struggle. At the beginning of the season official policy is announced. However, the real course of events develops only in the months afterwards. What happens during the year depends, among other things, on the behaviour of, and decisions taken by, officials and politicians, the activities of individual rice mill owners and the rice mill owners' association, officials' and politicians' need for money, paddy availability and paddy rates. The various actors in this process of negotiation and struggle deal with each other and make strategic decisions about what to do: sell levy-rice[2] or not, be friendly or not, accept bribes or not. In short, policy implementation can be characterized as a social process in which different types of actors participate whose day-to-day interaction is structured—constrained and made possible but not determined in a strict sense—by the existing social relations and official policies.

Rice, obviously, is the object of this struggle and negotiation. On the one hand, procurement agents try to get hold of it. In their attempt to do so, they make use of several means: persuasion, the law, or threats. On the other hand, rice mill owners and traders do their best to keep the amount of levy-rice to the minimum. In fact, this is a struggle about calories, profit and power. The government needs to procure rice in order to distribute this to the public; traders resent it because they fear that the profitability of their businesses is

[2] While paddy/rice traders and rice mill owners themselves usually say they have to 'give levy', I prefer the much less common phrase 'to sell levy-rice', to point out that rice millers and traders are compensated financially to some extent for this levy.

threatened, and to some extent it is, indeed, the government's objective to do so. The struggle over rice is also about power: who determines what happens with the foodgrains? Is it traders and rice mill owners who shape market and distribution processes, or is it the government? Thus, not surprisingly, it is not only the foodgrain itself, but also policies, rules and regulations laying down procurement practices that are at stake in the struggles and negotiations.

In this chapter I first give some background information on procurement policy in Karnataka (Section 4.1). This includes a discussion of the official and actual modes of procurement. Then I describe the different actors involved in procurement (Section 4.2). In the third section I discuss the various types of struggles and forms of cooperation that have developed in the process of procurement implementation. The fourth section discusses the effects of procurement policy on social relations among and between the principal actors involved in procurement.

4.1 THE SYSTEM OF LEVY COLLECTION

Each year in August–September, the Government of India decides, in consultation with the State governments, the quantity of paddy that should be procured in each State. The Food Corporation of India, a Union state organization, acts as procurement agent. The responsibility for implementation and enforcement of procurement policy rests with the individual State governments. It is up to these State governments to decide which mode of procurement they will employ.[3] In Karnataka, procurement started in 1966 with a levy on paddy growers. Farmers producing paddy were supposed to sell part of their paddy to the government. After 1981, this was replaced by mill point procurement.[4] Rice millers and traders who convert paddy into rice should surrender part of their produce as a levy in the form of rice. During the first years this was 50 per cent; in 1987 it was reduced to 33.3 per cent. This obligation to be levied is laid down in the Karnataka Rice

[3] See Acharya (1983), Chopra (1988: 223–54) for discussion about various modes of procurement.

[4] Karnataka was one of the last States to give up the system of levy on paddy growers. See Nadkarni (1987: 123–4) about farmers' protests against this type of levy.

Procurement (Levy) Order 1984, coming under Section 3 of the Essential Commodities Act.[5]

Not all State governments agree with the procurement target set for them by the Government of India. For instance in 1991–2 there was a dispute between the Government of India and the Government of Karnataka about the targets for Karnataka State:

In August 1991 the Karnataka target was fixed at 2 lakh (200,000) tonnes for the procurement season 1991–92. Shortly afterwards there was a unilateral GoKa [Government of Karnataka] Cabinet decision to reduce the target to 1.5 lakh tonnes. The GoI [Government of India] did not agree. It argued that due to irregular rains in some States production had been affected and prices would be rising. Hence, it is 'of utmost importance that our efforts are directed to procure maximum possible quantities of rice' (24.10.91). The GoKa replied that '[w]hile reviewing the achievement of the levy targets fixed during the previous years, and taking into consideration the area under cultivation of paddy, production of rice and the types of existing rice mills in the State, the Government has decided that it is not desirable to fix a higher target [than 1.5 lakh tonnes] without any expectation of achieving it' (23.11.91). The GoI is not convinced and suggests increasing the levy percentage. Furthermore, it states that '[y]ou will also appreciate that unless procurement is maximised, it will become difficult to meet the requirements of States/[Union Territories] including that of your State' (24.01.92).[6] This last remark is an outright threat: if you do not procure, we cannot guarantee supply for your PDS. Despite this threat the GoKa did not give in; the target remained 1.5 lakh tonnes. At the end of the season only 1.16 tonnes had actually been procured, that is 77 per cent of the target.

Yearly the procurement prices are fixed. The CACP calculates the average costs of production and recommends procurement prices. Procurement prices may vary slightly from State to State. CACP recommendations are always the starting point of procurement price fixation but some upward revision may take place, usually as a result of farmers' lobbies (see, e.g. Radhakrishna and Hanumantha Rao, 1994). As the procurement price for rice in south India is usually

[5] The Essential Commodities Act has the objective of controlling production, distribution and trade of/in essential commodities, including foodgrains. See Chapter 7 for its role and function in the public distribution system.

[6] Quotations from letters D.O. No. 167(5)/91-PY.I/SF/120/91 D.O. No. FTD 27 RPR 91 and D.O. No. 6(KARN)(6)/91-DR.I, respectively.

lower than the open market price—at least this was the case during the year of fieldwork, as well as during the preceding years—evasion of levy on the part of the miller/trader can be expected. Levy procurement, therefore, usually has elements of tax and compulsion.

The enforcement of levy is easier the more surplus an area has, as the supply is larger and the prices generally lower. Therefore, from the perspective of the levy collector, areas of surplus foodgrain production should preferably keep the surplus within the area. Movement restrictions, hence, form an integral and significant part of procurement policy. During the time of fieldwork, paddy movement from one State to another was prohibited, but transport of paddy within Karnataka was free.[7] Transport of rice, on the other hand, was controlled. It could only take place if the trader had fulfilled his levy obligations. When a trader or miller surrendered one levy load[8] of rice to the FCI he received two permits with which he could transport two loads of rice to whichever place he wanted. This could also be outside Karnataka. Transport and sales of rice were thus under intensive control. Each lorry load of rice transported and sold on the open market was to be accompanied by the proper documents. Each quantity of rice on the open market corresponded in principle with another quantity of half that weight sold as levy to the government.

In short, the Karnataka Rice Procurement (Levy) Order prescribes that each miller or trader should surrender one-third of his produce to the government, and the legal procedure is such that after delivery of each levied load, the miller/trader can apply for release certificates for two loads of levy-free rice, to be freely sold and transported inside or outside Karnataka.

However, to facilitate levy procurement, the administration has added its own regulations. After the Government of India has fixed targets for each State, the Director of the Karnataka State Food and Civil Supplies

[7] For example, in principle; free transport of paddy remained a contested fact in practice. In several ways the Karnataka government kept trying to restrict paddy transport. First, it made it obligatory that paddy in transport should be accompanied by a so-called non-objection certificate, to be obtained from the *Tahsildar*. Second, occasionally the Karnataka government reintroduced a government order that restricted paddy movement within Karnataka. Traders and rice mill owners always protested against these movement restrictions. All the government orders restricting paddy movement have been challenged and always struck down in the Karnataka High Court. Moreover, several large trading corporations had obtained individual stay orders from the Karnataka High court, exempting them from the necessity of obtaining non-objection certificates from the *Tahsildar* before being allowed to transport paddy.

[8] One (lorry) load is usually 100 bags of 100 kg, that is 10 tonnes.

Department fixes the target for each district. This decision is made mainly on the basis of paddy production figures. In each district the District Collector fixes the procurement target for each *taluk*. Then the targets per mill and per trader are fixed by the District Collector and the *Tahsildar*. This is done on the basis of criteria such as mill capacity and last year's performance, but individual and collective bargaining also play a role.

In this chain of target fixing some adjustments take place. The sum of all the individual targets is more than the *taluk* or district target. For instance the target of Akkipura district was 42,000 tonnes of rice in 1991–2. The total sum of individual traders' targets was 65,770 tonnes, and the total sum of individual mill targets was 66,080 tonnes.[9] This means that when each trader and mill owner surrenders about 65 per cent of his individual target the district target will be reached.

This overtargeting is an administrative trick. It increases potential pressure on sellers of levy-rice and thereby facilitates reaching the full district target. Although millers and traders may not know the extent of this overtargeting, they are aware of this phenomenon and realize it gives them some latitude to negotiate about their individual targets.

So on the one hand there is the levy order, a legal document prescribing that each trader/miller who converts paddy into rice should surrender one-third of his produce to the government; on the other hand there are administrative devices, the individual targets. These targets do not have a legal status. Originally they were dictated/prescribed, but since the rice mill owners won a High Court case concerning this issue, the District Collector or *Tahsildar* sends a note to the traders and rice mill owners stating their target and *requesting* them to cooperate in levy collection. Fig. 4.1 summarizes both systems.

The procedure followed in reality in Akkipura is a mixture of both systems. At the beginning of the levy season (October–November) each trader and each rice mill owner gets an individual target. For each levy load he receives in principle two permits for two loads of rice to be freely sold and transported. This is only in principle because often, especially at the beginning of the levy season, officials are

[9] There is both a trader and a mill point connected to each load levy surrendered to the FCI. The trader is the owner of the rice, the mill point is the place where the paddy is converted into rice. Often (but not always) the trader and rice mill owner are the same person as many rice mill owners are paddy/rice traders.

reluctant to issue these certificates. In order to enhance levy collection they sometimes start issuing these certificates only after a certain percentage of the target has been surrendered.

	Legal procedure	Administrative Instruments
Principle	One-third of produce should be surrendered as levy	The target should be surrendered as levy
Laid down in	The Karnataka Rice Procurement (Levy) Order, coming under the Essential Commodities Act	No legal basis. Based on negotiation, cooperation and threat
Operation procedure	For each levy load, the trader/miller receives 2 permits for 2 loads of free-sale rice	Free trade after the target is reached
Check	—On free market rice, whether the permits are in order —On account books, whether indeed 33.3 per cent is sold as levy	—Whether target is surrendered already

Fig. 4.1 Two systems of levy collection in Karnataka

The target is an important instrument to harass traders and rice mill owners—even though it has no legal status. It is much easier to prove that a trader has not yet surrendered his target so far, than to argue that a trader is not selling one-third of his produce as levy, this is so because it is nearly impossible to establish what the total produce of a trader/miller is. So in the day-to-day interactions between officials and traders/millers the administrative devices are very important.

But the legal procedure remains crucial. As I explained earlier, movement restrictions are introduced with the objective of making procurement easier by keeping rice in surplus areas. The government needs to have an instrument to control transport, which it finds in the legal regulations. Moreover, the legal regulations come under the Essential Commodities Act, whereas the administrative procedure has no legal basis. As the Essential Commodities Act is a strict piece of law, it is a powerful resource in the hands of officials imposing the levy. I will come back to this later in this chapter and also in Chapter 7.

Table 4.1 gives details of levy collection in the years 1986–7 to 1991–2 in Karnataka. In none of these years has procurement reached the State target, whether the target was set at 200,000, 175,000 or 150,000 tonnes. Column 5 gives procurement as a percentage of rice production. This percentage fluctuates somewhere around 5 per cent. The levy order prescribes that 33.3 per cent of paddy/rice dealt with by millers and traders should be sold as levy. In reality, not all rice produced passes through the hands of traders. Paddy converted into rice for farmers' own consumption—by so-called custom mills—is exempted from levy. According to my estimate, this is a relatively small proportion of all the rice produced,[10] but even if it were 50 per cent, actual levy collection is only a third of what it should be according to the one-third-principle laid down in the law. In fact, targets themselves are fixed at a rather low rate: about 7 per cent of the production figure.

Table 4.1
Levy collection in Karnataka 1986–1992

	1 Rice production (in tonnes)	2 Levy target (in tonnes)	3 Procurement (in tonnes)	4 3 as % of 2	5 3 as % of 1
1986–7	2,310,100	200,000	121,576	60.79	5.3
1987–8	1,890,000	200,000	66,407	33.20	3.5
1988–9	2,510,000	200,000	122,753	61.38	4.9
1989–90	2,380,000	175,000	156,297	89.31	6.6
1990–1	2,170,000	150,000	145,431	96.95	6.7
1991–2	2,288,750	150,000	115,754	77.16	5.1

Sources: Food and Civil Supplies Department, Bangalore; Directorate of Economics and Statistics, New Delhi.

[10] As far as I know there are no reliable estimates in Karnataka of the percentage of paddy/rice that is not marketed, i.e. that is used for farmers' own consumption and payment in kind. Due to regional differences it would be very difficult to make such an estimate. Clay et al. (1988: 23) estimate that 70 per cent of foodgrains is handled by private traders in India. My guess, as far as Karnataka is concerned, is that most paddy/rice is marketed. This is based on personal observations and information gathered about two major rice-producing districts in Karnataka, one of which is Akkipura. In these two districts paddy/rice production is commoditized to a large extent. These are

4.2 THE ACTORS INVOLVED IN PROCUREMENT

Functionally speaking, there are several main categories of actors involved in procurement: rice mill owners and traders who convert paddy into rice and are, hence, liable to levy payment; officials involved in the implementation of levy policy; officials involved in storage and conservation of the procured rice; transport companies; financial institutions; and party politicians, who decide about levy policy and who also play an important, though less clearly defined, role in the process of implementation. In my research on rice procurement in Akkipura district, I concentrated mainly on those liable to pay levy, officials directly involved in procurement and (local) politicians, as especially these categories of actors operate at the district level.

Such a classification of the different types of actors involved is straightforward; it is based on the position of the actors in the procurement process. However, it also has disadvantages. It suggests homogeneity within the different categories, while in reality there are important differences between various people within each category of actors. Furthermore, it suggests strict boundaries between the categories while in reality the boundaries are often blurred: rice mill owners may also be involved in politics, and there are some politicians (e.g. members of the Legislative Assembly) who, or whose family members, own rice mills or large trading companies. Nevertheless, aware of these difficulties, I use it here as a first subdivision of the various actors involved.

Rice mill owners and paddy/rice traders[11]

As explained, levy policy in Karnataka prescribes that rice mill owners and paddy/rice traders who convert paddy into rice should surrender one-third of their produce to the government as levy. This obligation

---

the districts that are important for levy collection; together they are good for about 50 per cent of the total procurement in the State. My idea is further supported by Nadkarni (1987: 124), who writes about one of the major rice-producing areas in Karnataka that 'there is evidence that a good part of the [paddy] output is sold even by small farmers'.

[11] In the following discussion about the actors involved, I concentrate mainly on activities and social relations that have anything to do with levy procurement. Other activities remain outside the discussion. This means, for instance, that I neglect the activities of politicians in fields other than rice procurement, and that I discuss rice mill owners only as producers of, and traders in, rice, and not as traders in by-products such as husk and bran. Also the relationship of paddy/rice traders with their suppliers (farmers or intermediaries) is left out.

to pay levy is what makes them one category of people. Within this category, there are rice mill owners and there are paddy and rice wholesale traders. Many rice mill owners are also paddy and rice traders. In 1991–2, 638 firms were registered as liable to surrender levy in Akkipura district. Of these, 149 firms (23 per cent) were rice milling cum trading companies; 150 (24 per cent) were milling firms without trading activities, and 339 (53 per cent) were involved in trading only.[12] As far as levy is concerned, the first category is the most important one. Although this category comprises less than a quarter of the total number of firms involved in levy collection, as trading firms they should collectively surrender 69 per cent of the target allotted to Akkipura district, while as mill points they are responsible for 113 per cent of the district levy target.[13] These firms, thus, play a key role in procurement.

Most of these firms have modernized rice mills, developed in Germany or Japan, with rubber rolls for the hulling process. This rubber roll technology increases the paddy/rice conversion rate from about 65 per cent to about 67 per cent. Furthermore, many of these modernized mills have oil-fired driers, cleaners, by-product separators, and polishers. The capacity of these mills varies from 1.5 to 3 tonnes of rice per hour.[14] All in all about 30 per cent of the rice mills are modernized in Akkipura district.[15] Most of my interviews have been with representatives from the milling cum trading firms, though I have also interviewed some traders without rice mills and some rice mill owners who are not involved in trading activities.

The rice milling sector is rather closed. It is a rare phenomenon that new people enter the rice milling business. Most of the rice mill owners have had their rice mills since the 1950s or 1960s. In the course of the years they have modernized their mills and expanded their business. The number of newcomers is small. Since the 1980s, new rice mills are more often the second or the third rice mill of an already established rice milling family rather than the start of a completely new firm. The most important reason for this impenetrability is that investments are relatively huge. The value of land, building and machinery of a modernized mill is about 1.5–15 million rupees (30,000–300,000 pounds). In fact, I have come across more people

[12] Figures from *Tahsildar* office, Akkipura.

[13] This can be more than 100 per cent because of the over-targeting explained above.

[14] See Harriss and Kelly (1982) on rice milling technology.

[15] Details from the Karnataka Food and Civil Supplies Department, Bangalore.

who have recently closed and/or sold their mills than people who have recently entered this business—which would suggest that concentration is taking place in this sector. However, this observation has no claim to representativeness.[16]

The profession of wholesale paddy/rice trader is more accessible than the profession of rice mill owner. The required amount of capital is less, though still considerable. Some firms have started as unlicensed traders doing some buying of paddy, custom milling and selling of rice on a small scale. These people do not necessarily have a trading background. Some of them apply for a licence after a couple of years and become registered wholesale traders; others continue their activities on a small scale without obtaining a licence. Although it is not difficult to get a licence to trade in paddy and rice, some traders decide not to apply because registration immediately involves extra obligations, in particular the obligation to surrender levy. The disadvantage of working without a licence is that expansion of the business is impossible; unlicensed traders can only work locally on a small scale.

In principle, the various milling and/or trading firms function as independent enterprises competing with each other, but there are economic and social relations between various firms. These relations may be based on family or caste ties, or they may be based on financial interdependencies. Traders who do not own a rice mill are usually associated with a rice mill owner; they hull the paddy in his mill and pay hulling charges. Most rice mill owners in Akkipura district do not dispose of sufficient cash and stock to run their machinery continuously. They need traders 'to do business in their mill'. Rice mill owners have developed different strategies to bind these traders to their mills. They may give them credit and act as moneylenders; they may reduce hulling charges; they may try to protect traders from harassment by officials and/or levy obligations.

Although these aspects of trader-trader and trader-miller relations are undoubtedly important for understanding the social intricacies of the paddy and rice market, they are less relevant for a study of levy procurement. What matters especially in this chapter are the relations between traders and millers, and the differences between them that are a result in one way or another of levy policy, or that would affect implementation.

Indeed, one can argue that levy policy influences the relations

[16] The observations are from 1991–2, when the sector was under intensive control.

among those paying levy and that organization and mobilization of these traders affects the implementation of procurement policy. Levy policy has both unifying and differentiating effects. In other words, it stimulates collective action, but it also introduces new dividing lines and additional forms of competition among those paying levy. The unifying effect exists because virtually all rice mill owners and traders regard levy policy, and officials responsible for enforcing it, as the main constraint undermining their business interests. It is an important frustration and it is a subject they can complain about endlessly. Whether it is true or not that their financial interests are damaged—and I have my doubts about that claim, but I will come back to this later—does not really matter now. What is important here is that leavy policy creates a shared frustration. The traders, in their own view, do their best 'to serve the people', while the government fails to appreciate their contribution but, instead, places obstacles in their way and regards them as proto-criminals. Let me illustrate this with a few quotations:

> We have to pay large bribes to the officials, but we are not at all respected. In the neighbouring district, the mill owners have a strong association. They still pay bribes, but they are respected. The officials say 'hello' and 'good bye'. Here, they are very impolite; there is only harassment (Rice mill owner).

> The food traders are treated as traders in heroin, while of course, they are very different kind of people. There is nothing wrong with their profession. So, why is there so much contempt and suspicion? Why is the law so strict and why are there so many checks? (Traders' advocate).

> We suffer from levy policy. The prices are very unfair. I am not against food distribution and levy, but why should we alone suffer? And you see what happens. We deliver first quality rice to the FCI. And then it is exchanged for bad quality rice, which is not even fit for human consumption, only for cattle feed and manure. While we go bankrupt because of this policy (Office bearer rice mill owners association).

In short, there is a shared feeling of being unjustifiably disadvantaged, treated with contempt or humiliated.

Sometimes the shared frustration gives rise to collective action aimed at government policy. Often the rice mill owners' association plays a crucial role in such actions. Rice mill owners in Karnataka are associated on several levels: *taluk*, district and State-wise. The district associations especially play a role in bargaining, collective action and brokerage between rice mill owners and officialdom. One of the office bearers of the rice mill owners association in Akkipura explained to me the objective of the association:

The purpose of the association is to fight the government. We fight for concessions, or we try to intervene in policy making. For instance we have protested when the District Collector tried to organize levy in such a way that we could only get permits after surrendering our full target. We have also protested against a levy obligation of 50 per cent; now they have changed it to 33 per cent. And two years back they fixed a very high district target. We sent a delegation and then they reduced it.

During my year of fieldwork in Akkipura district, I collected many accounts of collective action taking place at that moment: meetings with district officials, delegations to the Food Minister and top officials in his department, a meeting with the Chief Minister. The association functions as a lobby club to protect the shared interests of rice mill owners, which mainly have to do with levy policy.[17]

Apart from a unifying effect, levy policy also has differentiating effects on millers and traders. First, interests are divided along regional lines. This is because levy policy is not implemented uniformly in all districts. One obvious cause for this type of differentiation is related to district targets. These are based primarily on paddy production figures. But, and this is claimed by millers and traders in districts with high targets, paddy production does not automatically translate into paddy availability. Transport of paddy within Karnataka is free. Some of the biggest rice mills are located in districts where only small amounts of paddy are grown. These rice mill owners import the paddy from other districts. Due to the location of these mills the levy target is set at a low level—and in some instances this was probably one of the reasons why the mill owners constructed these huge mills in rice deficient areas in the first place. The rice mill owners of Padipura, a major rice-producing district, have even gone to the Karnataka High Court in 1992 to protest against their high district target. They demanded a more equitable distribution of targets over districts, something the Court granted.

A second differentiating effect of levy policy does not result in conflicts, but in some degree of sub specialization among the rice mill owners. This too, has to do with geographical differences. The FCI classifies rice into three categories, that is superfine, fine and common. This classification is based on the length-breadth (L/B) ratio

[17] The structure of sales tax and regulated marketing tax is another subject that has figured on the agenda of the Akkipura district association. Furthermore, the association has tried, but failed, to fix uniform hulling charges.

of the grains. Varieties having L/B ratios below 2.5 are classified as common, those having L/B ratios between 2.5 and 3.0 are fine varieties, and those with ratios of 3.0 and above are classified as superfine. There is a differential pricing system. Procurement prices are highest for superfine rice and lowest for common varieties.[18] As classification on the basis of L/B ratio does not necessarily correspond with consumer preferences and open market price differentials, traders who have to pay levy prefer to offer such varieties to the FCI as are classified superfine, but which are less profitable in the open market. In Karnataka State IR64 fulfils these criteria. Generally, consumers find it rather tasteless. It is cheap, but the FCI offers the highest price for it. IR64 is, however, not produced everywhere. There are regions where farmers grow other varieties. Rice mill owners and traders in these areas either import IR64 paddy from elsewhere or surrender levy elsewhere. It is possible for levy payers in these regions to make a deal with a rice mill owner elsewhere that the other surrenders levy in their name.

This practice of selling levy rice in the name of someone else is quite common, not only because IR64 is not produced everywhere, but also because some areas are too wet after harvest to produce rice with a low moisture content as prescribed by the FCI, or because there is no procurement centre in the vicinity. Of course, there are costs involved for the person in whose name levy is surrendered. The rice mill owner who surrenders makes some profit on the deal, and often there is a middleman as well, who brings the two parties together and who works on a commission basis.

In the wake of these regional differences, *de facto* functional specialization develops. There are some traders and rice mill owners who have specialized in the production of levy rice. For instance rice mill owner Siddanna who, together with his brothers owns two rice mills:

> In one of our rice mills we produce only rice for our own trading business. It is all exported to Kerala. In the other mill we produce rice for trade and rice for levy. There are about 10 traders working in this second mill; they have all specialised in levy. In the levy season we work day and night. During these 2–3 months we produce 2.5 loads of rice per day. We do not bother about open market prices. We only produce levy. The trader gets Rs 500 per load from the person in whose name the levy is paid. We get the hulling charges.

[18] Apart from variety, the FCI investigates moisture content, percentage of brokens, foreign matter, damaged grains, etc. It may reject offered quantities of rice, or it may reduce payment to the rice seller in case of substandard quality.

The advantage, you know, is that you don't need so much working capital. When you sell rice in the local market it will take at least 15 days before you get your money. You need a working capital of at least Rs 12.5 lakh (Rs 1.25 million). No interest is paid. It is just not feasible. But the FCI pays within 2–3 days.

Thus a small number of traders and rice mill owners have succeeded in turning levy into a source of income. A precondition to do so is that they dispense with good relationships with several other rice mill owners and paddy/rice traders elsewhere.

A third differentiating effect of levy policy is that new forms of competition are created among rice millers and traders. Due to intense regulation and control of the market that goes with levy procurement, it is of crucial importance for running a rice milling and/or trading firm to establish and maintain good relations with officials and politicians. Business success stands or falls with the strength of the social network, the quality of relationships established with other important actors involved in procurement. Some traders and mill owners are not able to cope with this. They lack the material or immaterial assets to do so, or they simply do not like to please officials. A few have gone bankrupt or closed their mills after considerable hardship. On the other hand, others see it as a challenge and thrive in this climate. Rice mill owner Shankar, for instance, says:

We don't have much problems with officials. Usually, when a new Food Assistant is appointed in the district, the former Assistant comes with the new one to our mill to introduce us to each other. Sometimes we give a party, both a farewell and a welcome party.... We contribute a lot to political parties and politicians. During the election campaign, we give Rs 15,000 to the ruling party, 8000 to the most important opposition party, 5000 to the third, 1000–2000 to independent candidates. We also give when there are special occasions. Or we offer meals or parties. We have to give that much; we are a big company.

Apart from donations, social functions, family relations and social status are important assets in business. Of the 19 major rice mill owners[19] in Akkipura *taluk,* 10 belonged to the dominant Lingayat caste; there were 3 Vaishyas, 3 Kurubas, 1 Muslim and 2 others.[20] At least eleven of the nineteen rice mill owners/firms are big property

[19] According to data from the *Tahsildar*'s office there are twenty-two rice mill owners in Akkipura *taluk* who have a levy target of more than 25 loads. I was able to collect information on nineteen of these mill owners cum traders.

[20] The Lingayat caste is the dominant caste in Akkipura district. Many government officials also belong to this caste. Vaishyas are the traditional traders. Kurubas belong to the lower castes.

owners. They either own several rice mills, oil extraction plants, theatres, a petrol station or substantive amounts of (mostly irrigated) land. There are ten firms that are well-connected in politics, mostly in Congress (I). There are only three rice mill owners out of the nineteen major ones who could not derive any influence from other assets or political connections. I interviewed two of them. They had both developed a very pragmatic view on bribing officials and politicians. 'Why should we complain', one of them said, 'we pay in ten thousands, but we earn in lakhs.'

Many of the small rice mill owners and traders lack these relationships and other assets. Although they are marginal in levy collection and, hence, remain somewhat outside the whole process, they are certainly not unaffected by the policy. In some cases, small custom millers—who are not the owners of the rice—are forced to sell levy-rice, although legally the rice hulled by them is exempted from levy. They often lack the influence and social relations to stand up against these unlawful demands. Although individual MLAs raise these issues now and then in the Karnataka Assembly, these custom millers lack a powerful medium that defends their interests.[21]

Levy enforcing officials

Officials from various departments—the Food and Civil Supplies Department, the Revenue Department and the police—are involved in levy collection. These departments are all part of the Karnataka government. In addition, there is the FCI, a Union state parastatal. The FCI is the procurement agent; it purchases rice and wheat. It has no enforcement authority. It has no means to pressurize millers for more levy. The only thing the FCI can do in order to increase levy is to convince politicians and officials in other departments that more of an effort should be made. There is frequent contact between the FCI and the enforcing departments. Regular reports about procurement progress are sent by the FCI to the Director of Food and Civil Supplies;

[21] The rice mill owners associations are, generally, completely dominated by the big milling cum trading firms and their interests. The office bearers of the Akkipura rice mill owners' association were all economically and politically powerful rice mill owners and traders. An example of the fact that the smaller firms are disadvantaged by the association is that when the rice mill owners association collects money in order to pay the Food Cell, small custom millers are asked to pay the same amount as big rice mill owners. In the eyes of the small custom millers this means they have to pay unreasonably large sums.

there are meetings about quality control, opening of procurement centres and other practical matters. In day-to-day interactions that make rice mill owners and traders surrender levy, the FCI does not play a significant role.[22]

The Directorate of Food and Civil Supplies is part of the Food and Transport Department. The Directorate has a head office in Bangalore and district offices in each district. The head office is headed by the Director, who visits the districts now and then to monitor procurement progress and keep an eye on other things, such as distribution, stock, etc. The Director is a member of the IAS. These high-level civil servants are so-called generalists; they are not specialized in a particular field. They are regularly transferred from one post to another. The district office is headed by a Deputy Director, who is generally called Food Assistant. Virtually all these Deputy Directors in Karnataka come from the Revenue Department; they work on a deputation basis in the Food Department. All other staff members below the rank of Food Assistant belong to the Department's own personnel. Like all other officials they are liable to transfers, but only within the Food and Civil Supplies Department.

While not all staff members of the district offices are involved in procurement activities, the Food Assistant along with some of his subordinates is. This entails, among other things, keeping records of who has surrendered levy and how much; issuing release certificates for free market rice; manning checkposts in the district where lorries transporting rice are inspected and visiting and/or raiding rice mills and trading companies to pressurize for levy. If they find any irregularities they may hand over the case to the police force for further investigation. The Deputy Commissioner may order the confiscation of the commodities.

The Deputy Commissioner, or District Collector as he is called in most other Indian States, is the highest official at the district level. He is also a member of the IAS, and he is ultimately in charge of procurement in the district. Within each *taluk* there is a *Tahsildar*, a member of the Karnataka Administrative Service (KAS). In the office of the *Tahsildar*, which is part of the Revenue Department—the most important task of this office is to collect taxes—there are one or two people responsible for procurement. They may be from the Food and Civil Supplies Department or from the Revenue Department. Their

[22] Before the mid-1980s, the Karnataka Food and Civil Supplies Corporation (KaFCSC) was also involved as procurement agent.

tasks are similar to the tasks of the officers working under the Food Assistant: monitoring procurement, visiting/raiding rice mills, manning checkposts, etc.

Since 1980, the police force has a special Food Cell, later renamed as Food and Civil Supplies Enforcement Department, but still known to the public as the Food Cell. Originally, the Cell was under the administrative control of the Home Department, but since 1989 it is part of the Food and Transport Department. The head office is in Bangalore, and it has five regional offices spread over Karnataka. The major task of the Food Cell is to safeguard the effective enforcement of the EC Act. Enforcement of the Rice Procurement (Levy) Order, one of the government orders issued in Karnataka under the Act, is one of the tasks of the Food Cell. Officials of the Cell conduct raids on rice mills and trading companies; they also control food transport. In case of irregularities, they hand over the case to the local police.

Thus in several offices people perform similar jobs. Procurement is administered and monitored by the Food Assistant and his staff of the Food and Civil Supplies Department, as well as by the Deputy Commissioner and *Tahsildar* and their staff from the Revenue Department. With regard to enforcement, even more people are involved, as officials from the Food Cell and the local police are also responsible. On the one hand, this means that there is overlap in the work: many officials have similar responsibilities. On the other hand, there is a division of tasks between these various people from various departments, which sometimes results in complicated procedures. For instance after a trader surrenders one load rice to the FCI he gets a voucher. He then has to go to the office of the Food Assistant to get two release certificates. Within thirty days he has to go to the *taluk* office to get two transport certificates, to be used within twenty-four hours.

Despite the different ranks and different departmental backgrounds, the various officials involved in procurement have several things in common. In the first place, they are all officials, posted temporarily in a particular post or 'station'. They are all transferable, some to other departments, others to other posts within the same department or to similar posts in other districts or regions. According to transfer rules the duration of a posting is about three years, and certainly not less than two years. In reality, however, transfers take place much more frequently. Table 4.2 shows that the average tenure of officials in the key positions as far as food matters are concerned varies between ten and fourteen months. Officials lower in the hierarchy are also often transferred.[23]

Table 4.2

Frequency of transfers in key positions related to food

Position	Number of people posted between 1980–92	Average tenure
Director, Food and Civil Supplies (IAS)	15	10 months
Deputy Commissioner, Akkipura (IAS)	13	11 months
Food Assistant, Akkipura	10	14 months
Supt of Police & Dy Director, Food Cell (IPS)	10	14 months

Source: Personal interviews and wallboards in the offices.

This fact of being transferable, and having to live with the uncertainty of transfer in the very near future, is a dominant feature of the professional life of each civil servant. It also has consequences for the way offices and departments function. It always takes some time for new officials to know the ins and outs of the department and the specific characteristics of the area they are working in. A lot of valuable knowledge is lost or never gained because of frequent transfers. The probability of a quick transfer also prevents people from digging deep into a matter. It stimulates a mentality of 'let's wait and see; it will last out my time'. And last, but not least, the frequency and uncertainty of transfers make people do many extra things in order to influence their next transfer. Traditionally, June in the transfer season, although many transfers happen outside the yearly rounds. In the weeks before transfers are announced many people do not work; they are running around trying to use influence to convince others in order to get favourable transfers. Many of the posts that have to do with levy procurement, certainly in a rice-producing district such as Akkipura, are very much desired. So here the officials are trying to exert influence *not* to be transferred to other less preferred places or posts. The Food Assistant of Akkipura district, for instance, was transferred

[23] The Karnataka F&CS Department is not exceptional in this respect. See Potter (1987, 1988).

to another place within one year of his initial posting, but after employing influence he was reposted to Akkipura.[24]

Officially, the higher civil servants decide about transfers of lower officials, while the government decides about transfers of top civil servants. In reality, politicians play a role in most transfers, even of office clerks and lower rank civil servants. It is an open secret that payment is an important mean of influencing transfer decisions. An Assistant Director in Akkipura, whom I talked with during a break outside the office, told me about the transfers:

> 'I think it is terrible. There is no continuity in the office, and we don't have peace of mind. We don't know about today; we don't know about tomorrow. Today I am working here, but what about tomorrow? I am having two children and I just shifted my family to this place. Now we have settled here, but what if I am transferred? As a father I have some responsibilities. Some people go without their families but that is very expensive; then we have to maintain two households. I shouldn't say this to you but sometimes people pay 1–2 lakh (Rs 100,000–200,000) for a transfer, and then without caring for the person who is doing the job at that moment there is a transfer. At the moment it is really too much....' I said I had heard about another district where a few months back the Food Assistant had been replaced four times within one month. 'That's right' he said. 'I was working there at that time.' I asked whether all these four people had paid for the post. He said 'You are correct; you are understanding the system. Afterwards I was posted to C; now I am posted here since three-four months. We don't know for how long.' I asked whether there is no way to protest. He answered, '95 per cent of the officials are very much against this government, and think there should be a change. But we can't do anything. If we complain the government does not like it. Without verification we are transferred.'

A second thing the various officials have in common is the fact that their job—enforcement of levy policy—offers good opportunities to make money. For a corrupt official it is very lucrative to get a post in levy enforcement in a district such as Akkipura. There are many rules and regulations to enforce; it is always possible to find some mischief. The people to control are moneyed people. They are able and willing to spend large amounts if they think their business would benefit from that. And in the case of levy, this is the case indeed. Depending on the difference between the levy price and the open market price, the losses caused by procurement varied from Rs 4000 to Rs 15,000 per levy

[24] See also Wade (1985) and de Zwart (1992) about the history, the effects and reasons behind frequent transfers.

load in the 1991–2 season.[25] It is no surprise that rice mill owners and traders are willing to strike a deal with enforcing officials. They have no objection to paying large amounts of bribes if that would result in fewer levy obligations or less levy-related harassment.

A third shared feature of officials involved in levy policy is the fact that they have to deal with contradictory tasks and instructions. On the one hand, they are responsible for levy collection. Rice should be purchased by the government, and they are the prime people to organize this. On the other hand they have to comply with incidental (but often frequent) instructions from politicians, which often hinder their work. This is illustrated in the following story:

In February 1992, the rice mill owners in Akkipura started to feel increasingly uneasy. The open market paddy price was high, and the loss on each load of levy was too much, they felt. Still, the district target was a long way ahead. Collectively, they had only reached 40 per cent of the target, much less than in the previous year on the same date. They considered collecting a large bribe to convince the Food Minister himself to reduce the target.

When the Deputy Commissioner heard of this plan he foresaw difficulties. If indeed the rice mill owners and wholesale paddy/rice traders would 'convince' the Food Minister that procurement was too harmful for their business, he—the Deputy Commissioner—would be in an awkward predicament. It would mean that political support for harassing and threatening rice mill owners and traders—the main pillar of levy enforcement—would be reduced. On the other hand, the blame for not reaching the district target would continue to rest on his shoulders. Hence he had to act quickly. Within one week he raided more than a dozen rice mills, and seized the paddy and rice present in the mills. The idea was that in due course these commodities could be used as a lever to safeguard the levy. However, a few days later the Chief Minister happened to visit the area. Through a middleman the rice mill owners sought contact and succeeded in arranging a meeting. The millers explained their case, and on the spot the Chief Minister ordered the Deputy Commissioner to release the seized commodities against only an indemnity bond.

So the officials responsible for levy procurement are faced with the difficult task of reconciling the official *and* unofficial instructions, which come from the same politicians or superiors and which are often contradictory.

[25] In reality, this financial loss may be much smaller, since traders and rice mill owners probably compensate for this loss both by giving less money to their suppliers and by selling open market rice at a higher price. It is difficult to estimate these price effects of levy procurement, but, according to some rice mill owners, both strategies are pursued in order to reduce the losses.

Politicians

The third category of actors involved in procurement is formed by politicians. There are various types of politicians. They may operate on a local or (Karnataka) State level; they may represent the ruling party or an opposition party. Here I concentrate on members of the Karnataka Legislative Assembly—including members of the Cabinet—as they are the most prominent politicians in Karnataka. In principle their role is twofold: (*a*) as legislators, involved in the process of policy making, pushing particular issues they or their party think important (*b*) as middlemen, acting on behalf of their constituency or mediating in local conflicts. This second role matters much more to most MLAs than the first one.

In order to investigate their role as legislators I interviewed about five politicians of various political parties during the election campaign in 1991. Some were (candidate) members of Parliament or the Legislative Assembly; others were MLAs or party workers. I also interviewed the present and previous ministers of Food and Civil Supplies on their ideas of food policy, and I collected background material from the political parties and their election manifestos. Two things emerged very clearly from this material. First, there were hardly any differences between the standpoints of the various political parties. Viewpoints differed, but that had more to do with individual preferences than with systematic party differences[26]. Second, apart from one or two exceptions, the ideas and opinions expressed by these politicians were not original or well thought out in any way. Often the viewpoints expressed in the interviews were contradictory. Most of the politicians were in favour of protecting farmers' incomes, which is not surprising in view of the strength of the farmers' movement and its hold over vote banks. Simultaneously, they were against raising consumer prices. Middlemen and traders should be kept short; yet the free market was regarded as the best solution. The less control the better. They were against a dual market system, but in favour of the

[26] Harriss did similar fieldwork before the State Legislative Assembly elections in 1980 in Tamil Nadu. She also concludes that 'with the exception of the CPM there is equally abundant policy confusion and ideological obfuscation within these political parties as between them' (Harriss, 1984 a: 276). It may, however, be that differences between the parties will become more explicit in the future. According to Vithal (1994: 205) the tenth General Election in 1991 was the first occasion on which the preparation of manifestos of different parties was given serious attention, because it was realized that these manifestos could possibly constitute the basis on which coalitions would have to be forged.

PDS, and depending on the question they were against the exclusion of certain categories of people from the PDS but in favour of targeting subsidies to others.

In the Karnataka Assembly, the issue of levy is only occasionally discussed. Politicians of the opposition party sometimes take the opportunity to accuse the government that the PDS is not implemented properly and that the ruling party is not able or willing to force traders to surrender levy. More often, individual legislators defend the interests of traders, big rice mill owners and small custom millers in their district/constituencies by arguing that there should be exemptions from levy in particular cases, or that the 'atrocities and unfair deeds' of officials go beyond conventional limits.

At the level of the constituency, politicians are much more present MLAs function as mediators in local conflicts, smoothers of policy implementation processes, resource brokers and gatekeepers regulating access to influential politicians. This, in fact, is what people expect from their representatives, as others have also observed. For instance, Potter (1986: 152) writes:

> An anthropologist[27] who worked in Orissa in the 1950s reported that electors in villages demanded two things of their MLA (Member Legislative Assembly). The first was his reliability in saying 'my constituency right or wrong'. The second was that the MLA 'should be effective, and by this they do not mean that he should make a mark in the legislature, but that he should be able to stand up to local officials in the interests of his constituents'. For a successful MLA is a 'fixer' in the eyes of many people, someone who can get a man a job, divert development monies into the constituency, help secure a contract, find a place in a school or a hospital.

This description still contains much truth. Several MLAs who represent constituencies in Akkipura district are 'fixers' indeed. They mediate in conflicts between rice mill owners and officials—for instance about individual targets or about seizures; they give some protection against bureaucratic harassment; they act as middlemen between rice mill owners and the Food and/or Chief Minister.

In most instances, it is in the interests of—and on request of—rice mill owners that these politicians intervene. Officials generally regard this intervention as unnecessary interference. They think it hampers administration because seizures, harassments and other things they regard as necessary are undone. The effect of political interference is that in the long run the prestige and authority of officialdom are

[27] Bailey (1962: 120).

undermined. It is relatively rare that Deputy Commissioners are able to withstand the pressure from MLAs. In the daily battles between officials and politicians, the latter usually get their way.

Why do MLAs so often take up the cause of rice mill owners and wholesale paddy/rice traders? Unfortunately, the material collected in my research gives only an incomplete answer, as my access to rice mill owners was much better than my access to politicians. But there are at least two mechanisms that seem to play a role. First, rice mill owners and wholesale paddy/rice traders and politicians are closely connected to each other. They are part of the same social networks. They belong to the same castes, sometimes to the same families. Several rice mill owners are party members and politically active at the local level. This increases their access to and ties with other more influential politicians. In fact, both professions—politician and miller/trader—are comparable jobs. They require considerable capital, as well as good personal networks. Notwithstanding the exceptions, many politicians and millers/traders have a similar class background. They belong to the entrepreneurial rich. All this means that when politicians take up the cause of millers and traders they (*a*) defend issues they are familiar with and (*b*) often defend their own kin, caste members or friends.

Second, there are considerable material benefits. Rice mill owners are moneyed people who spend large sums on donations to political parties. As a lawyer said in an interview: 'MLAs need lakhs of rupees to finance their election campaigns. Mill owners contribute to that.'

Also the effectiveness of political interference, the control of politicians over the bureaucracy, is an intriguing question which can only tentatively be answered here. MLAs have access to resources and to influential people in the Cabinet and top ranks of the administration that others do not have. If their requests are not fulfilled they may be able to mobilize even more powerful pressure. One of the implicit threats is related to their control over the transfer process. If a Deputy Commissioner is really stubborn and refuses to give in, he risks getting an unfavourable transfer. In reality, this means that many officials are only able to withstand political interference when they receive orders from above to do so.

4.3 COOPERATION, EXCHANGE AND STRUGGLE DURING IMPLEMENTATION

The description of the various actors involved in procurement, their different interests, strategies and means/tools leaves no doubt about the nature of the encounter. It is a battle in which the various actors involved all try to realize their own conflicting objectives. Traders and rice mill owners are competing with each other; collectively they fight and negotiate with officials and politicians. The government needs to procure sufficient amounts of rice; officials are responsible. Simultaneously, many civil servants are searching for additional sources of income, and politicians regularly interfere in the conflicts between those liable to pay levy and civil servants. To a certain extent the various interests and objectives are also compatible. While some encounters result in clear winners and losers, on other occasions all parties profit to an extent. In other words, there is both struggle, exchange and cooperation in the process of procurement implementation. Various types of interaction will pass in review in this section.

Levy and threat

Despite the fact that each load of levy means a loss of Rs 4000–15,000, that is in the conception of traders and rice mill owners, rice is sold as levy to the FCI. This does not mean that traders and mill owners cooperate with levy policy; it means that they are compelled to sell rice as levy now and then. Officials dispose over two forceful instruments to enforce levy policy, namely the EC Act and individual targets.

The EC Act dates from 1955 and has been amended several times since. Each amendment has made the law more strict. There is a minimum punishment laid down in the law; the burden of proof rests with the accused, that is the trader; and EC cases are tried in special courts. In Chapter 7, I will discuss the EC Act and the way it functions in more detail. Here I will only illustrate how it facilitates levy procurement.[28]

The order describing levy collection is the Karnataka Rice Procurement (Levy) Order, 1984. However, in the process of levy collection and in day-to-day interactions of officials and rice mill owners, other orders are more important. These are the EC (Maintenance of Accounts, Display of Prices and Stocks) Order that describes how traders in essential commodities have to keep accounts and display a price list of the commodities for sale, and the EC Licensing Order. These orders describe trading procedures in such detail that it is virtually impossible to comply fully with the rules.

[28] As with the rest of this book, this section is based on fieldwork conducted in 1991–2. Since then, various provisions of the ECA have been relaxed (*EPW* editorial 14 Nov. 1995, pp. 2900–1).

Both traders and officials agree on this. A highly placed official explained:

> You are asking me whether rice mill owners cooperate with levy policy. Well, we can't use the word cooperation in this context. Rice mill owners respond to the threat. We can exercise a lot of threat with the help of the Essential Commodities Act. Even for a well willing person it is impossible to follow all the regulations. There are sufficient possibilities to give trouble to the millers. And the millers, they respond. It is very easy to punish them. If we seize their commodities, the EC Act says: if the commodities are perishable—and they always are—and if there is a public demand for the commodities—and there always is a public demand in the case of rice—the Deputy Commissioner can decide to sell the commodities. The price to be paid to the miller is a fair price, that is the PDS price of controlled commodities. That is much lower than the open market price. This is such a threat for the rice mill owners; they will give the levy.

In addition, individual targets are a handy instrument for deciding who should be pressurized for the levy. As long as a miller/trader has not surrendered his target, there is a considerable risk of being harassed to sell more levy-rice.

Not only officials, but also millers and traders regard threat as a crucial element of procurement. As a rice miller remarked: 'When there is a seizure we have to do something. We usually have two options. Either we pay levy, or we pay bribes.' Or otherwise, as stated by the official, the Deputy Commissioner may decide to confiscate the commodities—which would involve a considerable loss—and a court case may even follow, often for an arbitrary contravention that has nothing to do with levy. In short, the various orders coming under the EC Act are very suitable instruments with which to threaten traders liable to pay levy. Procurement is achieved by using the law in improper and probably illegal ways.

Social networks and cooperation

As indicated earlier, some rice mill owners and traders consciously try to develop friendly and pleasant relationships with officials responsible for procurement. They pay their respects, organize parties or try to please the officials otherwise.

Another phenomenon is that sometimes officials start behaving as partners in trade. I collected a few examples where civil servants and rice mill owners seemed hand in glove.

Each load of levy is registered in the name of a trader and in the name of the rice mill in which the paddy is converted into rice. Often the trader and rice mill owner are the same person, but not always. Some rice mill owners do not have a licence to trade in essential commodities. In those cases they need another person, a trader with an EC licence, to surrender levy. In such cases officials sometimes act as brokers, mediating between the trader and the miller/job huller.

Murthy has a rice mill, in which he hulls paddy mainly for farmers. He has no EC licence himself, although he does (necessarily unaccounted) trading himself. His levy target for 1991–2 is 20 loads. Last year he surrendered 8 loads. He told me the following. 'Last year there was another Paddy Procurement Assistant [PPA] working in the *Tahsildar*'s office than the one who is there now. He did like this. He was very powerful. First he went to a trader who had not yet fulfilled his levy obligations, and he threatened and told him to surrender the levy. Then he went to a custom miller like me, and he said: 'I know someone who wants to give levy for you, for free.' Then I had to give him Rs 400. Last year I could give 8 loads in this way, through different traders depending on the PPA. My loss was very little. Now there is another PPA who does not yet understand these kind of things.'

In this example, the Paddy Procurement Assistant no longer regards himself as an outsider who inspects, controls and enforces. Instead, his involvement is such that he becomes a middleman in business transactions. As Paddy Procurement Assistant, he is knowledgeable about the extent to which various traders and rice mill owners have fulfilled their levy obligations. Moreover, as a result of his position he can easily exercise power over the others. Together, this gives him an excellent opportunity to earn some extra income through brokerage.

As compared to the relationship between civil servants and traders/millers liable to pay levy, friendship and cooperation is a more common characterization of the relationship between traders/millers and politicians. As described earlier, local MLAs often act as stand-bys to divert or undo seizures, or to help rice mill owners and traders out of other precarious situations.

Bribes

Virtually all the examples given so far show the ever important role of bribes. Whether officials threaten or act as middlemen, bribes are usually part of the deal. And officials are not the only bribe takers, politicians also accept donations from rice mill owners and traders, both during election time and outside it. It seems impossible to run a business without giving bribes now and then. In any case, I have not met one trader or rice mill owner who maintained throughout that he never gave bribes.[29] Several rice mill owners calculated on paper exactly how much they had to give each year to everyone, and how much this added up to in total. See Fig. 4.2 for an example.

As far as officials are concerned, it is possible for them not to take bribes. Although there is pressure on officials to pass money on to higher officials and politicians, it still seems possible not to participate in this chain of money collection. There are costs attached to opting out, of which the most obvious one is the probability of unfavourable transfers. Nevertheless, in the course of fieldwork I have met a few officials who claimed to have never participated in the transfer circus and who were often posted to the least attractive posts and regions.

From the perspective of the bribe giver, bribes can serve various functions. First, bribes are used to establish normal working relations. Without expecting any direct favour rice mill owners and traders tend to give money to officials. To give an example from my research diary:

In August 1991 I met rice mill owner Venkatesh for the first time. He told me that a new Food Assistant had just been appointed in the district. He had not yet met this new official. Three months later I met Venkatesh again. He recounted that he had visited the Food-Assistant the previous morning. 'I went to his house with Rs 1000.' I asked why. 'There is no special reason,' he said. 'It is just normal that we go now and then and pay Rs 1000. So, why not take the initiative myself?' Venkatesh had been accompanied by the PPA. But unexpectedly, the Food Assistant had refused the money. 'After some time, we have to wait a little bit,' he had said. Venkatesh had taken back his money and had left the room. The PPA had stayed for a short while. Afterwards the mill owner had asked the PPA why the Food Assistant had not accepted the money. 'He wants to see whether he can increase the amount. It he accepts Rs 1000 from you, that will be the normal amount. Maybe he wants more,' the PPA had replied. In March 1992 I met Venkatesh for the third time. Now he told me that the Food Assistant had demanded Rs 3000 from all the rice mill owners. Venkatesh had tried to negotiate about this amount, but had failed. So far he had only given Rs 1850, but, as he said, 'one of these days I have to settle the balance'.

[29] Sometimes traders/millers were reluctant to talk about these things. They first enquired of the person who had introduced me whether they could be frank with me and tell me all this. One or two rice mill owners kept saying till the end of the interview that they never gave bribes, and then off the record, in Kannada, they told my companion they give money to officials like all the others.

Seasonal bribes		***Rupees***
Food Assistant		3000
Tahsildar		3000
Food Inspector		1000
Paddy Procurement Assistant		1000
Food Cell		1600
Regulated Marketing Court (RMC) Secretary		1000
RMC Squad		2500
Other bribes in relation to RMC		2000
TOTAL		15,100
Annual bribes		
Pollution control		500
Boiler inspection		700
Labour inspection		300
Provident Fund Inspector		250
Factory inspection		600
Renewal EC licence (Food and Civil Supplies Department)		250
Renewal rice mill licence (Food and Civil Supplies Department)		250
Commercial Tax Office intelligence		3000
TOTAL		5850
Bribes depending on levy and free sale rice		
FCI	per load levy	500
Food and Civil Supplies Department	per release certificate	50
Checkposts	per lorry rice	10–20
Irregular bribes		
Deputy Superintendent of Police (1991–2 for the first time)		500
Superintendent of Police (1991–2 for the first time)		2000
Circle Inspector		not fixed
Commercial Tax Office		depends on turnover
Karnataka Electricity Board		not fixed
Additional bribe for the Food Minister in 1991–2 per rice mill fixed at		3000

Fig. 4.2 Overview of bribes 1991–1992 (Rice Mill Owner Lingaraju)

The bribe in this example does not serve any special purpose. It is meant to put things on good terms, to establish a pleasant relationship, which is seen by the rice mill owner as a necessary condition to run his business. It is clear that the relationship between an individual rice mill owner/trader and official is an unequal one. The Food Assistant dictates the terms. The bribe-giving party cannot do much except accept his demands.

A second reason for giving bribes is to get a certain, very normal and necessary job done at all. For instance when a rice mill owner surrenders one load levy to the FCI he should get a voucher. In order to get this voucher he has to pay Rs 500. Although this is illegal, it is the normal procedure. The price is fixed and the same for everyone, provided there is nothing wrong with the rice. However, if the seller of levy-rice has surrendered substandard rice the price may be higher. Here we see the third function of bribes: to buy a special favour. Bribes are given on an occasional basis to get a target reduced, to get substandard rice accepted as levy, to facilitate illegal transports, to avoid a seizure, etc.

The practice of bribe giving and taking is not always a matter between individual actors. Often the rice mill owners' association plays an intermediary role. The Food Cell, for instance, makes it known to the office-bearers of the association when it plans to visit the area. The secretary of the association is then supposed to telephone around and tell all the rice mill owners that they have to give a certain amount of money. The money is collected and handed over in a lump sum during the visit of the squad. Also the collection of the large bribe for the Food Minister mentioned at the beginning of this chapter was organized by the rice mill owners' association. As one of the office-bearers once remarked sarcastically in an interview: 'We are the brokers for the officials.'

Even though bribes are a very normal, daily and crucial part of the interactions in the procurement arena, there are risks involved. The bribe giver may hope to influence future events and anticipate a lenient attitude of the bribe taker, but he can never be sure about the result. To give a bribe differs from making a purchase. There is no legal contract backing the deal, and no receipt is given. The bribe taker can always decide not to fulfil the expectations created in the transaction. There is no right or entitlement the bribe giver can refer to to make a claim. Trust is important in the deal, and that makes the establishment and maintenance of extra-economic and extra-administrative relations so important. The better the social relation between the two parties, the more secure the deal.[30] Various traders and rice mill

[30] This may be one of the reasons why middlemen are often involved in bribery. For

owners do indeed develop strategies to establish or maintain such relationships, as was described above.

Legal struggle about the levy system

While the three types of interactions discussed so far all deal with the day-to-day practice of levy collection, there is a fourth type of interaction important in procurement. Both collectively and individually, traders liable to pay levy try to convince the government that the system of levy collection is unfair and detrimental to the rice milling industry. Appendix 2 contains parts of letters sent by the Karnataka State Rice Millers Association, in which the association requests the total abolition of mill point levy or the relaxation of levy policy.

Also in face-to-face encounters, rice mill owners and traders try to convince levy enforcing officials or politicians of the evils of the system. One strategic point of entry is, for instance, the target system of levy collection, which is a thorn in the flesh of most traders selling levy rice. The following excerpt is from an interview with a rice mill owner cum trader.

"Today, the Director (Food and Civil Supplies) came to Akkipura. There was a large meeting, with the DC, the Food Assistant, the FCI and some more officials, and 35–40 rice mill owners. Our chairman [of the Rice Mill Owners' association] spoke. He said that we are prepared to give one-third of our produce as levy, but we are very much against the target system". I was surprised. At present, the targets are fixed at a level much below one-third of the production. The mill owner resumed: "I know. Also the Director said that we would be in big trouble, that levy is now only 10 per cent, rather than 33 per cent. Of course, we know that. But you know, the levy order is unimplementable. The officials would lose all control. The target system is very convenient for officials. It makes us all defaulters, and then the Food Assistant can threaten. That is why we argue in favour of the levy order."

---

the bribe giver the middleman means an extra witness. Usually the middleman in known to both parties. His presence adds to the weight of the transaction. In other cases, the involvement of a middleman may have a different function, middlemen makes it possible that bribe giver and taker do not meet each other personally, which makes it easier to maintain the image of a clean unspoilt institution. For instance, in the case of bribing judges. Compared to other parts of the state the judiciary has a relatively clean reputation. To protection this image direct contact between bribe giver and taker is avoided; all contact is through middlemen.

Apart from sending letters and memoranda, and participating in discussions, rice mill owners have also gone to the Karnataka High Court. They have challenged maximum stock limits, transport restrictions, bureaucratic retardation, or their arrest after a seizure. Indeed, many of them have succeeded individually in obtaining favourable court orders on these issues. I even met one rice mill owner who had employed a manager especially for this purpose: challenging legal provisions and administrative orders in court. Sometimes groups of rice mill owners go to court together.

4.4 THE EFFECTS OF LEVY POLICY

Despite manipulations and lack of cooperation of those liable to pay levy, procurement does take place. In the years between 1986 and 1992, on an average between 60 and 90 per cent of the levy target has been collected. Thus in terms of sheer quantities, procurement policy is reasonably successful. The way in which this end result in achieved differs vastly from official procedures as laid down in the Karnataka Rice Procurement (Levy) Order. Not only have enforcing officials devised their own additional system of procurement, procurement policy is also imposed in a seemingly arbitrary fashion. Procedures vary from Deputy Commissioner to Deputy Commissioner, from district to district, from year to year, and they may even change in the course of the season. Some traders are exempted from certain legal procedures, either because they obtained a stay order, bribed the officials or are well connected to influential politicians, while others are faced with strict procedures and officials. Enforcement happens at unexpected moments, and often contains an element of threat and coercion. Although the Food and Civil Supplies Enforcement Department usually gives notice in advance when it plans to visit a certain area, many raids and seizures have a surprise element. Even rice mill owners who are well-connected to politicians are not completely safeguarded against raids or seizures.

This apparent arbitrariness is not coincidental. On the contrary, it is fundamental to the way procurement is achieved and it is consciously maintained. It is the essence of the attempt of the bureaucracy to control traders and millers, as it is thought that fear and uncertainty helps in the process of compelling the latter to sell levy rice.

As can be expected, this seemingly arbitrary implementation of procurement policy has consequences for the organization of the rice trade and differentiation among those selling levy rice. From the viewpoint of the trader, arbitrary implementation means uncertainty. It is often unclear which rice mill will be visited by officials to push for levy; bribes may help to divert a seizure, but not always; at the beginning of the season it is often not clear whether release certificates will be issued immediately or only after a certain number of loads have been sold as levy; the attitude of politicians is not known, whether they will be in favour of relaxation or in favour of strict implementation; officials in charge may be transferred in the course of the year and replaced by others with a different attitude and/or a different social network, etc.

The result is that paddy/rice traders and rice mill owners, who in different circumstances are powerful people, are made dependent on the administration and politicians. While on other occasions these traders and rice mill owners act as patrons and are in command, procurement policy implementation turns them into clients and bribes givers who hope to buy a favour.

I have already discussed the three functions of bribes from the perspective of the bribe giver. But there is a more general point to make in relation to arbitrary implementation and bribery. Threats and bribes are felt as humiliating by those who are harassed and pay bribes. They feel degraded; their social status is reduced. In the case of procurement policy implementation—where sometimes lower rank officials who are not always members of a dominant caste have to deal with economically powerful and politically well-connected traders—this is crucial. It means that officials responsible for policy implementation gain authority over these traders.

Thus from the perspective of civil servants, the system functions as a means to control traders and force them to comply, to some extent. Bribery is, hence, not simply in contradiction with policy implementation. In the case of procurement, it can also be seen as a crucial element of policy implementation, as it contributes to shifting the balance of power between those implementing the policy and those liable to pay levy and resisting it, in favour of the former.

Not all millers and traders are able to cope with this reduced status and uncertainty. Some clearly live with a lot of frustration and stress; a few even close their mills. Others, however, thrive very well in this climate of arbitrariness. Erratic implementation means that there is ample scope for obtaining individual treatment and getting round certain parts of the policy. Cultivating friendly relations with officials and bribing them has a high pay-off potentially. Involving politicians in the struggle and bargaining process can be very rewarding. Arbitrary implementation, thus, induces particular forms of competition between firms. The ability to maintain extra-economic and extra-administrative relationships becomes a very important asset for running a business and competing with others, perhaps to the same extent or even more than investment in technology or strategic market transactions.

This is not only true as far as the big milling cum trading firms are concerned. Also the small custom millers are affected. These firms often lack the social network to offer resistance against demands and threats for levy, while the rice mill owners' association is also more concerned with the big firms.

We may, hence, hypothesize that intense and arbitrary enforcement raises a barrier against entering the milling and trading business. A newcomer lacks the necessary contacts and is, therefore, more vulnerable. The effect of this would be that rice milling and paddy/rice trade develop into a production process cum market with oligopolistic characteristics. The rice price would become higher and profits would increase. According to some rice mill owners this is indeed the case:

> Jaganath and Narayanswami are two brothers who together own two modern rice mills. They are very influential people in the region, as they maintain good relationships with MLAs as well as religious leaders. When I interviewed them about rice procurement and their dealings with officials they told me frankly about all their frustrations and grievances. They had been involved in several court cases; they had had a big fight with the Deputy Commissioner who had threatened to confiscate their whole stock worth Rs 15 lakh (1.5 million), and they were very dissatisfied with their mill target, which was much too high in their opinion. At the end of the interview the person who had introduced me asked them for their opinion about levy policy. I anticipated that they would just continue their complaint, but to my surprise they answered: 'Well actually, we are earning a lot of money. We always complain, but if the government lifted levy policy, everybody would do the same business in the free market. There would be much more competition; and our profit would be less.'

This story of Jaganath and Narayanswami supports the hypothesis that arbitrary implementation of procurement policy contributes to a market with oligopolistic characteristics, and, hence, to an increase in economic power of some of the more successful traders and rice mill owners. But more research is necessary to corroborate this idea.

Apart from this effect on competition and the characteristics of the rice/paddy market, procurement policy also affects the bureaucracy, as it offers additional opportunities to enforcing officials to collect an extra income. As many of the traders paying levy are moneyed people, it is often a lucrative job to deal with them. The executive posts of Food Assistant and Food Inspector are, hence, desired and well paid for. Simultaneously, a proper execution of the tasks of the job themselves is often difficult due to political interference. As the descriptions in this chapter illustrate, this interference is a regular phenomenon, usually motivated by personal or political considerations. Often civil servants obediently carry out instructions from politicians. Some of the officials I interviewed complained about this situation, but many others regard it as a *fait accompli*, although it obstructs their work. Often they feel that they have no choice but to oblige.

In fact, this situation means these civil servants are caught in a doubly contradictory situation. In their dealings with those liable to pay levy, they have to balance and negotiate the diverse objectives of collecting levy and collecting bribes. They develop strategies and relationships in order to combine these two dimensions of their work. This situation is cross-cut by additional and incidental orders made by politicians, which often obstruct the slightly longer-term strategies they have devised to deal with the traders and rice mill owners. Given this double contradiction, it is no surprise that many civil servants develop a non-committed and indifferent attitude.[31]

To summarize, the struggles and interactions described in this chapter clearly illustrate that rice is a precious commodity. Levy enforcing officials aim to procure it, but traders and rice mill owners do not want to part with it because selling to the government at a fixed rate is less profitable than selling to others at a self-determined moment. The struggle is not about rice alone, but also about official rules and regulations and other norms defining command over the commodity. Government officials devise new rules and policies; traders and rice mill owners challenge these in court, and both categories of actors manipulate the official rule systems in order to get more out of them. The system of levy is the main reason for political mobilization of the rice mill owners and traders. Individually and collectively, they make many efforts to retain the rice and change

[31] Vithal (1994) also points out that political interference and the absence of clear-cut objectives result in erosion of discipline in the bureaucracy and decreasing efficiency.

levy procurement regulations. At the same time, some of the traders liable to pay levy seem to profit from the practices and social relations that have developed around procurement implementation. New forms of competition have emerged and/or intensified that centre around extra-economic and extra-administrative relationships. In this sense, levy policy influences not only the market in rice, but also the political process. It creates, reproduces and reinforces a political system in which influence is exercised primarily outside the electoral system or official bodies of consultation and negotiation, but through personal links and the ability to pay.

5

Food Distribution
About entitlement and access, rationing and appropriation

Mahatma Gandhi has never run a fair price shop

(*Kannada* expression)

Once rice and wheat are procured, they are stored and often transported to depots in other parts of the country. Thereafter, it changes hands from the FCI to a local (PDS) wholesale dealer, then to a (PDS) retail dealer, and finally it reaches the consumer/card holder. That at least, is, the official model of the organization of the PDS. This chapter describes and analyses day-to-day processes of food distribution. The main question is: how does food distribution policy work out in reality? What will become clear in this chapter is that the poorest and most vulnerable people are not among the prime beneficiaries of the PDS. On the contrary, the subordinate classes have limited access and benefit only marginally. The chapter analyses various mechanisms that lead to this situation.

First, I start with a presentation of official facts and figures concerning the PDS. How is food distribution organized, how much food is distributed and for what price? Then, Sections 5.2 to 5.4 take a closer look at actual distribution practices. Each of these sections has a different point of entry, namely (*a*) Consumers/card holders: their entitlements and use of the PDS (5.2), (*b*) the relationship of the public with the bureaucracy: the organization of 'access' and opportunities to voice complaints (5.3), and (*c*) ration dealers: their financial difficulties and the 'solutions' they have developed (5.4). Different mechanisms influencing (often restricting) the relevance of the PDS for consumers are revealed in this analysis. Finally, the fifth section draws some conclusions regarding the functioning of food policy in Karnataka and Kerala. In both States, PDS foodgrain is not only a nutritional and an economic commodity, but also a political one. But as a result of the different political-economic contexts in which the PDS is embedded, this political commodity character is different in these two States. Generally, while in Karnataka, PDS food contributes to the economic and political power of some of the already powerful actors involved, in Kerala, PDS food has become an issue in popular mobilization and public action directed at a more accountable implementation of government policies.

5.1 SOME FACTS AND FIGURES

The system of distribution

Both in Karnataka and Kerala, food distribution is a complex mixture of public and private agents and responsibilities. The FCI, a central government body, sells the foodgrains to wholesale agents. In Karnataka, the (KaFCSC)[1] is the biggest wholesaler, with 119 outlets. In addition, there are 148 wholesale depots run by cooperative societies, who also get their supplies from the FCI.[2] Since 1984–5 there have been no private wholesale agents. In Kerala, there are private authorized wholesale dealers and cooperative wholesale dealers. The (KaSCSC) is not active in the field of PDS wholesale, but the FCI itself has a small number of wholesale outlets. So PDS wholesale is performed by private, public and cooperative actors. The same holds for PDS retail. In Karnataka, there are fair price shops run by the KaFCSC, cooperative societies and private persons. In Kerala, again the Corporation is not active in this field, but there are private and cooperative authorized retail dealers (ARDs).

Although non-cooperative and non-public wholesale and retail dealers are referred to as private agents, their businesses are almost fully conditioned by government policies. Monthly quantities to be sold and profit margins, are both fixed. So the earnings of the dealers are fixed. It is an income rather than a profit. Entrepreneurial skills are hardly required.

The mixed set-up of PDS wholesale and retail means on the one hand that public, private and cooperative agents compete with each other over the volume of trade, while on the other, the government is able to contract out tasks it is not willing or able to do itself.

[1]The KaFCSC and the KeSCSC are public enterprises run by the Karnataka and Kerala governments respectively. See Chapter 6 for a more elaborate discussion and evaluation of their activities.

[2] Figures relate to 1993–4 (*Economic Survey 1993–94*, Government of Karnataka, 1994).

Competition to increase market share takes place especially with regard to PDS wholesale. It is regarded as profitable, and various parties (private, public and cooperative) are willing to take it up. PDS retail, on the other hand, is regarded as less attractive. In Karnataka, the government contracts out this task. The Corporation is only willing to run fair price shops in city areas when the amount to be distributed through a shop is substantial, i.e. when at least 800–1000 cards are attached to a shop. Otherwise, it is regarded as a loss-making business and left to others. In Kerala, the Corporation is not involved at all in PDS retail. Both the KeSCSC and private ration dealers regard PDS retail as financially unsustainable.[3]

Prices, aggregated and average quantities

How much foodgrain is distributed and for which price? To start with the situation in Karnataka, the quantity distributed varies from year to year, as can be seen in Table 5.1. On average, in the period 1986–94 approximately 840,000 tonnes foodgrains were distributed yearly: 590,000 tonnes rice and 250,000 tonnes wheat. The population of Karnataka is about 45 million. This means that on average 18.7 kg per person per year, that is nearly 1.6 kg (about 5500 kcal) per month were distributed.[4] If the foodgrain requirement is taken as 500g per person per day,[5] PDS would provide on average foodgrains for three days a month. In other words, PDS in Karnataka contributes to about 10 per cent of the total foodgrain requirement.[6]

[3] It is for this reason that the association of ration dealers demands full nationalization of the rationing system. Ration dealers argue that the fixed profit margin is insufficient. They would prefer to have a wage employment contract, instead of a quasi-private business whose turnover and profit/loss are fully laid down by the government.

[4] This calculation is based on the assumptions that (*a*) PDS foodgrains are distributed equally among the whole Karnataka population, and (*b*) that no diversion of foodgrains from the PDS to the open market takes place.'

[5] The establishment of energy and foodgrain requirements is a disputed subject. See, for instance, the debate between Sukhatme, Dandekar and Krishnaji in the *Economic and Political Weekly*, 1981. See also n 13 of this chapter. Based on the assumption that people eat more than foodgrains only, I take foodgrain requirement as 500 g per capita per day (1725 kcal). This figure more or less corresponds to the average consumption of cereals in India. In the 44th round (1988–9), the average daily cereal consumption in rural India was 485 g per person (NSS, 1990). Also the reliability of NSS data is disputed (see Chandrasekara Naidu, 1983; Hill, 1984; Vaidyanathan, 1983). Hill (1984; 495) states that the 'all India National Sample Survey is perhaps the most remarkable example of wasted statistical effort in the whole world.'

[6] According to NSS estimates (42nd round), PDS accounts for 22 per cent of all

Table 5.1
Distribution of foodgrains through PDS in Karnataka (tonnes)

	Rice	Wheat	Total
1980–1	74,000	21,000	95,000
1981–2*	354,000	37,500	391,500
1982–3*	332,000	48,000	380,000
1983–4	300,126	91,274	391,400
1984–5	305,337	68,927	374,264
1985–6	464,454	93,838	558,292
1986–7	639,433	166,817	806,250
1987–8*	680,770	166,996	847,766
1988–9	559,000	171,900	730,900
1989–90	520,600	251,100	771,700
1990–1	504,700	319,600	824,300
1991–2	435,100	338,600	773,700
1992–3	755,450	291,155	1046,605
1993–4*	636,742	257,983	894,725

Note: * Extrapolation on the basis of figures for 8 or 9 months.
Source: *Economic Surveys*, Planning Department, Government of Karnataka.

In reality, PDS foodgrains are not distributed to individuals, but to families holding ration cards. There are two types of card holders in Karnataka: green/tricolour card holders[7] and other card holders.[8] Green card holders are subsidized by the Karnataka government (see Section 3.3). Rice and wheat meant for these card holders are cheaper than rice and wheat for other card holders. Green card holders are entitled to 10 kg of subsidized foodgrains per month. About 40 per cent of card holders in Karnataka hold green cards.

---

purchased rice and 50 per cent of all purchased wheat in Karnataka (NSS, 1989). This is much more than the percentage I calculated. The difference between what I calculated and the NSS estimate may be due to the fact that the latter refers to foodgrain *purchases* only—cereal supplies through other than market channels are excluded—while my own calculations are based on foodgrain *requirements*.

[7] As mentioned in Chapter 3, in 1991–2 all green cards were replaced by tricolour cards. As the card is still known as the green card, I continue to use this name.

[8] There are several categories of card holders within this broad denomination of 'other card holders'. By far the largest group is included in the informal rationing scheme. This category of card holders does not receive any subsidy from the Karnataka government.

Figures 5.1 and 5.2 show the development of the prices of PDS and open market rice and wheat in Karnataka. It is clear that all prices increased considerably over the years. The price of green card rice remained stable for the first five years after 1985, but from 1990 onwards it started to rise. The price of PDS rice for other card holders has tripled between 1985 and 1994. As the figures show, the open market prices of rice and wheat also doubled or tripled in the decade 1985–94.

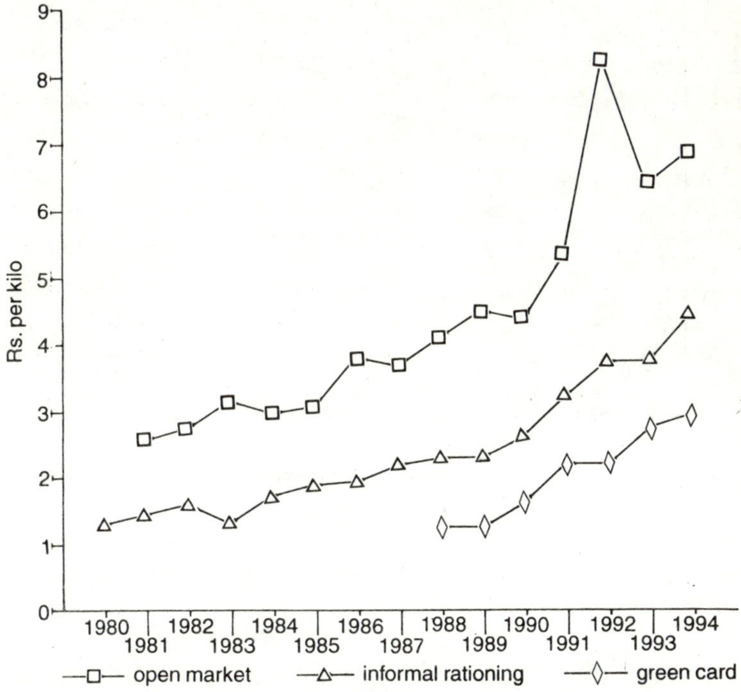

Fig. 5.1 Rice prices* in Karnataka 1980–1994

Note: * All prices are nominal prices.

Sources: Department of Economics and Statistics, Bangalore; Department of Food and Civil Supplies, Bangalore.

At the time of fieldwork, ration rice was distributed at Rs 3.50 (green card) and Rs 5.10 (other card) per kg. The average open market price of rice was Rs 6 in 1991. PDS wheat was sold at Rs 2.20 and Rs

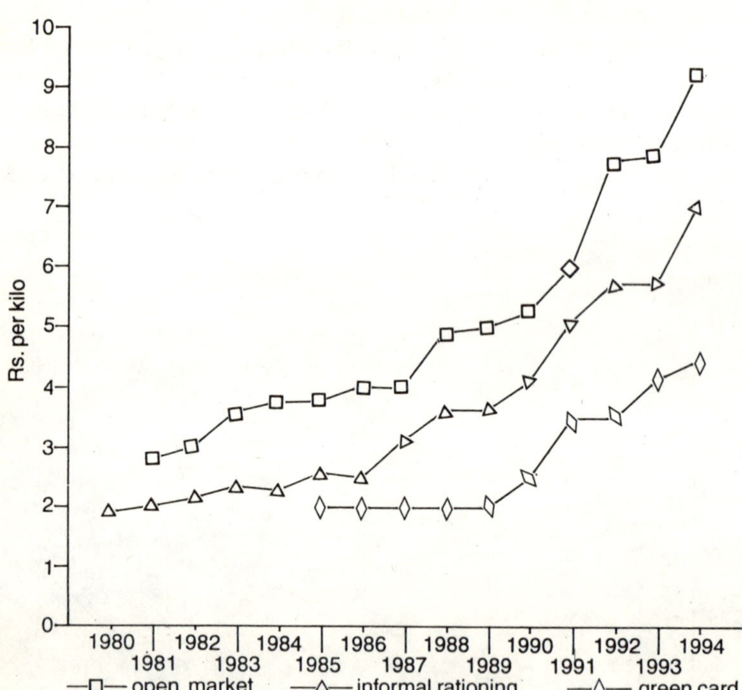

Fig. 5.2 Wheat prices* in Karnataka 1980–1994

Note: * All prices are nominal prices
Sources: Department of Economics and Statistics, Bangalore; Department of Food and Civil Supplies, Bangalore.

3.20 per kg, while wheat cost Rs 5.33 in the open market. This means a green card holding family would on average receive a monthly indirect financial assistance through PDS of approximately Rs 25. Households not included in the green card scheme would have an average monthly benefit of about Rs 12.

Compared to Karnataka, more foodgrain is distributed in Kerala (see Table 5.2). On average, in the period 1986–93 approximately 1,800,000 tonnes of foodgrains were distributed yearly, that is, 1,600,000 tonnes rice and 200,000 tonnes wheat. The total population of Kerala is about 29 million people. This means that the per capita distribution of foodgrain through PDS in this period was 62 kg per year, which comes to 5.2 kg (almost 18,000 kcal) per month.[9] This is about one-third of the foodgrain requirement.[10]

Table 5.2

Distribution of foodgrains through PDS in Kerala 1980–1993 (tonnes)

	Rice	**Wheat**	**Total**
1980	0,769,540	47,679	0,817,219
1981	1,064,410	43,839	1,108,249
1982	1,158,696	58,913	1,217,609
1983	1,288,114	201,810	1,489,924
1984	1,325,308	147,475	1,472,783
1985	1,384,275	110,020	1,494,295
1986	1,554,983	98,441	1,653,424
1987	1,597,962	104,208	1,702,170
1988	1,661,064	153,409	1,814,473
1989	1,270,857	194,915	1,465,772
1990	1,649,273	232,332	1,881,605
1991	1,671,398	332,706	2,004,104
1992	1,804,212	271,505	2,075,717
1993	1,646,819	218,630	1,865,449

Source: *Economic Review*, State Planning Board, Government of Kerala.

In Kerala, the PDS ration is the same for everyone. Virtually, the whole population has a ration card. There is only one type of card; the only qualification made is with respect to the number of adults and children depending on the card.

[9] See n 7 of this chapter.

[10] This calculation is again based on a daily cereal requirement of 500 g per day. The NSS (1989) estimates that PDS rice accounts for more than 50 per cent of rice purchases in Kerala, while PDS wheat even accounts for over 90 per cent of purchased wheat. This estimate is much higher than that in the text. However, as said before, the NSS data leave out cereal supplies through other than market channels. Moreover, it may be that the 500 g daily requirement is too high. As compared to the rest of India, cereal consumption is very low in Kerala, i.e. approximately 325 g per capita per day, as compared to 485 g in India as a whole (again NSS (1990) data; cereal supplies through other than market channels are not included). One of the reasons for this low cereal consumption is probably that cassava is an important staple food for some categories of people in Kerala.

Figure 5.3 gives an overview of PDS and open market prices of rice and wheat in Kerala. PDS rice has steadily become more expensive, but especially after 1991, prices have risen sharply—as has the open market rice price. Open market wheat prices were not readily available.

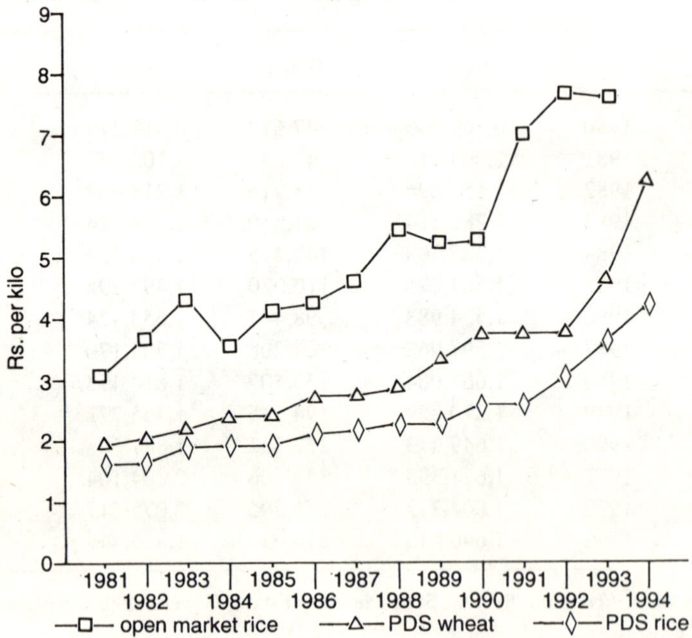

Fig. 5.3 Wheat and rice prices* in Kerala 1980–1994

Note: * All prices are nominal prices.
Source: Kerala State Civil Supplies Department, Thiruvananthapuram; Government of Kerala, *Economic Review* (various years).

When we look at rice distribution only, at the end of 1991, the indirect financial transfer through the PDS per person was about Rs 15 per month. For an average household this comes to approximately Rs 75.[11] This is three-six times as much as in Karnataka.

Although these official figures and estimates give some indication of the relevance of the PDS, it is necessary to look at actual distribution

[11] The average household size in Kerala consists of is 4.98 members in rural areas and 4.86 in urban areas (NSS, 1990).

practices in order to understand what happens in reality, who benefits and in what way.

5.2 CONSUMERS AND CARD HOLDERS

As there are several tens of millions of beneficiaries in Karnataka and Kerala together, while, moreover, their dependence on and benefit from the system varies substantially, it is impossible to give a summary of *the* relevance of food distribution for *the* card holder. Instead, this section describes the relevance of food rationing in two different localities: Naguraj in Karnataka and Pattambi in Kerala. Both are rural places. In my description, I am especially concerned with the ways in which the poorest people acquire their food, and to what extent the PDS contributes to this.

Food security in Naguraj, Akkipura, Karnataka[12]

Naguraj is a village of approximately 2,400 inhabitants, located about 10 km from Akkipura town. Part of the land cultivated by the people of Naguraj is irrigated wetland, on which paddy, sugar cane and areca nut are grown. Cotton is the main crop in the drylands. The agricultural population of Naguraj can be divided into three categories; landless or marginally cultivating households, peasant households which own up to 5 acres of land and which rely largely on family labour, and capitalist farmers who own 5–50 acres and who employ people to work on it. Often part of the land owned by the latter two categories of producers is irrigated wetland.

This grouping of households on the basis of landownership also proved relevant with regard to food consumption and household food security. Rice is the principal staple food of villagers in Naguraj. The poorest people eat some *ragi*, a coarse grain cheaper than rice, but once a day at most. Vijverberg calculates that on average landless and marginally cultivating households consume 3.7 kg rice and/or *ragi* per adult per week, that is about 500g (approximately 1725 kcal) per day. Peasant households eat about 600g foodgrains per adult per day, while in households of capitalist farmers an average adult consumes approximately 650g per day. As the diet of landless and marginally

[12] This section draws heavily on Vijverberg (1994). Vijverberg's study was conducted in June–September 1992, and was supervised by me.

cultivating farmers is poor in other ingredients, the amount consumed is hardly sufficient to meet the estimated minimum physiological needs (Vijverberg, 1994: 22).[13]

Table 5.3 gives an overview of the average expenses on food in the various households. As the reader may notice, the variation within each category of households is substantial. Peasant households all produce their own paddy, so they hardly purchase any rice. Also some of the landless and marginally cultivating households produce paddy—either on very small plots owned by themselves or on rented wetland. But while peasant households can generally feed themselves from their own produce, marginally paddy cultivating households do not produce enough or are forced to sell their produce in order to redeem financial obligations. Many of these poor households take a crop loan from a paddy merchant, on the condition that they sell their produce to this merchant (Vijverberg, 1994: 55–61). Also most capitalist farmers produce paddy, but some of them sell their entire paddy crop and purchase rice of better quality and higher price (ibid.: 1994: 60–1). Because of their easier access to formal credit markets, these farmers incur lower costs in the production of paddy than marginal farmers, and get a better price as well.

With regard to food purchase also, the poorest households are comparatively disadvantaged. Because of their economic situation, they have to buy their foodstuffs in small quantities in village shops for relatively high prices. Some of these local shops sell on credit. On the other hand, peasant households do their shopping on a weekly basis at the weekly market in Akkipura city, where the prices are low but the quality is not always good. Households of capitalist farmers are even able to purchase several foodstuffs on a monthly basis from wholesalers, who sell good quality food at low prices (Vijverberg,

[13] This is a controversial subject. Cut-off points for nutritional requirements are not easy to establish and are contested in academic and policy circles. According to the FAO-WHO, the recommended intake is 3000 kcal/day for a well-fed man and 2200 kcal for a well-fed woman. The minimum physiological requirement, corresponding to a critical limit of adaptation, is estimated as 1800 kcal per day for a man, and 1500 kcal for a woman (Pacey and Payne, 1985; 55–6). These figures date from 1973 and 1977 respectively. Since then several studies have suggested that there are large variations between individuals, gene pools, age groups, ecological conditions, seasons etc. Moreover, it has been discovered that populations surviving on a very low food intake adapt their energy requirements, which undercuts the whole possibility of establishing absolute uniform cut-off points. These adaptations have to do with long-term adjustments, particularly in body size, and short-term responses in conversion efficiency of energy in the body or behaviourial changes (ibid.: 51–94).

1994: 31). Moreover, as indicated earlier, some of these farmers are almost self-sufficient as far as rice is concerned.

Table 5.3

Expenses on food of various households in Naguraj, Akkipura, June–September 1992

		Average expenses per person per week	Range
Landless and marginally cultivating households	Rice and ragi	Rs 17	Rs 11–25
	Vegetables	Rs 4.5	Rs 3.3–6.7
(N=26)	Other*	Rs 10.5	Rs 5.6–20
	Total	Rs 32	Rs 25–50
Peasant households	Rice and ragi	—	—
(N=8)	Vegetables	Rs 4.6	Rs 2.5–7.5
	Other*	Rs 32	Rs 20–42.5
	Total	Rs 36.6	Rs 25–50
Households of capitalist farmers (N=8)	Rice and ragi	Rs 19**	Rs 18–20**
	Vegetables	Rs 9.3	Rs 3.6–17.5
	Other*	Rs 40	Rs 17–72.5
	Total	Rs 68.3	Rs 38.6–110

Notes: * This includes pulses, edible oil, spices, sugar, jaggery, etc.;
** This is based on only two households.

Source: Table 4.1a to 4.1c in Vijverberg (1994: 23–4).

According to Vijverberg, the relevance of public food distribution is only marginal. Although most landless and marginally cultivating households have a green card—which entitles them to 5 kg of rice and 5 kg of wheat for a price substantially below the open market price—the actual benefit is small. The ration has to be purchased at once, as the shop sells the rationed commodities only during the last week of each month. Although the food is subsidized, this still means green card holders who buy their rice and wheat quota have to spend nearly Rs 30 at once, a considerable investment.[14] Buying on credit is not possible. The local fair price shop made it compulsory for green card holders to buy their rice and wheat ration together. In other words, one cannot get rice without also taking wheat. Since most landless households hardly ever use wheat this is a big disadvantage to them. Nonetheless, whenever these households had enough money, they bought rice and wheat. Sugar was often not purchased.

Peasant households hardly used their ration cards. They produced their own rice and preferred jaggery to sugar. Households of capitalist farmers generally purchased wheat and sugar every month. Some of these farmers, especially influential ones, could get more wheat and sugar than their ration. As Vijverberg (1994: 30) recounts, a former president of the cooperative society could get 15 to 20 kg of wheat and as much sugar as he wanted every month.

In short, foodgrain consumption of the poorest households in the village Naguraj is hardly sufficient. So, from a nutritional point of view, there is certainly a case to make for public food distribution. Unfortunately, in reality the relevance of the system is limited. The quantity distributed is small and the organizational set-up (compulsory off-take of wheat, no possibility to buy on credit, limited opening of the shop) does not fit consumption habits and shortage of cash of many poor households. These limitations are not uncommon, in fact they were reported in other locations as well.

Food distribution and card mortgaging in Pattambi, Madhyapura, Kerala

As indicated earlier in this chapter, the overall situation of the PDS in Kerala compares favourably with the rest of India. The per capita amount of PDS food is more than elsewhere, almost all households have a ration card, and the bureaucracy functions relatively well.

[14] In 1992, in Naguraj, the daily wage for casual agricultural work was Rs 15 for women and Rs 25 for men (Vijverberg, 1994: 63). The availability of work fluctuates considerably over the year. During certain months of the year, it is very difficult for agricultural labourers to find work.

The case study presented here is rather exceptional. It describes the relevance of the PDS for ultra-poor people, temporary squatters in a remote, hilly area about 30 km away from *taluk* headquarters, a group which is very difficult to reach in any government programme.

Pattambi is a ribbon-like settlement. These kinds of settlements are not uncommon in Kerala, although the situation in Pattambi is extreme. Just in between the road and a rubber plantation there is a small strip 2 or 3 m wide on which ninety-five households have built their dwellings. To illustrate their own living conditions I was told the following story by these people that one night last year a lorry passed by along this road. Because the driver noticed an unexpected object lying on the road he stopped the vehicle and got down to have a look. It turned out to be a small child who had rolled down from one of the huts while it was asleep.

These settlements are illegal. In fact many dwellers live here for only a few years and then move on to another (illegal) settlement. Nearly all the inhabitants of this settlement are Sambawars, one of the formerly untouchable subcastes. Apart from the Sambawars there are also a few Muslims residing in the locality. More than 80 per cent of the people are involved in working with bamboo; they make several types of bamboo baskets which are sold for a few rupees.

I surveyed thirty out of the ninety-five households. The average daily staple food consumption (that is rice, wheat and tapioca) was only about 1600 kcal per day per adult equivalent (children counted as half an adult).[15] This is very low because staple food is by far the most important source of energy and protein for these people. Another thing that struck me was the relatively large number of households not covered by the PDS, as compared to the other villages in Kerala. Of the thirty households six, that is 20 per cent of the sample, did not possess a ration card at the time of survey. All of them had had a ration card at some time in the past, but they had lost it for a variety of reasons: a flood, a family split or moving to a new locality, etc. Four of these six families had recently applied for a new card, but they had not yet got it. One person said that the cost of getting a ration card was too high. It requires at least one, but probably more, bus trips to the *taluk* supply office, which is about 30 km from the settlement. So

[15] I did not ask the age of the children. Both adults and children are self-reported adults and children.

poverty and physical inaccessibility of the bureaucracy is a reason for not having a ration card. Furthermore, the fact that this is an illegal settlement may also explain the relatively large number of people without a card. Some of the people live only temporarily in this place. When the government starts creating problems about their settlement they shift to another locality. Getting, and keeping a ration card, requires some residential continuity.[16]

Of the twenty-four families with a ration card eight had mortgaged their card at the time of the survey, i.e. they had given it to some one else as a collateral for a small loan. Therefore, only sixteen families were in a position to use their own ration card at the time of the survey. In five families it was admitted that they had pledged their ration card at least once during the last five years (see Table 5.4). In nine households, people claimed never to have mortgaged their ration card. 'The card is too valuable,' one woman said, 'so we prefer to take other kinds of loans.[17]

Table 5.4

The practice of card mortaging in Pattambi, Madhyapura

	Number of households
No card at the moment	6
Card presently mortgaged	8
Card not mortgaged now, but at least once during last 5 years	5
Card mortgaged long ago	2
Card never mortgaged	9
Total	30

Households who were in possession *and* in command of their ration cards were all using it. Ration rice was purchased by all households. Only in one household was I told that no rice was purchased in the week preceding the survey because it was regarded as substandard. Many households bought some wheat when it was available. Sugar

[16] In fact, keeping all this in mind, it is perhaps a remarkable achievement that 80 per cent of the people still did have a ration card.

[17] As an example, this woman said she sometimes borrows Rs 100 with a monetary monthly interest of Rs 10.

was bought by most 'when we have money', but often part of it was re-sold at a higher price. None of the houses had electricity, so everybody bought kerosene for lighting purposes. For cooking purposes firewood was used.

For none of the sixteen household was the ration supply sufficient. In all the households additional rice was purchased on the open market, as well as wheat products and/or tapioca. In caloric terms, on average the ration supply contributed to 50 per cent of the total staple food consumption. If we assume that, in the absence of food rationing, households would purchase the same amount of rice and wheat on the open market, food rationing means a financial benefit of just over Rs 20 on average per household per week.[18] Although I cannot relate this amount to the total money available in these households I think it can be concluded that for the people studied here, the PDS indeed means a substantial household subsidy.[19]

As shown in Table 5.4 card mortgaging is a widespread phenomenon. One woman said that her present pledge was the fifth or sixth. The most common reason for mortgaging the card is to cover medical costs: hospitalization or tablets.[20] This was mentioned twelve times by people who had mortgaged their cards. Other reasons, mentioned only once or twice, were of domestic nature (that is to buy food), house repairs, advocate's fee or the purchase of school books for children.[21]

[18] I have taken the ration rice price as Rs 3.95 (the highest possible price in the ration shop) and the open market price as Rs 7.50 (the lowest price mentioned by respondents).

[19] Rs 20 per week means Rs 1000 per year. Compared to the official poverty line in India in 1991–2 (sometimes taken as Rs 3600, sometimes as Rs 6400 per household per year), this is 15–25 per cent (or more) of the income of people classified as poor.

[20] Officially public medical care is free in Kerala. In reality, however, doctors always ask for some money. Moreover, not all kind of tablets are available in the public health care centres and, hence, have to be purchased from (private) medical shops. Furthermore medical treatment often requires travel expenses.

[21] Compared to other Indian States, Kerala has a very high morbidity rate. These morbidity figures are based on self-reported illnesses, so it may well be that a relatively greater awareness is the reason for this high rate (Drèze and Sen, 1989: 222). Compared to people elsewhere in India, Keralites may be more inclined to seek medical help. Sometimes it is half seriously joked that people from Kerala are so conscious of their health that with the first cough they rush to the doctor, (see e.g. Govindan Kutty, 1990, about 'medicine as staple food'). The material collected in this small survey does indeed support the idea that disease and health matters have a high priority in Kerala, even for the very poor. However, on the basis of this small survey, I would certainly not conclude that there is an over-awareness. All diseases mentioned as a reason for taking a loan were quite serious: heart complaints, severe skin disease, leprosy, typhoid and tuberculosis. Many people were still not cured at the time of survey.

Most of the people pledged their cards with relatives or people in the neighbourhood, who themselves were not really well-to-do. One woman who had taken a loan of Rs 50 said that the moneylender himself could not afford a bigger loan. Only two people had given their cards to someone who takes cards more often. In one case this was a retail rice merchant.

The conditions of the mortgage vary widely. One man said that he could still use the pledged card. Two households received a share of the ration commodities. Most households with pledging experience could not claim any of the rationed articles, and in two cases the moneylender even charged an additional monetary interest. In most cases the total interest paid on these loans came to an incredibly high percentage. The weekly loss (calculated as the difference between the ration rice price and the open market price, plus the extra earnings through the sale of the sugar quota) came to about Rs 20 per household. The loan was usually not more than Rs 100. This means that the interest on a yearly basis added up to the incredibly high rate of 1000 per cent. We are not talking here about short-term loans, which usually carry a high (though not this high) interest rate. The average duration of the five reported pledging experiences in the past was twenty-four months.

The interest rate of course varies, with the amount borrowed and the value of the card, that is the number of household members registered on the card. There was no tendency at all among people with pledging experience to bargain for a higher loan to bring down the interest rate. On the contrary, most households were keen to keep the loan as small as possible because they realized that the bigger the loan the more difficult repayment would be.

One might expect that card pledging would affect food consumption. Gulati, in her study of card mortgaging in a peri-urban settlement around Trivandrum found that this was indeed the case: households with the lowest per capita daily consumption of cereal or cereal substitutes are precisely those that mortgage their ration cards (Gulati, 1977). In my survey this relation could not be established. It may be that the size of the sample was too small and that the method chosen to establish household food consumption (through interviewing about last week's purchases) was not precise enough to uncover differences in food intake. It may also be that there are other ways of coping when the ration card is not available. One way may be to buy on credit. This indeed seems to happen. Unfortunately, I did not collect systematic data about this issue, but the three people who told me that they purchase open market rice on credit were all members of households that were not in command of their ration cards. Another way to 'solve' the problem of the absence of the card may be to shift consumption from rice and wheat to tapioca. The price of 1 kg rice was at least Rs 7.50, while an equal amount (in caloric terms) of tapioca cost Rs 4.40.[22] Indeed, I found that in households which have mortgaged their ration cards, more than one and a half times as much tapioca is consumed as in households which are in command of their ration cards. This may mean that households which have mortgaged their ration cards shift their food consumption partly from foodgrains to tapioca. However, it may of course also mean that in households with a relatively high tapioca consumption one is less reluctant to mortgage the ration card.

By way of conclusion, in Pattambi we must distinguish between the relevance of food rationing proper and the relevance of the ration card itself. All households in command of a card used it to purchase their rations. This gave them a financial benefit of Rs 20 on average per household per week. For these very poor people who are often short of cash, this is probably a substantial subsidy. The relevance of the ration card itself goes beyond food only: it is used as a loan collateral. Although this may sometimes solve financial problems in the short run, the long-term costs are often considerable, as the interest rates are exceptionally high. It may be hypothesized that mortgaging of ration cards happens especially (*a*) among the very poor who are desperate for cash and have nothing else to use as a loan collateral, and (*b*) when ration cards have some value, where the people in command of cards should be sure to get the ration and where the amount of food distributed per card should not be negligible.

The PDS and food entitlements

The two case studies in Naguraj and Pattambi suggest that the PDS is regarded as a welcome addition to household food security. In both villages, card holders usually purchased their rations whenever they

[22] The caloric content of rice is approximately 345 kcal per 100 g. The caloric content of tapioca varies greatly with the water content. Fresh tapioca tubers contain 35 per cent carbohydrate, less than 2 per cent protein and 63 per cent water (Gibbon and Pain, 1985: 131), which means the caloric content is 148 kcal per 100 g (2.3 times less than rice). The caloric content of dry tubers is much higher. As I do not know the water content of the tapioca consumed in Pattambi, I have used the same conversion rate (2.2) that Gulati (1977) used in her study on card mortgaging and food intake in Kerala.

were in a position to do so. In Naguraj the organizational set-up of the system disfavoured the poorest consumers. In Pattambi the function of the PDS for ultra-poor people went beyond the distribution of food. As the ration card is one of the very few valuable assets of these people, the card was also used collateral in order to obtain small loans. As explained, this situation has advantages, as well as disadvantages for the people involved.

Apart from these location-specific observations, a more general point can be made about the form of the PDS intervention. Especially for poor people the food situation is more secure the more sources they can rely upon. Or in other words, the more the (exchange) entitlement relations, the less vulnerable is one. Both in Naguraj and in Pattambi the food security situation of the poorest households is precarious. Yet, there is an important difference. In Naguraj, marginal households have been able to diversify their food base to some extent. Some produce cotton, the profit from which is used mainly for food. If they have a little irrigated land at their disposal they produce some paddy for their own consumption. They work as agricultural labourers, and they invest in kinship and other social relations to rely on in times of emergency (Vijverberg, 1994: 42–78). The population in Pattambi, however, depends almost exclusively on the sale of bamboo work. As soon as the market for bamboo baskets collapsed the food situation of these people would come under serious pressure.

The effect of the PDS is that it strengthens the existing exchange relationships. In itself, it is not an additional relationship—like a dole or a public work employment contract. The PDS affects the exchange rate between money and foodgrains, not the relationships through which cash is obtained. In a situation where the most vulnerable people have several strategies to obtain an income, there is less need for an additional entitlement relation than in a situation where they depend on one source mainly. In the latter case, a diversification of exchange entitlement relations—or put more generally, a broadening of the economic base—would, in fact, contribute more to the food security of these most vulnerable people than a change in the terms of exchange only. In such a situation, the PDS would, hence, not be the most suitable intervention in food security. As far as these consumers are concerned, the subsidy should have a different form, i.e. to introduce an additional type of exchange entitlement relationship that enables people to diversify their food base.

Apart from the argument mentioned earlier that generally the more exchange entitlement relations one is involved in, the less vulnerable is the person, such a broadening of the economic base would also make mortgaging of ration cards unnecessary. Close to Pattambi I interviewed some very poor tribal people to whom the Kerala government had given a small portion of land. I was told by these people that card pledging had become a thing of the past since they now owned two or three coconut trees, which could be used as loan collateral. The suggestion made is, hence, that as far as people with a very small economic base are concerned, there are perhaps other types of interventions that contribute more to food security than cheap food rationing. I will come back to this in Section 8.3.

5.3 THE PUBLIC AND THE BUREAUCRACY: CARDS AND VIGILANCE, ACCESS AND VOICE

How to get a ration card?

In almost all States, rationing is organized with the help of ration cards. In Karnataka and Kerala, consumers have to become card holders in order to become entitled to a certain amount of PDS foodgrains, kerosene and sugar. An important issue, then, is the procedure of inclusion, of becoming a card holder.

Both in Karnataka and Kerala, there are official procedures: applicants should be able to produce a surrender certificate of a previous card (if any), a certificate related to the house the applicant owns/rents, an employment certificate (in case of regular employment; otherwise a sworn affidavit to that effect), sometimes photograph(s), and a filled-in application form.

These bureaucratic rules and requirements themselves already raise a barrier in the accessibility of the system. Not everybody lives in a house, let alone one that is properly registered; many people are unemployed or work in the so-called informal sector; a photograph involves an investment before there is any certainty about future benefits.

In reality, access is sometimes even more problematic because official bureaucratic rules are implemented arbitrarily or imperfectly and are mixed up with other systems of access regulation (Schaffer and Wen-hsien, 1975: 16). This is illustrated by the following entry in the diary of my research assistant:

> Today, I visited one of the regional offices of the Food and Civil Supplies Department in Bangalore. On my way, I met a client who wanted to apply for a card. She was not able to read or speak *Kannada*, so she asked me to fill in

the form. She told: 'Last year, we came to Bangalore. First, we did not bother about a card. But now we feel it is necessary as we need it for each and every purpose. Even the government asks for it.' Then, a fat fellow came and took the application. I asked who he was, and she said it was their own man. Only afterwards, I understood he was a middleman.

Later, I talked to Mr Ali, who is a petty merchant. He applied for a ration card. He said he had to give Rs 250 to a person (he showed the person) who is a 'social worker' named Dorai. Dorai is a full time broker, and he is famous in the locality. Ali said 'If you come to this place and ask for Dorai, anybody will show him. All the work is done by the social worker himself. Other wise, we (people who want a ration card) have to wander for getting the cards.'

I also talked to one Mr Joseph, who is working in a press. He had come here to get his ration card transferred from a far-away depot to a depot nearer to his home. Joseph is only bothered about kerosene, not about the other commodities. What happens now is that Joseph or one of his family members will go to the far-away shop. By the time they arrive, the kerosene is finished. Now, Joseph was trying already for 5 days to get his card transferred. Yesterday, the Food Inspector had told him to get a certificate from the *Tahsildar*, and today he had said to get a renewal certificate. Then Joseph had asked the Food Inspector how much money he wanted and he had shown 100 rupees. 'I don't mind giving money', Joseph said, 'instead of wandering every day, since now I am losing income because I have to take leave. But the food inspector did not take the money. He said to come tomorrow anyhow with the certificate.' According to Joseph it is impossible to get the work done without extra money. 'But the officials do not ask straightaway for it. That is their dignity. If someone gives money and gets the work done, next day he may tell this to some one else. So what they expect is that you go through brokers. And then, they get their share.' The brokers ask money and share it with the officials. In this way, the officials get the money easily with out asking for it. 'Nowadays,' Joseph said, 'this system is increasing since everybody requires a ration card. It shows that someone belongs to a certain State. People are afraid that if they don't have card, one day they may be pushed out of the State because they wouldn't belong to Karnataka.'

Joseph also said that the stamp vendors make a lot of money. One has to give 5 rupees plus the costs of the stamps, and then they fill in the application form, 'which takes hardly 10 minutes'. Even educated people cannot fill in their own application form. 'Today morning, what happened was that a person filled in the form himself and gave it to the DD (deputy director). But the DD said there were a lot of mistakes in it, so the client had to get the application filled in by the stamp vendor.'

Then, I spoke to Mr Raju, who is a coolie worker. He said he had been trying to obtain a ration card for 6 months now. He had come to Bangalore long back, but half a year ago he started to feel the need for a ration card. So, in the last six months, he had wandered several times around the offices. Every time he had come to this office the officials had asked him for one or the other certificate. Raju had become fed up and had given the application form to his brother who is working in a government office. This brother had kept the application for one and a half month, and only yesterday he had returned it with a signature on it of one of the superior officers. So far, Raju had not given any money, but his expenses might have crossed 150 rupees, because of the number of times he has come here, sometimes even by auto (rickshaw).

This lengthy entry illustrates a number of important things. First, for these would-be card holders, the ration card is a precious document. They undertake considerable effort, pay large sums and accept humiliations in order to get one. The reason for this is not only the value of the foodgrains, sugar and kerosene, but also the fact that the ration card has the function of an identity card. For many people it is the only official document that proves that they exist. It is cheaper and easier to get than any other identity paper. People need it to get their children admitted to school, register their scooter, get a driver's licence or obtain a passport. Second, it seems as if the officials in this Bangalore office made the bureaucracy inaccessible on purpose. They made the clients come and go, sometimes for months and months. What they obviously preferred is to work with gatekeepers—stamp vendors, 'social workers', brokers or others. That provides them with an easy way to earn extra money without demanding bribes themselves. Third, generally the clients accepted this kind of behaviour. They may have been used to it, or they felt they were not in a position to protest. They may have felt it a tiresome procedure, but they obliged. It may be that their frankness towards my assistant should be interpreted as a sign of protest, but then it is a weak protest.

In other words, access is restricted not only by the official bureaucratic rules, but also by the unofficial procedures involving considerable waiting-time, additional financial costs, passing gatekeepers and brokerage. It is difficult for applicants to know how they can best proceed. In fact, it is only in the course of their efforts to obtain a ration card that the rules applicable to their particular case take shape. In terms of 'access theory',[23] this situation can be characterized as a 'complex queue'. While in a simple queue the admission rules are universally known, unambiguous, not discretionary and finite, a complex queue deviates in one or more respects from

[23] Although the main contributions to 'access theory' were written 20–25 years ago, (e.g. Hirschman, 1970; Schaffer and Lamb, 1974; Schaffer and Wen-hsien, 1975), I prefer to use this literature and terminology rather than to the inclusion-exclusion dichotomy that is in vogue in the mid 1990s, (e.g. Stiefel and Wolfe, 1994; Wolfe,

this ideal type (Schaffer and Wen-hsien, 1975: 24–26). In the situation described, the queue is complex because there is more than one gate (as the example of Raju indicates), brokerage is a normal phenomenon, the procedures are vague and dependent on the discretion of the officials, and the waiting-time depends on the priority attributed by the responsible officials and gatekeepers.

This observation from a Bangalore regional office is a rather extreme example of how difficult it may be for 'the common man' to get a ration card. In Akkipura, however, the bureaucracy was significantly more accessible. While about half of my respondents in the villages said that they had paid Rs 10–25 to the village accountant as 'good will', many green card holders claimed that no bribe or gift had been required. A factor restricting access in Akkipura, however, was the limited time span in which green cards could be obtained. Green cards were only issued during the first months of the scheme and during a short re-survey in 1991–2. The distribution of other cards was, however, not restricted in time.

In Madhyapura in Kerala, not even one of my informants reported having paid more than the official card fee. Getting a ration card was certainly a time-consuming affair: usually when I visited the Madhyapura *taluk* supply office, it was crowded with people all queuing to get their cards adjusted or renewed. But I suspect that the rules defining admission were more transparent then in the Bangalore situation. In any case, almost all villagers interviewed in Madhyapura had succeeded in obtaining a ration card, which is more than in Akkipura or Bangalore where 5 to 20 per cent households visited did not have a ration card. I only found some families without ration cards in Pattambi. Of course, there are other ultra-poor and remote localities like Pattambi, but generally a very large percentage of the rural population in Kerala has a ration card.

The reason for the rather extreme situation in Bangalore may have to do with the anonymity and lack of social control in city offices—as compared to the visibility and the more public character of dealings of village accountants. Another factor may be the greater proximity

---

1994). The authors writing about 'access', 'voice' and 'exit' tried to develop analytical tools to understand organization-client relations, while the concepts 'inclusion/integration' and 'exclusion' mainly serve as new catchwords in development discourse. Their meaning is both broader (exclusion can have many dimensions, including exclusion from social services, livelihood, consumer culture, political choice, bases for popular organization and understanding) (Wolfe, 1994), as well as conceptually less elaborated.

of the Bangalore office to the (Karnataka State) centre of political power and corruption. It may well be that Food Inspectors and Deputy Directors in Bangalore are expected and more pressurized to surrender a higher percentage of their illegal incomes to their superiors than their colleagues in more remote areas. Moreover, an executive post in Bangalore (e.g. Food Inspector) is a position desired by many people. Relatively large amounts of money are paid for such positions. In due course, these amounts have to be earned back. In addition, it may be that the importance of the ration card as identity card is greater in a metropolitan city such as Bangalore than in smaller places such as Akkipura where people generally know the whereabouts of other people. The nearly 100 per cent coverage in (rural) Kerala, without any bribing practices, has probably a lot to do with the high literacy rate and the well-developed sense of rights and entitlements, which makes people more assertive and apt to resist unlawful procedures restricting access.[24]

What do card holders do when the service fails?

While getting a ration card is the first important type of interaction between clients or recipients and the food bureaucracy, public vigilance of the ration shops is the second. In both States, card holders complained about black-marketeering, various other malpractices, and the low quality of rationed food. In the interviews I held in the villages, I often heard: 'What can we do; there is no unity in our village. When I make a complaint there will be repercussions for me, so I keep quiet.'

Still, there are substantial differences between Akkipura in Karnataka and Madhyapura in Kerala, which have to do with public awareness, the local balance of power and the bureaucracy's responsiveness.

In Karnataka, there are officially organized vigilance committees. Both their membership composition and tasks and duties are prescribed from above. In fact, the whole idea of establishing these committees was a top-down affair, reinvented by various governments in various forms. The latest idea, popular at the time of fieldwork, was that each fair price shop should have its own committee, consisting of three women, one scheduled caste member, one scheduled tribe member

[24] It would be interesting to compare the situation in Bangalore to that of big cities in Kerala such as Thiruvananthapuram or Kochi, but unfortunately I do not have the data to do this. In general, all the hypotheses ventured in this paragraph need further investigation.

and two others, all of them card holders. This committee should supervise the dealings of the fair price shop, the timing of stock arrival, the quality of goods and possible black-marketeering. In reality, things did not work out this way. As a local politician somewhere in Akkipura explained:

> The committee has to sign after the stock has arrived. But often, the ration dealer collects only part of his allotment, while according to the books he collects all. The members of the committee get a bribe. How much depends on their status. Sometimes it is money, sometimes sugar. These committee members only cause problems. They come to the shop and ask for sugar. They are misusing their power. Often, the committees are completely dominated by the ruling party. If people have genuine complaints, they do not go to this committee, because it does not have real authority.

In Kerala, there are no such formally organized vigilance committees, but vigilance is organized through existing political and bureaucratic channels. If individual card holders, local branches of political parties or other grassroot organizations have a complaint they may inform the responsible officials. The minimum action on the part of these officials is to order a suspension of the ARD. Both officials and ration dealers say that 'even anonymous complaints may result in a suspension', and suspensions may take place immediately, before a proper inquiry is carried out.[25] The Rationing Inspector or the Taluk Supply Officer (TSO) have to follow up such complaints. If they do not, card holders could seek justice from a superior official or a local politician. Both options are bad for the TSO or the Inspector.

In short, in Karnataka the vigilance committees, although officially meant as a forum for redressal, do not work as such. Instead, they are part of the local political structure in which criticism or opposition to the local elite is not a common practice. Neither are there other ways in which the Karnataka card holders voice their complaints. In Kerala, it is more common to speak up should the service fail. Frequently, the route taken is not a direct appeal to the administration, but a detour is made by forming an alliance with local politicians who then act as spokesmen. The result is that the food bureaucracy is forced to behave somewhat accountably and to perform tasks for which it was established.[26] In the minds of the ARDs this situation creates a

[25] Clause 45, subclause 8 of the Kerala Rationing Order 1966, indicates that 'if considered necessary [the enforcement officer] may suspend the appointment of the authorized retail distributor temporarily pending enquiry'.

[26] See also Mencher (1980), Nag (1989), and G. Sen (1992) on the relation between public awareness, government accountability and the provisioning of (mainly health) services in Kerala

permanent fear of the officials. Although many of them have never experienced a suspension themselves, they regard it as a routine matter for officials.

5.4 RATION DEALERS: PROFITS AND DIVERSION TO THE OPEN MARKET

Shivu is about 35 years old. Together with his father he runs a (normal) provision store as well as a fair price shop in Akkipura town. 'My father works mainly in the provision store and I am usually in the fair price shop. There are four labourers as well, three in the provision store and one with me. We are in this business already for a long time, the provision store since twenty-eight years and the fair price shop since sixteen years. That was when PDS started in Akkipura.

Sixteen years back, not many people were interested in running a fair price shop. Now it is very different; it has become difficult to get a licence. In those days, most fair price shop owners had private provision stores as well. Now, estimate only 20 per cent of the fair price shops in Akkipura city are combined ration and provision stores. Earlier, usually the shops were kept in the same premises, but now one has to have separate accounting, separate cash and a separate godown.

Our income from the fair price shop is minor, maybe Rs 1000 per month. That is why my brother and I suggested to stop this business. But my father has done it already for sixteen years and he wants to continue.

As compared to most ration shops, Shivu's shop is a relatively profitable one, with more than 500 cards attached to it and located in a city area. Yet he complains about his low income. There is nothing unusual about this. Both in Karnataka and Kerala, ration dealers often complain about low incomes. And indeed, it is true that the average net income through legal transactions is small. On average, this income came to about Rs 600 per month in 1991–2.[27] This is more than an agricultural labourer earns on average, and comparable to the lowest office staff.

The financial situation of ration dealers is especially precarious because they have to make large investments relative to their small

[27] In Karnataka in, 1991–2, 773,700 tonnes foodgrains were distributed through 17,364 fair price shops. On average, each fair price shop sold 44,558 kg of foodgrains in 1991–2. That is just over 3700 kg per month. The profit margin for the retailer is fixed; in 1991–2 this margin was Rs 10 per 100 kg. This means that by selling PDS foodgrains the fair price shop dealers could earn an average monthly income of Rs 370. There are additional sources of income. Fair price shop dealers also sell ration

earnings. In Karnataka, dealers have to collect the allotted quantities of foodgrains and sugar once per month only.[28] This means they have to dispose of a relatively large amount of money: the value of one month's stock, which comes to approximately Rs 15,000. The gross profit/turnover ratio is only 5 per cent,[29] which is much less than a private retail foodgrain trader makes on average.[30] Also the profit/investment ratio is low. During a large part of the month, the fair price shop trader's working capital is not invested in any trading. In rural areas, the stock in the fair price shop is usually sold out within a few days. The trader has to wait nearly one month before he can reinvest the money in his trading business. In Kerala, distribution is organized on a weekly basis. Each week the ARDs have to collect the commodities, and the card holders get their ration on a weekly basis. The expenditure locked in investments of an average ration dealer is about Rs 9000 as far as foodgrains are concerned. The quantity for one extra week is stored in the ration shop. Thus Rs 18,000 are

---

sugar, as well as the gunny bags in which the rationed commodities have been stored. The profit margin on sugar was Rs 3.50 per 100 kg. On average there was 800 kg sugar per month per fair price shop in 1991-2. The price of used gunny bags was Rs 7. This means that the total monthly gross income of a fair price shop owner came to Rs 750. The expenditure (rent, labour, travel expenses to and from the warehouses, small tips and bribes, electricity and stationary) came to Rs 200 on average. The net income would be about Rs 550–600 monthly. In Kerala in 1992, 2,075,717 tonnes foodgrains were distributed through 13,142 authorized retail depots. This means that each shop distributed 158 tonnes yearly, that is a little over 13 tonnes per month. The retail margin in 1992 was approximately Rs 11 per 100 kg foodgrains. This means that from the sale of foodgrains alone an average ration dealer in Kerala earned just over Rs 1400 monthly. There are additional income sources from sugar and gunny bags. The expenses Kerala ration dealers had to meet were much higher than in Karnataka, especially transportation and labour costs. Transportation of foodgrains from the wholesale depot to the retail outlet was organized and financed by ration dealers themselves. The shops were usually open during the whole month. At least two workers are required (usually one licence holder/shop owner and one other person). The net average monthly income was probably comparable to that in Karnataka. According to the Kerala Ration Dealers Association itself, an average dealer makes a monthly loss of about Rs 750 (Circular 3/91, dated 31 August 1991 by the Kerala State Retail Ration Dealers Association, *taluk* committee Kollam).

[28] There is no official rule prescribing that all monthly allotted commodities should be collected at once. However, due to late arrival of stocks, subsidized transport of the commodities once a month and bureaucratic obstinacy, many fair price shop owners are forced to collect and pay for the whole monthly allotment at one time.

[29] The monthly gross income is Rs 750, while the monthly turnover is Rs 15,000.

[30] The gross profit/turnover ratio of a private retail dealer in foodgrains was estimated as 10 per cent by the Kerala Sales Tax Department, and as 10–15 per cent by a representative of the Karnataka Retail Foodgrain Dealers Association.

permanently invested in foodgrains. Once a month sugar and occasionally edible oil are allotted to the shops, which means an additional investment of Rs 5000–15,000. The capital required to run a fair price shop in Kerala is thus more than in Karnataka. The invested capital is utilized continuously; there are no breaks as in Karnataka.

Despite the relatively low income and the in-built financial difficulties,[31] there are always people eager to enter this business. I heard several stories that candidate traders were willing to pay between Rs 10,000 and 50,000 for a licence. These may be exaggerations, but it is a fact that people are fighting to get licences to become ration dealers (see, for instance, an example of a court case concerning this issue as described in Section 7.3).

There are at least three reasons why the profession is seen as an attractive one. First, although the income is small, it is still better than nothing. Especially in situations of widespread un(der)employment it is not surprising that people are willing to take this opportunity. Moreover, in Karnataka, being a fair price shop owner is generally no full-time job. It can be easily combined with cultivating land or other activities. In Kerala, that is different. Shops are usually open during the whole month, and one or two persons have to be present.

Second, even when financial earnings are small there may be other advantages, such as prestige and local influence. As one local politician in Akkipura in Karnataka explained to me:

> Fair price shop owners are important people, not only in their villages, but also for politicians from outside. In case we, politicians, want to know something of a particular village we go to the fair price shop owner. They are in close contact with the people and a source of information. Sometimes they are influential as opinion makers or they act as intermediaries. That is why politicians usually support them. For instance, when there is a problem between the party and a leader of a certain colony, we ask the fair price shop owner to give some extra commodities to this leader, so that the whole colony again turns in favour of us.

I also met several fair price shop owners who were active local politicians. Running a fair price shop and distributing food favours adds to their political capital. This is especially true in Karnataka, where political awareness is less developed and card holders are

[31] In both States, ration dealers can get a permanent cash credit bank loan of Rs 25,000 maximum. Only a minority of shopkeepers make use of this opportunity. More often, they take loans from private moneylenders, sometimes on the condition that part of the foodgrains is sold to these moneylenders, as I will explain later in this section.

generally not organized enough to voice their complaints against the (mis)use of PDS food for the maintenance of political/clientilist relations.

Third, the real income of ration dealers is often much higher than the Rs 600 per month calculated above. In Kerala, it is a widely acknowledged fact that ration dealers make their 'adjustments'. 'Through the front door we are making losses, but through the back door we are making profits,' as ration dealers themselves say. This is not even an open secret, but rather a tacit agreement between ration dealers and the government. Sudharshan, the secretary of a Kerala ration dealers association, told me that:

> ...everybody knows that ARDs can only survive because of their manipulations. Also the government knows the commission is not sufficient. We have told them several times. Our association has negotiated with several ministers in the course of the years. But they say: If we increase your commission, consumers have to pay more. It is all a game of politics. The ministers say: We all know this, but how can we help you? As soon as we raise the commission, the press and the opposition will say that we have taken money from your association.

The implicit deal is that the government does not raise the commission, but looks the other way when ARDs sell the excess stock unclaimed by card holders to others at a higher rate. There are other manipulations as well, such as selling common rice for the price of superfine or giving slightly less than is paid for. These practices happen in both States.

How do illegal sales take place? Let me take Akkipura *taluk* as an example. Here the bulk of illegal sales takes place at an early stage in the distribution chain, though there are also some illegal sales at the local level (fair price shop owners who sell locally to people who are not entitled to buy the commodities, often at a higher rate).

Figure 5.4 schematically shows the organization of the distribution of foodgrains. Transport from the warehouse of the FCI to the *taluk* wholesale depot is done by a private transport contractor. In each district, there is a yearly tender procedure to decide who will be transport contractor. Because of opportunities to sell the goods illegally this transport is a profitable job. The transport contractor in the district discussed here was a powerful person, who paid others not to participate in the tenders. He was also close to several important members of the Karnataka Assembly.

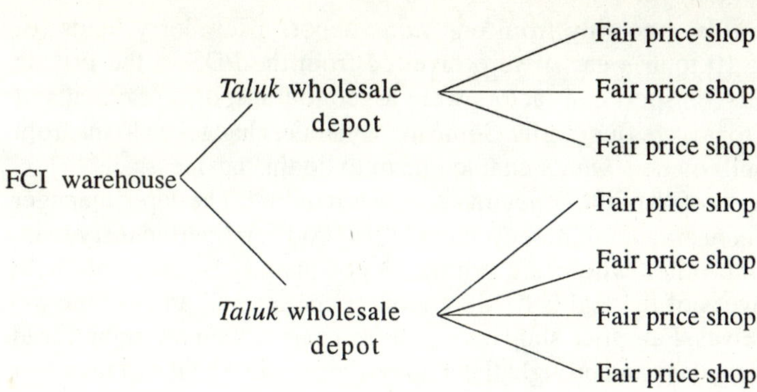

Fig. 5.4 Organization of food distribution

In rural areas, transport of foodgrains from *taluk* wholesale depots to fair price shops is organized by the government. In fact, this 'doorstep delivery' is one of the special features of the PDS in Karnataka.[32] This transportation is also done by private contractors who get the contract after a tender procedure.

Illegal sales of foodgrains cannot take place without the involvement of managers of *taluk* wholesale depots and fair price shop owners. Account books have all to be in order so as to minimize risk or bribes in case of a sudden inspection. This means the cooperation of all the links in the chain is required. This is no problem as we will see.

At the time of stock arrival, fair price shop owners make their financial arrangements. In the Akkipura depot, there were private, independent moneylenders. They lent Rs 5000–15,000 to fair price shop owners on the condition that the latter left a part of their allotment at the wholesale point. That is, with the help of moneylenders fair price shop owners paid for the full allotment, but they did not take all; they sold part of the allotment, mostly wheat, to the moneylender, and they left it at the *taluk* wholesale depot. Moneylenders had similar deals with several fair price shop owners. From each a few bags meant

[32] Doorstep delivery is generally regarded as a guarantee against illegal sales. A previous Prime Minister, Narasimha Rao for instance, while inaugurating the thirteenth meeting of the Advisory Council on Public Distribution on 23 August 1991 said: 'I would also urge you to take up the door delivery system [in the selected blocks of the 'Revamping the PDS' scheme]. Door delivery system exists in a few States, albeit too few. The system will not only ensure the reach but will also provide a safeguard against diversion of PDS foodgrains and other essential commodities by anti-social elements.'

that in total (monthly from one *taluk* depot) a few lorry loads (of almost 10 tonnes each) were diverted from the PDS to the private market. Transport contractors were asked to transport these loads of wheat to private flour mills. Some moneylenders had taken loans from flour mill owners which enabled them to do this business.

Cooperation of the depot manager was required. The depot manager got a fixed amount of money, namely Rs 1000 per diverted lorry load. At some other wholesale points, depot managers, most of them employees of the KaFCSC were more 'experienced' and did the job themselves. Fair price shop owners took a part of their allotment, sold it in a few days and brought the money afterwards. The depot manager gave them a bill as if they had taken the full quantity. He asked the transport contractor to go straight from the FCI godown to private flour mills, rather than first delivering the goods at the *taluk* depot. The profit for the transporter was about Rs 2000 per load. According to one of my informants, who had been involved in this business as a moneylender, on average in the whole district about 50 loads (approximately 500 tonnes) were diverted each month in this way.

The transport contractor had to make monthly payments to the district manager of the Food and Civil Supplies Corporation. Also the depot manager and the flour mill owner paid fixed amounts monthly. In turn, the district manager had to bring monthly amounts to Bangalore, which were shared with his superior officers. Officials who were unwilling to participate in this chain of money collection would most probably never be posted to a position such as depot manager, for which candidates were willing to pay in advance.

At the time of investigation in Akkipura district, about 40 per cent of the wheat and 10 per cent of the rice was sold illegally. Also in Madhyapura in Kerala, illegal sales of rice and wheat took place on a similar scale. In 1992, there was a special scheme in Kerala in which one-third of the PDS wheat was milled by private flour mills. Private flour mill owners interviewed by me estimated that more than half of the other two-thirds was also sold to them, mainly by authorized wholesale dealers.

It is difficult to estimate the value of the losses incurred by the government and the damage done to the card holder. Extrapolation of the figures presented here is impossible. One can only guess that similar practices occur in other districts and States as well, but one never knows for sure.[33] Moreover, the volume and profitability of this illegal trade are directly linked to the difference between the open market price and the subsidized price and, hence, will fluctuate. The smaller this price difference, the more PDS foodgrains are likely to reach the card holder (but the smaller the impact per kg for the card holder). The system of diversion described here was widespread at the time of investigation. However, a few months later PDS prices were raised, and consequently, the profitability and volume of this illegal trade came down.

5.5 CONCLUSION: THE DISTRIBUTION OF BENEFITS

In this chapter, I have described several mechanisms influencing the distribution of benefits of the PDS. In Section 5.2, I analysed the relevance of the system in two villages/settlements in Karnataka and Kerala. It was argued that the organizational set-up of the system (compulsory off-take of wheat, no possibility to buy on credit, limited opening of the shop) as well as the type of intervention (changing the exchange rate between money and foodgrains, rather than broadening the economic base) restrict the usefulness as far as the most vulnerable consumers are concerned. In Section 5.3, the organization of access—how to become a card holder—and the opportunities to voice complaints were discussed. It was shown that crucial differences exist in these respects in the two States, which—I suggested—have to do with the formal and informal rules governing bureaucracy and the degree to which consumers are eager and in a position to mobilize themselves politically. In Section 5.4, it was explained how and why part of the PDS foodgrains never reaches the card holders, but is instead diverted to the open market.

All these mechanisms imply a restriction of the suitability, accessibility and relevance of the public distribution system, in particular as far as the most vulnerable and less resourceful consumers are concerned.[34] In this way, this chapter has revealed an important link between food policy and politics. The system of distribution is

[33] Ahluwalia (1993) estimates leakages for the whole of India as 38 per cent for wheat and 36 per cent for rice. He calculates leakages as a residual by subtracting the total quantities of wheat and rice that were actually bought from the PDS between July 1986 and June 1987 (NSS 1989) from the quantities that the Government of India supplied to the system in this period. The calculated leakages include both physical losses incurred in transport and storage and diversion to the open market. The estimate seems very crude, especially since the reliability of NSS data is debatable (see n 5 of this chapter).

[34] On the basis of NSS data, Jha (1992) also concludes that food subsidy disproportionately favours the richer deciles of the population. Mundle and Govinda Rao (1991) draw a similar conclusion about subsidies generally.

organized in such a way that it favours the 'haves' rather than the 'have-nots'. This is not to argue that the system is irrelevant for this last category of people. As I have argued, these people too regard the PDS as a welcome addition to household food security. But the point is that the system suits other, less needy categories of people a good deal more. I am not refering only to more wealthy consumers/card holders. The system also provides a legal and illegal income to officials, private and cooperative ration dealers, as well as moneylenders, brokers and private traders. Furthermore, it contributes to the political power and legitimacy of those in command of the foodgrains. Food distribution sometimes contributes to the reproduction of existing social relations and hierarchies. This is especially the case in rural Karnataka. Influential people are able to obtain more than their quota or do not require a ration card at all. Fair price shop owners sometimes function as middlemen in solving local political conflicts or accommodating sections of the population with food. Positions in the official vigilance committees are given to people associated with the ruling party. Although such committees do little to improve the performance of the PDS, for the members it adds to their political capital and their ability to distribute food favours.

In other words, in Karnataka the operation of the PDS has adapted itself to the local power structure. PDS food has become a political commodity because it is a means through which power is exercised. Locally influential people have often succeeded in getting command over PDS foodgrains and are able to reproduce or reinforce their dominant positions partly with the help of this PDS food. PDS food is a resource for them in their interactions with less privileged and more needy people.

In Kerala, the situation is rather different. Although here also private flour mill owners, some government officials and ration (wholesale) dealers are among the prime beneficiaries, PDS foodgrains are also the subject of local political struggles in which 'the general public' participates. Villagers/card holders sometimes take the initiative to launch a complaint against a ration dealer involved in misconduct. In this way, the bureaucracy is forced to take some action. On other occasions local political parties take the initiative and make the struggle for a proper implementation of the PDS part of a much wider struggle for political followers and legitimacy.

Although the social relations giving rise to and conditioning the situations in Karnataka and Kerala are very different, there is one common characteristic: food insecurity. In both States the food security of many households is marginal or insufficient, as is the security in many other respects—employment, housing, health, etc. This means the PDS matters. The effects, though, of food insecurity are very different in these two States. In Karnataka, food insecurity seems to contribute to the continuation of relations of patronage. Insecurity inhibits people from protesting against malpractices in the distribution system. Participating in the existing local relations seems more rewarding than standing out against them. In Kerala, food insecurity does not only lead to subordination, but also to political mobilization. Food has become a central point in political struggles. At the local level, observed malpractices are reported and the food bureaucracy is forced to take action. At the level of the State, food insecurity has contributed to the development of articulated claims and demands for cheap subsidized food.

The different effects of food insecurity and the different meaning of 'food as a political commodity' in these two States is a result of the different types of social relations at the local level, the different political constellations and the different historical trajectories. As explained earlier (Sections 1.3 and 3.2) Kerala has a long history of political mobilization, as well as of welfarist policies. In Karnataka, on the other hand, populist policies were introduced 'from above' rather than as a result of active involvement and struggle of the population. These different political-economic contexts shape the final characteristics of the PDS, and ensure that, despite a similar blueprint, the actual outlook of the PDS is very different in different circumstances.

6

State Trading

The Food and Civil Supplies Corporations

According to the Ramayana saga, Maveli was an ancient king who ruled over a large territory. During his reign, there was no scarcity; everything that people needed was in plentiful supply. People were happy and worshipped their king. As a result, Maveli became such a popular and powerful ruler that it aroused the jealousy of the Devas, the celestial beings. One day they put their heads together and decided to complain to God Vishnu. After hearing their grievances, Vishnu took the appearance of a dwarf, Wamana, and came down to earth. He went to Maveli, who was pleased to see him and asked what he could do for his guest: 'All I have is at your disposal, money, jewels, the wide earth and all it inherits.' Wamana, however, answered that wealth was of no use to him. All he requested was three paces of land, as paced by himself. The king smiled, looked at the small legs of the dwarf, and said: 'So be it; pace and take it.' The little dwarf then suddenly assumed giant proportions, and with one step he measured the earth and with a second the entire heavens. There was no room left for the third step that had been granted, except on Maveli's head, and that was what Wamana did.

This was the end of the kingdom of Maveli. However, since he was not a bad ruler he was permitted to come back to earth once a year. This is celebrated at Onam, a festival in August/September that is observed particularly in Kerala.[1] For people in Kerala, Onam is by far the most important festival of the year.

[1] This is the version of the Maveli saga that I have often been told. See also Rajagopalachari's version of the *Ramayana* (published by Bharatiya Vidya Bhavan, Bombay, 1983), p. 31–2. However, there is also an older folk version of the story in which Maveli (or Bali) is not in exile, but living in another empire from which he comes over once a year. The introduction of Vishnu and the idea of exile is a Brahminical addition and reformulation of the older folk version.

This story of Maveli and the abundance during his reign has been taken up by the Kerala State Civil Supplies Corporation. Since 1980, the Corporation has organized special Onam markets where bananas and vegetables are sold. It has also opened permanent shops, so called *Maveli* stores, selling rice, edible oil, pulses, sugar and other essential commodities. Starting a few years ago there are now also *Maveli* supermarkets, as well as one or two *Maveli* hypermarkets.

This chain of markets and stores illustrates some of the activities that state trading corporations can undertake. In the whole of India, there are many state trading corporations. This chapter deals with the food and/or civil supplies corporations only, but there are other corporations dealing with other commodities. The largest corporation dealing with food is the FCI, a central state organization employing almost 70,000 people (Bhalla, 1994:145) and operating in the whole of India. In addition to this central food corporation, almost all State governments have established trading corporations working in the respective States. Most trading corporations perform tasks that are closely related to the PDS, (e.g. procurement of foodgrain or wholesale distribution). But there are some corporations—such as the one in Kerala—that undertake other or additional activities.

In line with public distribution generally, the overall objectives of state trading corporations are to protect the consumer and to discipline private trade. But apart from these publicly stated objectives the corporations serve various other functions. Food distributed by these corporations gives individual politicians and political parties an opportunity to increase their popularity. It supports governments and particularly Food Ministers. Moreover, the corporations themselves function as a small financial treasure that is (mis)used by concerned ministers. The foodgrain distributed by the corporation is a political commodity, and the corporation functions as an arena and resource for those in charge to reproduce and reinforce their influence.

While the FCI was established in 1964, most State trading corporations date from the first half of the 1970s. For instance the Tamil Nadu Civil Supplies Corporation was founded in 1972, the KaFCSC in 1973, and the KeSCSC in 1974. The political and ideological climate in the beginning of the 1970s was in favour of expanding state activities, also in the field of market interventions. In 1972, the Indian government even decided to take over wholesale wheat trade. The policy failed and was soon abandoned, but it illustrates the political climate at the time.

In the twenty to twenty-five years that have passed since then, the political climate has changed dramatically. Now, in the 1990s, state corporations and public enterprises are seen in a much gloomier light. They are regarded as inefficient and as a significant burden on government budgets and scarce resources. According to the World Bank (1995: xi), 'Public enterprises hinder growth, impede liberalisation, and thus both directly and indirectly limit efforts to reduce poverty.' The FCI is regarded as an inefficient and very expensive organization, because of its 'excessive staffing [and] inefficiencies ... in purchase, storage and transport operations' (Bhagwati and Srinivasan, 1993: 60). The FCI is held responsible for at least a considerable part of the huge subsidy bill, and an argument is made for decentralization and debureaucratization (Gulati and Hashim, 1994: 380; Vyas, 1994), if not for dismantling.[2] So far, the various State food and/or civil supplies corporations have escaped such harsh criticisms, but these corporations are also now regarded with greater suspicion and scepticism than at the time of their inception.[3]

This chapter is about the KaFCSC and the KeSCSC. In the first section, I describe the functioning of both Corporations. Since their foundation they have both met several crises, related to their very identity (what should the Corporation do?) as well as to their financial viability. So, at first glance, it seems there is some truth in the critique ventured by advocates of privatization or dismantling of public enterprises. For both Corporations the beginning of the 1990s was a financially difficult period in which they made losses—although 1992–3 was a good year for the Karnataka Corporation. (See Table 1 of Appendix 3 for some financial details of the two Corporations.) The next three sections focus on reasons behind the problematic functioning. The argument developed is that the Corporations have to operate within a normative political and economic environment that pulls and pushes them to various sides. Apart from the fact that they have to reconcile various conflicting objectives, they are regarded as private property rather than as public enterprise by some of the

[2] According to Vyas (1994: 126–7) 'The FCI, as it is organized now, is not able to perform [its] functions effectively. It is a centralized, bureaucratic, high-cost apparatus. The centralized way, in which it operates, makes the states complacent about managing their food economy. This also imparts a rigidity in decision-making, which puts it in a disadvantageous position in trading operations. Its unwieldy establishment adds to the costs of procurement and distribution of foodgrains and other agricultural commodities. Reorganization of FCI should be undertaken to correct these defects.'

[3] See Ghosh (1994) on the ideological assault on public enterprises.

politicians and officials in charge. The last section summarizes the argument and suggests that the solution would not be privatization, but rather making the Corporations *less* 'private' than they are now.

6.1 THE KaFCSC AND THE KeSCSC: A SHORT OVERVIEW

The KaFCSC and the KeSCSC share the same overall objectives: to exert a downward effect on prices and to discipline private trade. But the two Corporations also differ in several respects. The main function of the KaFCSC is to act as a wholesale and retail agent in the PDS, while the KeSCSC has organized a third parallel market, apart from the open market and the PDS: the *Maveli* stores. The Karnataka Corporation has not assumed special tasks pertaining to festivals or other celebrations.

The KaFCSC

The KaFCSC was established in 1973 by then Chief Minister Devraj Urs. According to the memorandum of the Karnataka Corporation, the main objective is' to engage... in the production, purchase, processing, storage, transport, distribution and sale of foodgrains, foodstuffs and such other essential commodities as it may choose.' Devraj Urs became the first chairman of the Corporation Board. Between 1973 and 1992, the Corporation has had twenty-one different chairmen. Some of them were ministers; others were secretaries to the government or relative outsiders—though usually with links to the ruling party.

The activities undertaken by the KaFCSC have changed over time (see Table 6.1). Initially, its main activity was procurement of foodgrains. Immediately after the KaFCSC came into being, the FCI, which had been responsible for procurement till then, ceased its procurement operations in the State. Apart from procurement for the centrally administered PDS, the KaFCSC also made purchases of paddy, *ragi*, *jowar* and rice, as open market purchases and support price operations. From 1984 onwards, the FCI again took over procurement. For the KaFCSC this meant that it suddenly lost its main task, and its main source of income. It had to find substitute activities, and these were found in wholesale, and to a lesser extent retail, of PDS commodities.

Till the mid-1980s, the wholesale of PDS commodities had been virtually the exclusive domain of the cooperative and private sectors. Private PDS wholesale was abolished in the mid-1980s, and gradually the KaFCSC became more and more active in this field. In 1993, the KaFCSC managed nearly half of the PDS wholesale points in the State. Also the number of retail outlets (fair price shops) run by the KaFCSC has increased, although the Corporation does not aspire to become an important actor in this field.

Table 6.1

Main activities of the KaFCSC 1973–1992

	Procurement (PDS)		Other purchases*		Distribution activities	
	Paddy (tonnes)	Rice (tonnes)	PSO** (tonnes)	OMP*** (tonnes)	Number of wholesale outlets (of total)	Number of retail outlets (of total)
1973–4	173,987	—	1314	6810	—	—
1974–5	188,169	—	—	17,459	—	—
1975–6	260,552	—	—	133,736	—	—
1976–7	97,606	—	—	—	—	—
1977–8	64,804	—	9999	—	—	—
1978–9	140,911	—	49,649	—	—	—
1979–80	87,807	—	24,349	—	—	—
1980–1	102,981	4543	7562	—	—	—
1981–2	83,703	82,743	42,221	—	—	—
1982–3	72,689	—	992	—	—	—
1983–4	142,871	—	—	24,925	46	45
1984–5	—	—	—	115,742	—	—
1985–6	—	—	—	36,896	58 (196)	—
1986–7	—	—	240	55,246	100 (270)	—
1987–8	—	—	—	4263	103 (266)	—
1988–9	—	—	—	—	112 (267)	—
1989–90	—	—	—	—	114 (267)	—
1990–1	—	—	—	—	124 (273)	261 (16,980)
1991–2	—	—	—	—	133 (282)	273 (17,364)

Notes: *Other purchases refer to the following foodgrains: paddy, rice, *ragi, jowar* and maize; **PSO means price support operation; *** OMP means open market purchase.

Sources: KaFCSC, Food and Civil Supplies *Annual Reports*; Dept. of Food and Civil Supplies *A decade of dedication to the consumer*; KaFCSC, 1983

The wholesale of PDS commodities is a relatively simple activity. The supply of the commodities is fixed and more or less secure. There is a certain fixed quantity allotted monthly to the State. The KaFCSC has to see that the allotted quantities are transported from FCI godowns to the KaFCSC warehouses, and subsequently to the fair price shops. The wholesale margins are fixed by the State government.

Table 6.2 gives a rough indication of the relative importance of this foodgrain market intervention in total foodgrain availability in Karnataka. It shows that the KaFCSC deals with approximately 7 per cent of the foodgrain available in the State.[4]

Table 6.2

Foodgrain production in Karnataka and amounts of foodgrain handled by the KaFCSC 1985–1993

	(1) Foodgrain production (million tonnes)	(2) Foodgrains handled by the KaFCSC (million tonnes)	(3) Foodgrains handled by the KaFCSC as percentage of total production 2/(1+2) (%)
1985–6	5.789	0.384	6.22
1986–7	7.338	0.403	5.21
1987–8	6.280	0.486	7.18
1988–9	6.732	0.285	4.06
1989–90	7.058	0.408	5.46
1990–1	6.244	0.468	6.97
1991–2	7.901	0.625	7.33
1992–3	8.600	0.547	5.98

Sources: Karnataka Food and Civil Supplies Corporation; *Economic Survey*; GoKa (Table 1.1)

Since the mid-1980s, the income earned in PDS wholesale is by far the major source of income of the KaFCSC. See Table 2 of Appendix 3 for the amounts handled by the KaFCSC. In 1991–2, sales of rice, wheat, sugar and palmolein oil together accounted for

[4] The table gives only a rough indication as it compares foodgrain production with the quantities handled by the KaFCSC. Foodgrain imports and exports are not included. Import and export figures are not readily available. In Karnataka, import and export quantities are small as compared to production figures.

95 per cent of the Corporation turnover.[5] Other potentially profitable essential commodities, such as kerosene, LPG gas and cement are handled by private wholesalers. The Corporation does, however, extend its activities into a number of other commodities, such as *sooji* and *maida* (both wheat products), yellow lentils, soap, tea, salt and notebooks. The significance of these commodities in total sales figures of the Corporation is very limited.[6]

The financial structure of the Corporation is as follows. The share capital is Rs 22.5 million (used and paid up; the authorized share capital is Rs 30 million). All shares are owned by the government. The Corporation can further draw a loan from the State Bank of India up to an amount of 100 million (in 1992). Since 1991–2, a second line of credit has been established (for items other than rice and wheat) through a consortium of bankers. The maximum loan on this second line is 41.5 million and the interest is higher than on the SBI loan and dependent on the general rate of interest in India. At the beginning of the 1990s, this interest rate was around 20 per cent. Since its inception, the Corporation has functioned without a subsidy. All its assets, among which there are two oil sachet factories, and the whole salary bill are paid for by the Corporation itself or with the help of regular loans.

The Corporation is managed by a Board of Directors, consisting of twelve members. The Managing Director is the chief executive and works under control of the Board. He is of IAS cadre.[7] In 1973–4 the total staff strength was 229; the salary bill came to Rs 1.5 million. In

[5] Palmolein oil is the oil made from the kernels of the fruits of the oil palm. Oil extracted from the fruits themselves is called palm oil. Palmolein oil is white or yellow, while palm oil is red. Generally, the food and/or civil supplies corporations in India have distributed palmolein oil. Palmolein oil is more expensive than palm oil, and regarded as a better quality oil.

[6] In 1991–2 there was a half-hearted attempt to expand the activities of the KaFCSC when the Karnataka Chief Minister Bangarappa announced his intention to step up sales of non-controlled commodities under the so-called Vishwa scheme. The idea of this scheme was to give loans to rural unemployed youths in order to help them to become entrepreneurs. The Corporation would purchase their products and distribute the commodities to fair price shops. The scheme has not got off the ground. In fact, it was more of a populist promise to the rural unemployed and a reason for granting loans to some favoured participants than a serious attempt of the Corporation to diversify its activities into new directions. The scheme came to an abrupt end when Chief Minister Bangarappa had to quit at the end of 1992.

[7] Since the inception of the Corporation, the Director of the Food and Civil Supplies Department used to act as ex-officio MD of the Corporation. This set-up was abandoned in 1990, since when the Corporation has had its own MD, who is in charge of the Corporation only.

1991–2 the staff total comes to nearly 1500, while the salary bill has increased to Rs 38.5 million. Originally all officials were drawn on secondment from other departments, in particular from Food and Civil Supplies. Over the years, however, the Corporation has been conducting its own recruitment. Apart from a few managers of IAS and KAS cadre, the personnel now solely belong to KaFCSC only. The staff has its own independent labour union, which is committed not only to the individual employee's interests but also to the well-being of the Corporation in general.

The KeSCSC

The Kerala State Civil Supplies Corporation was established in 1974. The memorandum setting out the objectives of the Corporation is very similar to the memorandum of the Karnataka Corporation. Both mention procurement, distribution, trade, storage, transport, etc. of foodgrain and other essential commodities as the main tasks. Yet the two Corporations have developed in different directions.

Initially, it was difficult for the Kerala Corporation to define a proper niche for itself. Kerala had a fairly well-developed PDS with a network of about 270 wholesale dealers and more than 10,000 fair price shops. There was no reason for the newly established KeSCSC to interfere in the existing situation. Therefore, from the start onwards the goal has been to develop the KeSCSC into a trading organization that would undertake activities parallel to both the existing PDS and the open market.

One fundamental requirement for such a trading organization is to establish a proper distribution network. During the 1970s, the Corporation experimented with several modes of distribution before it settled down to the present system (see Koshy, 1989). In 1975–6 it opened its own retail outlets, but the system broke down because of lack of stock and infrastructure. In 1979, a new scheme, the so-called Kerala Stores, was launched, but this scheme also did not prove viable. It was only after the inauguration of a new Left Democratic Front government in February 1980,[8] that the Kerala Corporation developed into a dynamic agent intervening in the Kerala market. (See Table 3 in Appendix 3 for an overview of the sales of the most important commodities since the inception of the Corporation.)

[8] In the 1980 Assembly elections, the Left Democratic Front consisted of the CPI(M), the CPI and various other parties, including the All India Muslim League. It won 93 out of 140 seats (Suresh, 1986).

This change in 1980 can be put, largely, to the account of the new CPI Minister for Civil Supplies, E. Chandrashekar Nair, who took office in 1980. Although this government remained in power less than two years, it left a major mark on the Civil Supplies Corporation. E. Chandrashekar Nair himself recounted in an interview:

Kerala is a very food deficient State. Since the food scarcity in 1964, we receive foodgrains from the Centre through PDS. The problem is, however, that this FCI rice is of very bad quality. We are here at the receiving end; we have to accept it. Apart from PDS, open market prices are uncontrolled. The prices are set by important traders in Bombay and elsewhere. Our own Kerala traders are relatively small compared to the large companies outside the State. Anyway, we felt that we had to organize a countervailing power against the traders. In 1980, when we came to power, prices were rising and the opposition claimed that we cooperated with the traders and that we tolerated hoarding. My idea was that one cannot solve economic problems with coercive power. We had to find an economic solution. I thought, if we have a market share of 10–15 per cent, that would be sufficient to control private trade. In principle, PDS can have this function, but the quality is not good enough. PDS has a downward effect on the price of low-quality rice. But so far nothing has happened to good-quality rice. The KeSCSC could fill that gap.

A second motive was the general price rise during festivals. Here, Onam is the most important festival. During this festival people change their usual eating habits. They prepare different things. What happens is that the prices rise very much. In 1980 the Corporation started to organize temporary shops and vegetable fairs, where people can purchase all the special requirements for the festival.

In 1980, the Corporation opened the first *Maveli* stores, and started to organize Onam markets. In 1992, there were about 500 *Maveli* stores. The number of commodities for sale in these stores fluctuates. In principle, it includes *Maveli* items such as rice, edible oil, various types of pulses, dry chillies, spices, and so-called non-*Maveli* items such as tea, soap, toothpaste and stationery.

The number of Onam markets in 1992 was 142. These markets are of different types, ranging from big fairs that last for three to four weeks, where a variety of commodities are sold, to small *chanda's* lasting for four to five days with mainly vegetables. Apart from the 142 markets, approximately 2000 cooperative societies were involved, conducting sales in 3000 different places. During festival months, sales figures are two-three times higher than in the rest of the year. The normal provision items (especially rice, oil and sugar) remain the most important commodities. These commodities constitute 75–85 per cent of the sales figures of the Corporation at the Onam markets.

Although vegetables and bananas contribute only 15–20 per cent, their supply involves a major effort. The commodities are easily perishable and have to be dealt with quickly. In general, the Onam markets require a well-thought-out scenario and personnel willing to put in extra hours and to perform tasks different from their usual work routine. Generally, these conditions are met: the markets are well-organized and supply is more or less continuous.

Apart from *Maveli* stores and Onam markets, the Corporation also supplies rice and other essential commodities to the midday-meal programme for schoolchildren, to prison institutions, mental hospitals, etc.

Most *Maveli* items are sold at a price below the economic cost.[9] The only exceptions are palmolein oil, on which the Corporation makes a profit, and some non-*Maveli* items. Rice is the most burdensome commodity for the Corporation. The price is fixed by the government at a low level and cannot be adjusted by the Corporation.[10] In respect to most other commodities the Corporation is expected to sell at a price approximately 20 per cent below the open market price, but price adjustments can be made by the Corporation itself.

Table 6.3 gives a rough indication of the contribution of the KeSCSC to total rice availability in the State. It is clear that the 10–15 per cent contribution aspired to by the previous minister E. Chandrashekar Nair is still is distant dream.[11] The Corporation deals only with 2–6 per cent of the rice available in Kerala.

[9] The economic costs are the costs per kg incurred by the Corporation. Apart from the purchase costs, they include taxes, transport costs, storage losses, interest on purchase costs, administrative expenses, etc. The Corporation calculates these costs partly on the basis of fixed estimates, (e.g. administrative expenses are set at 3 per cent of the purchase costs plus taxes) and partly on the basis of costs really incurred.

[10] This policy changed in 1993. In that year, the Kerala government decided that the Corporation was free to fix the selling price of rice, provided that this price was approximately 10 per cent lower than the open market price.

[11] This table gives only a rough indication as rice imports and exports by private traders are not included. These figures are not available. Rice import is considerable; rice export is much less. This means that the contribution of KeSCSC rice to overall rice availability is even less than the percentages in the fourth column indicate. On the other hand, E. Chandrashekar Nair was talking about 10–15 per cent of the *marketed* rice. As only part of the rice that is produced in the State (column 1) is marketed—the remainder is used for own-consumption—the contribution of Corporation rice to total marketed rice is higher than the contribution to total available rice.

Table 6.3

Rice availability in Kerala and rice handled by KeSCSC 1980–1993

	(1) Production (million tonnes)	(2) Imported from FCI (million tonnes)*	(3) Handled by KeSCSC (tonnes)	(4) Rice handled by KeSCSC as percentage of available rice 3/(1+2+3) (%)
1980–1	1.27	1.62	31,855	1.09
1981–2	1.34	1.57	42,966	1.45
1982–3	1.31	1.20	42,397	1.66
1983–4	1.21	1.30	156,592	5.87
1984–5	1.26	1.36	69,587	2.59
1985–6	1.17	1.46	45,393	1.69
1986–7	1.13	1.65	64,998	2.28
1987–8	1.03	1.66	51,223	1.87
1988–9	1.01	15.5	91,731	3.46
1989–90	1.14	1.27	136,623	5.36
1990–1	1.09	1.65	81,528	2.89
1991–2	1.06	1.67	75,783	2.70
1992–3	1.08	1.80	48,577	1.66

Note: * Figures in this column refer to calendar years.

Sources: Economic Review, Government of Kerala (various years); KeSCSC.

The KeSCSC does not receive any regular institutional subsidy. As with the Karnataka Corporation, it started with an initial authorized share capital of Rs 30 million. In 1982, this was increased to 150 million, of which approximately 80 million has been used. This amount is mostly fixed in assets. In 1992, the working capital of the Corporation consisted of a loan of nearly Rs 210 million from the Government of Kerala, plus a loan of 350 million from a consortium of bankers. There was an accumulated loss of Rs 350 million. In the beginning of the 1990s, the Corporation received two grants from the Kerala government, together worth Rs 130 million. This amount has been spent on cash losses. This means the net working capital of the Corporation is Rs 210 million, which, in 1991–2 was more or less the value of the stock. There was hardly any solvent capital. For all special transactions the Corporation had to enter into new loan arrangements. Since 1990, the Corporation has had to take additional loans each year to finance the Onam markets. In 1992, the Corporation imported almost 15 thousand tonnes of palmolein oil, for which it had to enter into a short-term loan with the Kerala cooperative banks. In 1992, the financial problems were fairly acute. Sugar allotted by the Central state was not collected any more because of the lack of solvent capital.

Like the Karnataka Corporation, the Kerala Corporation is managed by a Board of Directors. Unlike Karnataka, the chairman of the Board has never been a minister. The Corporation is headed by the MD, who is of IAS cadre, as is the General Manager. The total staff strength of the Corporation in 1992 was 2586. All salesmen and shop holders, as well as a number of managers are directly recruited, while virtually the whole middle cadre is on secondment from the Civil Supplies Department.[12]

An interim evaluation

The stated rationale for establishing the Karnataka and Kerala Food and/or Civil Supplies Corporations was to augment availability of essential commodities of sound quality at affordable prices. By doing so, it was envisaged, the Corporations would help reduce prices and discipline private trade. To what extent have the Corporations succeeded in these objectives? I shall look at price reduction first, and then at the impact on private trade.

It is very hard to say what the impact of the Corporations has been on prices of essential commodities, at any rate as far as Kerala is concerned. In Karnataka, things are relatively simple. The KaFCSC restricts its activities by and large to the wholesaling of PDS commodities. Since the allotment of PDS commodities to the state is not dependent on the fact that it is the KaFCSC that undertakes the wholesaling, the Corporation's effect on foodgrain availability is nil.

[12] This situation means that there are two categories of staff: seconded personnel (deputationists) and directly recruited personnel. These two categories have different interests regarding the set-up of the Corporation. Directly recruited salesmen and shop helpers are in favour of a full separation of the Corporation and the Department. In the present set-up they have no opportunity to get promotion within the Corporation because all the higher positions are occupied by deputationists. In contrast, for the seconded staff and for staff from the Civil Supplies Department generally, the present situation means that they have more promotion possibilities than they would have had otherwise. Although most of them dislike the secondment period itself, on the whole they prefer the present set-up. There is some resentment between the two categories of staff. Seconded staff look down upon 'manual work' in the Corporation, while directly recruited staff blame the other party for not putting its shoulder to the wheel.

Also the prices of controlled commodities do not depend on the Corporation: they are fixed by the government. In other words, as it functions now, the Corporation does not have an impact on the food situation in Karnataka. The allotted PDS commodities could, in principle, also be dealt with by the cooperative sector (as is happening in respect to part of the foodgrains in Karnataka) or by private PDS wholesale dealers (as is happening in Kerala). The legitimacy of the Karnataka Corporation is fully based on the claim that the Corporation is better able to perform this task of PDS wholesale than other potential wholesalers. (In practice, PDS wholesale can be problematic anyway, whosoever the wholesaler, as was discussed in Section 5.4).

In Kerala, the Corporation does affect the total availability of foodgrain in the State. The KeSCSC procures rice in Andhra Pradesh and other States; it purchases vegetables in Tamil Nadu. These activities are additional to private trade and the PDS, and may have an effect on open market prices. Whether such an effect does indeed occur is hard to say. This would require an analysis of various series of data regarding prices, supplies and qualities of a number of commodities in a number of markets, something which goes far beyond the scope of the research project reported in this book. Nevertheless, it is still possible to develop some hypotheses. Market intervention will be especially effective when the prices of distributed commodities are relatively low—compared to the open market—quality is good and supply is continuous, or at least timely. Regarding vegetables, these three criteria are fulfilled. During Onam season, the Kerala Corporation sells relatively cheap, good-quality vegetables. It is plausible that this intervention helps reduce open market prices, or prevents them from rising any further. Regarding rice and palmolein oil the same cannot be said. In particular, the third criterion is not fulfilled: supply is very irregular. There are long periods in which the Corporation does not sell any rice or palmolein oil, either because it cannot afford to sell rice or because palmolein oil is not available. This means that, at best, the Corporation can have short-term effects on the open market prices of these food items.[13]

[13] In 1992, the functioning of the Kerala Corporation was evaluated by a team of Tata Consultancies. Unfortunately, I have not been able to get hold of a copy of the final report but in 1994, one of the previous managers—who worked in the Corporation in 1992 but was transferred later on—told me that one of the conclusions of the report was that the Corporation was not able to control the markets or have any impact on the general level of prices, except during Onam season. This supports the hypotheses expressed in the text.

Ideally, in view of the objective of influencing open market prices, the Corporation should be able to respond quickly to open market price fluctuations, and glut the market in case of a sudden price rise. Such quick reactions have been absent in the case of Karnataka. In Kerala they are rare, but have happened occasionally. Neither of the Corporations maintains considerable buffer stocks to draw upon in case of sudden price rises.

In short, we can safely assume that one should not be too optimistic about the ability of the two Corporations to affect open market prices. Perhaps, occasionally, in specific locations their activities have an impact on the level of prices, but it is not likely that they have a permanent impact on the level of open market prices.

As far as the second objective, to control private trade, is concerned, the success of the Corporations is hard to measure too, and again, probably limited. In both States, the traders whom I interviewed themselves claimed not to experience any negative or positive effect of the activities of the Corporation. In Kerala, however, this has not always been the case, as the following story illustrates:

In 1980 and 1981, just after the first steps had been taken to set up *Maveli* stores, a vehement conflict broke out between the traders in Trichur and the headload workers. There were several issues in this conflict, in particular the power of the headload workers union, whether traders/employers are allowed to bring in outside workers in case the regular workers are on strike, and the wages to be paid. During the climax of the conflict in 1981, the headload workers went on strike, while the merchants closed their shops. The merchants anticipated that an indefinite closure of the shops would create a situation of scarcity and public resentment against the headload workers. All in all the shops remained closed for more than 50 days and a number of traders went bankrupt. After some time, when the food situation in Trichur became precarious indeed, the Kerala State Civil Supplies Corporation decided to intervene by opening a number of *Maveli* stores. The traders reacted by opening so-called *Wamana* stores, but their position had crucially weakened as a result of the intervention by the government, and finally a settlement was reached. One of the important long-lasting effects of this conflict was the push it gave to political organization of the traders. In 1981, an all-Kerala traders' association, the Vyapari Vyavasayi Ekopana Samithi,[14] was established, which has since developed into a major political force.[15]

Since 1981, the Kerala Corporation has not been involved in similar

[14] The literal translation is: United Organization of Merchants.

[15] This reconstruction is based on several interviews with people involved in the strike and breaking of it, as well as the M.Phil. thesis of Vijayasankar (1986).

conflicts with traders, and by 1989, one of the representatives of the Kerala Chamber of Commerce confessed that:

> ... at present, the merchants are a very powerful category of people. We almost form a parallel government. In any case, we can make or break the Kerala economy. The government is very dependent on us. For instance, each year before the Kerala Budget is presented, there is a pre-Budget meeting with us. The merchants are so important in Kerala because they provide the major source of state income, the sales tax.[16]

Both the Karnataka and Kerala Corporations have financially gone through very difficult periods. In the case of Karnataka, the profits or losses of the Corporation are, basically, dependent on administrative and/or political decisions. The income of the Corporation is directly related to (*a*) the quantities dealt with, and (*b*) the fixed wholesale margin. The Government of India decides the allotted quantity, while the Government of Karnataka decides the wholesale margin. The financial well-being of the Corporation lies in the hands of these two governments. In this sense, the Karnataka Corporation is not comparable to a commercial trading undertaking. Volume of trade and margins are fixed. Management decisions within the Corporation are of minor financial importance. The real decisions affecting profits and losses are made elsewhere.

This is different in the case of the KeSCSC. To some extent this Corporation is comparable to a commercial wholesale trading business. The KeSCSC has to procure at minimum prices and costs. The quantities dealt with are not fixed. Speeding up sales and circulation time of capital means that more commodities can be supplied to the *Maveli* stores. What is different from private trade is that retail prices are fixed by the government, at least for the most important commodities. These prices are less than open market prices. This does not necessarily mean that the Corporation needs a subsidy or makes losses. (I will come back to this below.) In reality, however, the financial situation of the KeSCSC has been difficult during several years and fairly problematic at the beginning of the 1990s.

In short, both Corporations concentrate their activities on a small number of commodities (the KaFCSC even more so than the KeSCSC). They accomplish only minor market interventions. Their ability to react quickly to open market price fluctuations is limited, and their impact on private trade is probably small. In addition, they face financial problems.

[16] See also Section 1.2 about the importance of sales tax in government tax revenue.

The question now is: why is this so? Is there something inherently problematic with state enterprises, as the advocates of liberalization want us to believe, or are there other reasons that explain the problematic functioning? In the rest of this chapter, I take the negative evaluative remarks as starting points for a further investigation. What are the reasons of the poor performance of the two Corporations? What are the dilemmas they face, and in which way is performance determined by the environment in which they operate?

6.2 SOCIAL OBJECTIVES VERSUS PROFITABILITY

To paraphrase Schumacher's apt description of public enterprises: the Food and Civil Supplies Corporations are somehow expected to sell essential commodities at a rate far below current market prices and also to show a substantial profit at the end of the year.[17] The Corporations have been established primarily with a social objective in mind: distribution of food at reasonable prices. But, on the other hand, both Corporations are expected to do so without subsidy, not necessarily making profits, but at least breaking even.[18] In other words,

[17] The original statement was: 'The nationalised enterprises are somehow expected never to charge more than the costs of production and also to show a substantial profit at the end of the year' (B.P. Schumacher, quoted by Ashok Rao, 1987: 57).

[18] In Karnataka, subsidy is not an issue. I have not met anybody arguing that the Karnataka Corporation should be subsidized. In Kerala, the issue of subsidy is debated and contested. According to the Corporation, there was a commitment by the government between 1982 and 1987 to subsidize losses made on rice. The reimbursement of the loss accumulated between 1982 and 1987, however, never happened, and the KeSCSC still claims a sum of Rs 340 million from the government. The Kerala government disputes this claim. And, indeed, the initial government order is ambiguous. G.O. (MS) No. 24/82/Food dated 12 Nov. 1982 sanctions a particular purchase of rice and states that 'the loss if any on account of sale of *this* rice at subsidised rate as fixed by the Government will be met by Government'. It further states that the Corporation may effect further purchases of rice, and sell these at economic cost. 'If, however, on the basis of Government's directions this rice has to be sold at subsidised rate, the question of reimbursement of loss on the score will be *considered* by Government later' (both emphases added). A telex message No.1113/08/87/F&CS dated 15 may 1987 states clearly that 'government will not pay any subsidy for rice... purchased'.

Whether subsidy is desirable is another contested issue. The viewpoint of many former managers and responsible politicians is that as soon as subsidy is a possibility, the discipline and commitment to try to manage without subsidy will erode. On the other hand, some people within the Corporation complained that it was very unfair that the government insisted on a low selling price for rice, while it was not willing to subsidize rice sales.

there is a dual set of objectives for the corporations to fulfil: social and financial.[19]

Often it is difficult to combine the two sets of objectives. The cheaper the food supplied (social objective), the less profit or more losses for the Corporation. In principle, however, a combination of the two sets of objectives is possible. I will outline the conditions under which such a combination is possible, and discuss to what extent these conditions are fulfilled in the States under review.

The first possibility is to deal with a fixed market segment. Purchase and sale prices are fixed, and the margin is sufficient. There is guaranteed demand and the quantities dealt with allow breaking even or making some profit.

The Karnataka Corporation, which deals with PDS commodities, is an example of this mode of operation. It buys foodgrain from the FCI, for which it pays a fixed issue price, and sells these foodgrains to retailers. The margin is fixed and sufficient to break even. The disadvantage of this set-up, i.e. as it operates in Karnataka, is that there is little flexibility to carry out additional market interventions which in certain periods would be very useful from a social perspective. For instance if there is a sudden rise in the price of rice, the Karnataka Corporation is not equipped to perform an extra, spontaneous market intervention.

In Kerala, the Corporation has no fixed market segment. It is not involved in PDS wholesale.[20]

[19] This contradiction between financial and social objectives has also attracted the attention of several other scholars studying public enterprises, although it has sometimes been phrased in a slightly different way. For instance Ray (1989: 78) writes that 'the objective [of public sector enterprises] are not clearly spelt out.' This lack of clarity is the 'reason why it is often seen that the private sector criterion of profits is used in a somewhat round about manner for evaluating performance of public sector enterprises' (78–9). Krishnaswamy (1980: 13) mentions the 'multiplicity of responsibilities'. According to him there were opportunities to make profits, but 'the association of public sector enlargement with socialistic or welfare objectives naturally meant that such temptations should be resisted and public sector enterprises treated somewhat like public utilities in the traditional sense' (12). According to Chakravarty (1987: 30). 'The government did not possess enough clarity of objectives for the public sector'. Surplus created in this sector was supposed to flow back to the state, but this never happened to the extent envisaged because the idea was that the public sector ought not to make profits. Bagchi (1994: 399) mentions 'deliberate underpricing of public sector goods and services' as one of the reasons for the failure to generate surplus/savings.

[20] In fact, the transfer of PDS wholesale from the private sector to the Corporation has been considered, but this idea has never found sufficient support. In particular, private authorized wholesale dealers, have lobbied against such a takeover.

The second possibility is to compensate loss-making activities with profitable activities. This strategy is pursued by both Corporations under review. The most important commodity for cross-subsidization is palmolein oil, not in the last place because the government holds a monopoly in palmolein trade, but also because palmolein oil is relatively cheap as compared to coconut oil. Other commodities used for cross-subsidization in the past have been cement and liquor. In the 1980s, the Kerala Corporation made more profits on cement than losses on rice.[21] When the Government of India decontrolled cement trade in 1989, this cross-subsidization came to an end.

The third condition under which the Corporations could combine the two sets of objectives, is when the cooperation would function more efficiently than private trade. This could be due to economies of scale, or because private traders make excess profits or function inefficiently. This condition is only relevant to the KeSCSC. The KaFCSC does not compete with private trade.

As far as the Kerala Corporation is concerned, Fig. 6.1 to 6.4 show that the Corporation works relatively efficiently as compared to private trade. The figures compare economic costs (of the KeSCSC) with open market retail prices (and *Maveli* retail prices). In the case of rice, economic costs are, on average, Re 0.5 below open market retail prices. In other words, the KeSCSC would be able to supply rice to the market at a rate 10 per cent under the open market price without making losses. In the case of green gram, *toor dhal* and chillies the differences are less permanent. Sometimes economic costs are higher than market prices, and sometimes market prices are higher.[22]

[21] This statement is based on a rough calculation on the basis of purchase and sales values. In the period 1980–9, the sales value minus purchase value in the case of cement was Rs 290 million (which means an average annual 'profit' of Rs 32.2 million); in the case of rice it was minus Rs 78.4 million (an average'loss' of Rs 8.7 million). These figures are not real profit and loss figures, as storage, handling, administrative costs, etc. are not included.

[22] The assumption in these figures is that the quality of products sold in *Maveli* stores and in the open market is similar. This is especially doubtful in the case of rice. There are huge differences in the quality of rice. The *Economic Reviews* published by the Government of Kerala give only one average retail price for open market rice, and do not indicate the quality of the rice. It may well be that the quality of this open market rice is, on average, higher than the quality of rice sold in *Maveli* stores, but I do not have any data on this issue. The quality differences as far as other commodities are concerned are likely to be less significant.

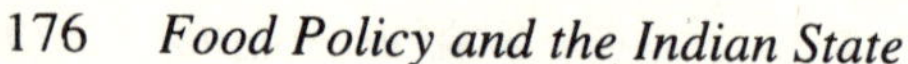

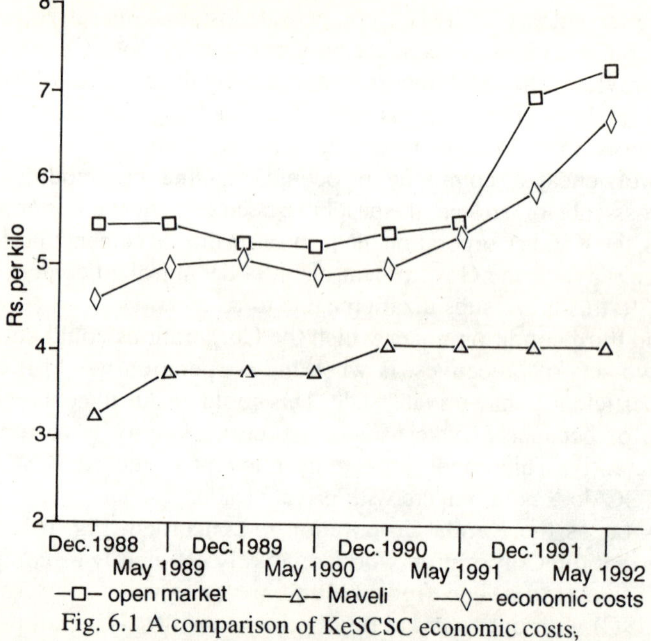

Fig. 6.1 A comparison of KeSCSC economic costs, *Maveli* prices and open market prices: rice

Source: Monthly Price Bulletins, KeSCSC; *Economic Reviews*; GoKe.

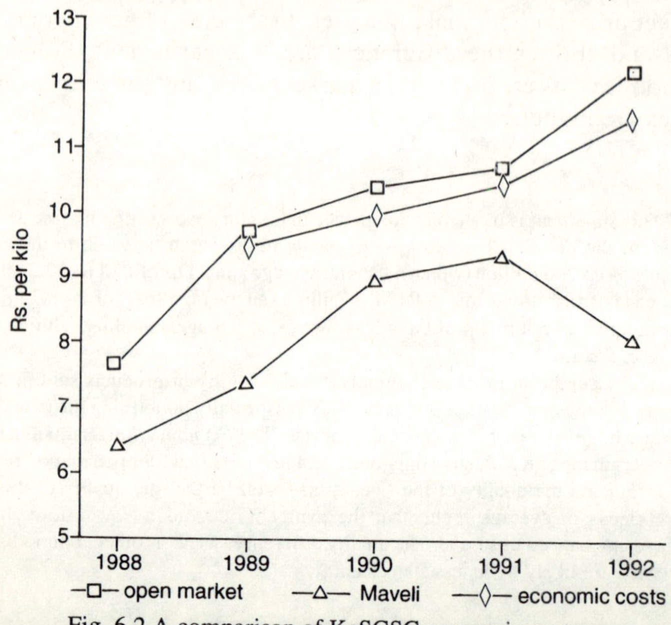

Fig. 6.2 A comparison of KeSCSC economic costs, *Maveli* prices and open market prices: green gram

Source: Monthly Price Bulletins, KeSCSC; *Economic Reviews*; GoKe.

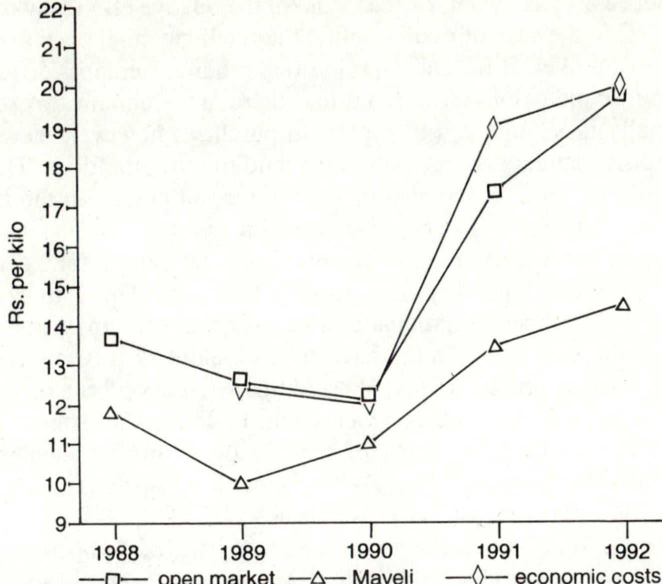

Fig. 6.3 A comparison of KeSCSC economic costs, *Maveli* prices and open market prices: *toor dhal*

Source: Monthly Price Bulletins, KeSCSC; *Economic Reviews*; GoKe.

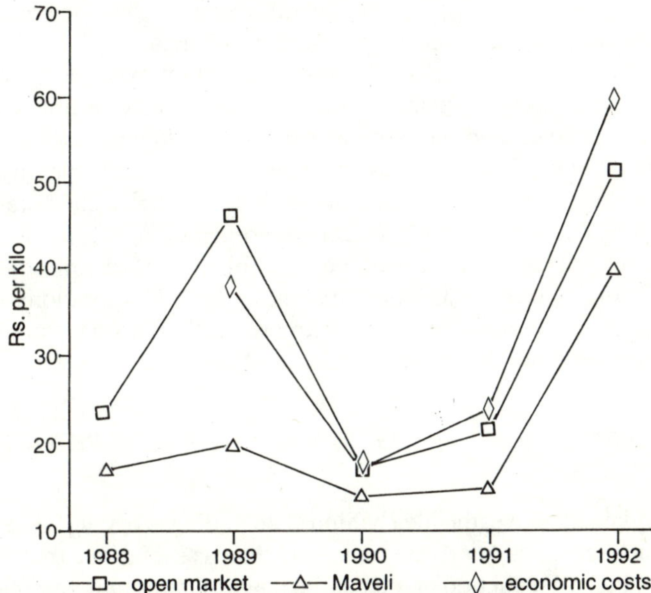

Fig. 6.4 A compression of KeSCSC economic costs, *Maveli* prices and open market prices: dry chillies

Source: Monthly Price Bulletins, KeSCSC; *Economic Reviews*; GoKe.

It is not easy to say what the reason is for the relative efficiency of the KeSCSC in the case of rice, or rather the relatively high open market price. Moreover, different commodities require, perhaps, different types of explanations. It may be that there are economies of scale, especially in storage and transport. In purchase, however, there are scale disadvantages. Large purchases tend to push up prices. This is true not only of rice, but also of vegetables and pulses. In the latter case, the slab system has become common practice. This means that the contractor delivers the first quantity, say 100 tonnes, for a certain price; the second quantity costs slightly more, etc. This slab system has been developed to anticipate price rises that occur as a result of large-scale purchases. On the basis of my fieldwork it is impossible to say whether private trade makes, at times, excess profits or works inefficiently. Several other researchers in India and South Asia, however, have found evidence of speculation, or similar phenomena (see Harriss, 1984b;). It is likely—but further investigation is necessary—that these phenomena exist in Kerala as well.

In any case, whatever the precise characteristics of the open market, the Corporation is able to supply at a similar or even cheaper rate without incurring losses. This means that it would be possible for the Corporation to combine its social objectives—to increase the availability of reasonably priced food—with financial viability. This would, however, imply sale at economic costs rather than at prices much lower, as was happening at the time of fieldwork.

To conclude, low prices and a large market intervention cannot be easily combined with financial autonomy. If one gives primacy to the social objective, then the issue of subsidy is a logical consequence. On the other hand, if one gives primacy to the financial objective, it is odd to demand that the Corporation should sell rice far below the economic cost price, as the Kerala government did in 1991–2.

Nevertheless, there are some possibilities of reconciling the conflicting objectives to some extent. In both Corporations under review these possibilities are not explored fully. This has, mainly, to do with two other dilemmas the Corporations face.

6.3 COMPETITION VERSUS COOPERATION WITH PRIVATE TRADE

As explained above, the idea behind state trading is that it can develop into an alternative to private trade, and that, as such, state trading can contribute to a reduction of mercantile power. One of the consequences of this idea is that, in as far as corporations have to deal with private traders and/or middlemen, a healthy distance should be preserved in order to prevent any entangling of interests. The Corporations have formulated various procedures—in particular, sets of rules prescribing purchase—meant to guarantee such distance.

In practice, however, the Corporations are not only competitors to private trade, but they also work closely together and need to do so. First, private traders are their main suppliers and, second, Corporations have subcontracted out some of their tasks to private firms. These relations and practices of Corporations are, however, constrained by the official rules and procedures. Especially because opposition parties are sometimes eager to blame the ruling party or the Corporation of conspiring with private interests, the Corporations have to remain on the *qui vive* not to develop too close connections with their suppliers or subcontractors. All in all, this situation implies that Corporations have to negotiate various contradictory demands, something I will explore in more detail.

To start with procurement,[23] the first issue is whom to buy from: producers, private traders, cooperative societies, market federations, or sister Corporations in other States? In almost all purchases the Corporation deals with private firms: traders, millers, commission agents, or other middlemen. There are very few examples of purchases from other than private traders or through other than private middlemen.[24]

This brings me to the second issue: how to purchase? The procedures are officially prescribed in the Store Purchase Rules of the government—which prescribe that all purchases should be made by tender—and in the procurement manual—describing the details of the tender procedure. The idea behind the tender system is that it is the best way to guarantee fair trade. A tender allows, in principle, no scope for collusion among suppliers because each of them fixes his own price on the basis of an individual assessment of margins, quality, availability, etc. In addition, the system should foreclose opportunities for collusion between private traders and corporation managers.

A rigid preference for tender procedures does also have disadvantages. It precludes the possibility of making a principled choice to

[23] This part of the discussion focuses especially on the KeSCSC. The KaFCSC does not undertake much procurement.

[24] An exception to this general rule is bananas for the Onam market, which are sometimes bought directly from producers. Another exception is a very modest attempt to start purchasing from market federations or sister corporations.

deal primarily with market federations, cooperative societies, or sister corporations.[25] Tenders involve high transaction costs; there is bureaucratic hassle and they often take time. Consequently, there is a tendency to tender for large quantities. For instance in the case of rice, it is much less time-consuming to have, say, three to six large tenders per year then to have ten to twelve small tenders. But large tenders tend to push up open market prices, as the market is affected by a sudden huge demand. Large tenders mainly attract well-established large trading firms, capable of dealing with large quantities. Because large firms tend to get the orders rather than smaller suppliers, an oligopolistic market market structure is reinforced. Furthermore, tender purchase does not easily combine with the flexible market intervention. There is always a considerable time span between the decision to float a tender and actual delivery. Moreover, the larger the tender the more bribe sensitive, as the stakes are high. In addition, there is substantial risk of default as suppliers may not have the quantities ready in stock. Entering into long-term relations with suppliers is impossible. While in private trade this so-called vendor development is a widely practised strategy to guarantee steady supply of certain quality, the tender system means that each purchase more or less starts from scratch.[26]

Although the rules prescribe that all procurement should be made by tender, in reality spot purchases have also taken place occasionally. A former manager described rice purchase as follows:

> What we did was the following. We floated a tender, and we purchased some quantity from the lowest bidder. In addition, we did spot purchases. We went to see whether there were other suppliers who could deliver at Rs 5 per quintal less than the lowest tender price. In this way also the relatively small suppliers came into the picture. They all possessed readily available stocks, while the large traders who participate in tenders still have to buy after getting the contract. We could develop contacts with some seven or eight small wholesale traders who supplied regularly to the Corporation.

This mode of operation is against the rules and risky in two respects. One is that such semi-permanent contacts develop into a collusion of

[25] It is doubtful whether an increasing emphasis on transactions with market federations, sister corporations or cooperative societies would contribute to overall profitability. It would, however, mean that the Corporation would remain more true to one of its original reasons of existence.

[26] Only small initiatives have been taken to build upon previous experiences. The Kerala Corporation, for instance, keeps records of potential suppliers. Firms that perform badly are blacklisted.

interests between suppliers and the managers of the Corporation. Although initially these contacts may start with the explicit purpose of guaranteeing steady supply at a relatively low price from reliable traders, the relation may change over time. So long as the Corporation's managers identify fully with the objectives of the Corporation there is no risk of spot contracts developing into network trade or of prices rising above prevailing open market prices. If, however, the managers develop their own private interests, there is an obvious risk of joining hands: the semi-permanent suppliers increase their selling rate and pay a bribe to purchasing managers.

A second risk is that of allegations. As soon as this mode of operation is known to others, the responsible officers and politicians risk being accused of favouring certain private parties, regardless of whether this is true or not. This is not only a hypothetical risk. The activities of the Kerala Corporation are, indeed, closely watched by opposition parties. The accusation that the ruling government is hand in glove with private trade is very common. At the time of fieldwork, there was an investigation pending in relation to a large-scale import of palmolein oil, to be distributed by the Kerala Corporation. The government was accused of having accepted kickbacks in the course of this transaction. Also an inquiry pertaining to irregularities in rice purchase in the mid-1980s is still fresh in the memory of many Corporation managers. It is for this reason that most managers and politicians in charge of the Corporation refrain from such a mode of procurement, despite the fact that it could be profitable for the Corporation.

But also, given the tender system of purchase, there is a third issue: how to monitor, supervise and control the suppliers? Here also, the Corporation has to strike a compromise between an obliging sympathetic attitude towards traders, and an uninvolved distance. Take, for instance, regulations regarding payment for goods delivered. In the case of rice, a certain percentage of the value is usually paid after the first quality check in the place of origin and after arrival of the railway receipts in Kerala, that is after loading of the goods. The remaining amount is paid after arrival of the full quantity, after a second quality check and after completion of all administrative procedures. This may last up to a few months. It is in the suppliers' interest to increase the percentage of the first payment. This percentage varies between 90 and 100 per cent. Sometimes, in order to cultivate goodwill among traders and also in order to anticipate lower tender quotes, this percentage is increased. At other times, when the Corporation feels it needs more security, this percentage is reduced again. Another example is punishment policy in case of default, which can be strict or more relaxed. A strict attitude fits in with the Corporation's objective not to give concessions to private trade, while a more relaxed attitude is preferable from the viewpoint of maintaining good relationships. A third examples refers to negotiations with the tenderers. If negotiations are a regular practice, suppliers may anticipate them and quote a higher rate. At the same time, occasional negotiations may help to reduce the purchase price. Apart from prices, other issues may also arise in these negotiations, related to packing of commodities, quality control or the already mentioned percentage to be paid in the first instalment. In general, the Corporation is afraid of a too harsh attitude rebounding on the Corporation itself, notably in the form of higher prices. On the other hand, it cannot permit itself to relax too much, not only because it should prevent its suppliers from acting opportunistically, but also to avoid allegations of playing into the hands of private trade.

Apart from procurement, there is a second way in which Corporations depend on private trade: they contract out some of their tasks to private entrepreneurs. The Karnataka Corporation, for instance, has entered into arrangements with private transporters, labour suppliers/ recruiters, rice millers and warehouse owners. In this way, the Corporation has manoeuvred itself into a paradoxical situation. How do you compete with, or develop into an alternative to, your own subcontractors?

In reality, many of these arrangements are problematic. They are profitable for private firms but detrimental to the Corporations and the public at large. A first example is the practice of contracting out transport of PDS foodgrains in Akkipura district. For several years, the KaFCSC gave the transport contract to a powerful contractor who paid others not to participate in tenders, and was himself involved in large-scale diversion of PDS foodgrains.

A second example relates to the storage and hulling of paddy and rice. In the second half of the 1970s, the KaFCSC entered into an agreement with several rice mill owners to store and hull paddy on behalf of the Corporation. This led to a long-lasting conflict between the Corporation and the rice mill owners. Some rice mill owners sold the paddy illegally or exchanged it for a lower quality substitute. Moreover, there was disagreement between rice mill owners and the Corporation about the terms of agreement. Fifteen years later these cases were still pending. Describing exactly what happened would require many pages; it is a long story of a number of criminal and civil cases, stay orders, attempts at arbitration and delay. Traders have succeeded in delaying and obstructing the cases almost endlessly and the Karnataka Corporation has not been able to respond adequately.[27]

In sum, the relationship between food and/or civil supplies corporations and private agents is of a contradictory nature. On the one hand, the Corporations depend on the private sector for supplies and because they have subcontracted some of their responsibilities to private firms. On the other hand, cooperation is restricted by certain norms and procedures meant to prevent too close contacts, and by the fear of being blamed for playing into the hands of traders. When we look at actual practices and the long-term effects, it may be hypothesized that Corporations sometimes contribute to a strengthening of the larger trading firms relative to the smaller, thereby contributing to a more oligopolistic market structure. In case conflicts arise, the Corporation is often not the strongest party, but is overruled by private traders' interests. The findings support Harriss' conclusion that parastatal trading organizations 'have come to depend on the very private mercantile sector that state trading officially seeks to challenge and to eliminate' (1984b: 72).

6.4 FLEXIBLE MANAGEMENT AND BUSINESS-STYLE VERSUS ACCOUNTABILITY, CONTROL AND POLITICAL INTERFERENCE

Food and/or civil supplies corporations are public enterprises and, therefore, controlled by various external bodies, such as Parliament and the Comptroller and Auditor General of India. Parliament has a monitoring role as custodian of public interest, while the Comptroller and Auditor General seeks to control the audits every year. Also within the Corporations there is control and supervision. The Board of a Corporation, consisting of various representatives of government,

[27] Apart from conscious efforts on the part of traders to obstruct the course of events, several other reasons were mentioned to me explaining the weakness of the Karnataka Corporation, or rather the government, in this conflict: frequent transfers of the responsible managers of the Karnataka Corporation and a tendency in the top management to postpone difficult decisions, unwillingness of the Minister of Food and Civil Supplies to accept a settlement that did not involve financial advantage for him personally, a rift between the Minister and rice mill owners because the latter had supported a candidate from another political party, lack of courage on the part of (junior) judges to act decisively.

supervises the activities of the Corporation. Officials higher in the hierarchy check activities of officials lower in rank. Many of these checks are necessary. In a democratic state, public enterprises should be accountable to the public or its representatives. What has happened to the two Corporations under review, however, is that this control has developed in such a manner that it stands in the way of flexible management and autonomous decision-making. Supervision has resulted in centralization of power, public accountability in political interference, while effectiveness of management has suffered.[28]

Five different, but related, mechanisms creating this contradictory situation can be discerned. The first mechanism is that official rules and regulations of government organizations stand in the way of flexible management and the development of an entrepreneurial style or working.[29] Take, for instance, purchase policy. Although the tender system reduces, in principle, the possibilities for collusion of interests and offers more opportunities to control purchases, the reverse side is that it will not always guarantee the lowest price.

The second mechanism is that the bureaucratic culture that has developed within the Corporations does not provide the right environment for an entrepreneurial spirit. As one staff member within the KeSCSC described the situation:

[28] Other investigators of public enterprises in India have also pointed at this dilemma. Shiva Ramu (1989) conducted a study of management problems of state public enterprises. The four most important problems, according to managers of twenty-three Karnataka State public enterprises, are appointment at the top of inappropriate persons, interference of unions in matters of discipline, political interference and interference by the ministry (ibid.: 93). Ray (1989) analysed the multiple control institutions, and concluded that there is 'chaos and confusion' (p.80). In the present set-up 'it is difficult to secure performance based on 'outcomes over procedures'(ibid.: 85). According to Chaudhuri (1994: 1345), the public enterprises, 'may be considered to be controlled by the ministers and bureaucrats—representing the government—and the top management'. But, he continues '[a] necessary condition for the profitable operation and the growth of the [public enterprises] is that those who run them should be interested in such objectives.' And this is exactly where the shoe pinches. According to Chaudhuri, public enterprises are sometimes used by top decision makers to further their own private, or other, interests. Iyer (1994: 2246) writes that 'the central problem that has both constrained and distorted the performance of [Public Enterprises] ... is an unhealthily close, dysfunctional relationship between them and the government—the absence of a proper *operational distance* between them.'

[29] The term 'entrepreneurial—or business style of working' refers to an archetypical style of working and management characterized by the ability to take decisions and organize the work in such a way that the tasks can be carried out, and the financial viability is secure. I realize that some private firms do not live up to this criterion, although it may be the objective of the managers to do so.

We work as a government organization, not as a trading firm. Once I visited a Super*Maveli*; the manager was very nervous. I asked 'What's the matter?' and he said he was worried because the sales were so high. You see, the more sales, the more responsibilities and the more activity. In a bureaucratic organization as ours it is best to do as little as possible; you won't get any questions and you won't get any difficulties. If I write a sales report, I get a lot of questions. If I don't write it, nothing happens. Decisions that you take with good intentions often work out against you. So, it's better to do nothing. When people start working within the Corporation they are motivated and have good ideas sometimes, but in the course of the years it becomes less and less. Their position is secure anyway. Even when you do nothing, nothing happens.

There are many levels of hierarchy within the Corporations, and little delegation of decision-making. From the perspective of the staff it makes no sense to do more than is strictly necessary. For the managers also, even when they might want to, it is difficult to change this bureaucratic culture. There are no means to reward people who are ardent, have good ideas or great commitment. Similarly, it is impossible to take action against those who 'simply sit in the office'.[30] In Kerala, there is the additional difficulty of seconded staff; these people generally do not like the period of secondment and are sure that they will return to their parent department within a few years.

The third mechanism contributing to lack of entrepreneurial spirit on the part of management is the fear of allegations. Corporation managers know they always run the risk of allegations that they have overlooked procedures or favoured suppliers because they were motivated by corrupt practices. This fear is especially strong in Kerala, where the political arena with its two opposing blocks is more polarized than in Karnataka, and makes management a stressful activity. In a sense, this keen interest of politicians and the public is justified. As a former MD of the KeSCSC described:

To be frank, it is very easy to earn extra money. If you want, there is a lot of scope for bribery. It is virtually impossible to reduce these possibilities; it all depends on the officials in charge. If they want, they can always earn more money.

On the other hand, fear of allegations of favouritism and corruption also inhibits effective management. Playing for safety has a shadow

[30] This was the answer of a FCI official when I asked him what he was doing when there were nc procurement activities. He himself was responsible for quality checks of levy rice. During the eight months of the year in which there is hardly any procurement 'I simply sit in the office', he told me, which indeed tallied with my own observations.

side, as is illustrated by the following statement of another former MD:

> Once we had to purchase a number of vehicles. We undertook an elaborate study of several companies, four of them Japanese, and one Indian. We had more than twenty criteria, and we did a comparative study of all the different vehicles. However, in the end we just decided for the cheapest vehicle, which was certainly not the best, just to avoid difficulties and criticisms.

The fact that civil supplies corporations are regularly (mis)used by opportunistic politicians is the fourth mechanism preventing them from functioning in a more business-like way. The fixing of *Maveli* prices can serve as an example. As discussed above, the Kerala government fixed the *Maveli* rice price far below the economic costs. The result was that the KeSCSC made large losses on rice sales, and hence reduced these sales. During 1990 and 1991, there was no regular supply of rice. In fact, this was a deadlock situation. The ruling party felt it could not afford to increase *Maveli* prices, the result of which would have been a public outcry. Opportunistic party political motives prevented a price rise, but sales were reduced to minimum. Political opportunism stood in the way of a more rational policy, that is of having a steady supply of rice at a higher price, but one that is still below the open market price. While politicians were primarily to blame for this bizarre situation, they themselves went scot free. The blame was on the Corporation for not being able to supply rice.

The fifth mechanism obstructing an entrepreneurial working style is the widespread practice of illegitimate interference of politicians in administrative matters. In both States, the Corporations are misused by politicians. The Corporations offer politicians another arena in which they are able to reproduce relations of power and patronage. In Karnataka, at the beginning of the 1990s, the Food and Civil Supplies Minister himself interfered regularly in decisions about transfers of officials, not only of top managers, but also of operational level personnel of the Corporation, whose transfers are officially dealt with by the Corporation's management. Dynamic directors are sometimes transferred just because they are dynamic and pursue their own vision rather than that of the Minister. The result of this political interference is widespread corruption within the Corporation. Officials pay large sums in order to be transferred to a desired post, such as depot manager. This money has to be recovered before the next transfer is due (e.g. by black marketing some of the PDS commodities). In Kerala, political interference in transfers was much less, but there were instances of interference regarding recruitment of personnel to staff *Maveli* stores, as well as regarding the location of new *Maveli* stores.

These five mechanisms have all to do with the reverse sides of checks, controls and supervision. Although checks and controls are necessary, in reality these controls have led to a lack of autonomy for the Corporations, centralization of powers and short-sighted and illegitimate interference in corporations' affairs, which has harmful effects upon the mode of operation of these organizations.

Many of the managers and operational-level staff are fully aware of these problems. As the various quotations in this section illustrate, it was often their own diagnosis that something was wrong with the bureaucratic culture as it had developed, the political interference and lack of autonomy. The Karnataka Corporation has an active labour union which has protested on several occasions against the misuse of the Corporation by the Food Ministers. It has sent letters and organized strikes to protest against various 'irregularities'. To illustrate, in a letter to the Managing Director of the KaFCSC (dated 19 July 1991) the labour union formulated the following eight questions:

> 1) Whether the Corporation is an undertaking of the government, or whether it is a private institution; 2) Whether the Corporation is having its own rules and regulations and administrative set-up; 3) Whether the Corporation is following the Karnataka Civil Service rules of the government, or whether it is run by influential persons; 4) Whether there is any provision or rule as to re-instate any person who has misappropriated thousands to lakhs of rupees; 5) Whether, in a situation that there is a case registered against such a delinquent official by the police, and the case is before a court, it does not amount to contempt of court to re-install such official; 6) Whether an officer who makes such an unethical order, deserves a KAS or an IAS degree; 7) Whether—in case the management says 'yes'—the management will also reinstate all the other 50 people who are also involved in court cases for similar breaches of law without taking any action against them for their misappropriation; 8) Whether the management passing such unethical orders will have any morals to impose a fine of Rs 50–100 to sales assistants and weightmen who come late by 5 or 10 minutes to open their retail outlets?

While the labour union can criticize these malpractices fairly openly, the management is caught in a contradictory situation. On the one hand, it is held responsible for operations and activities of the Corporation. The managers are blamed when the performance of the Corporation falls short of expectations. On the other hand, they are faced with government decisions and illegitimate interference which are difficult to combine with sound management. They can react to this situation in different ways. One strategy is to develop extra-cautious behaviour, e.g. to respond to ministerial demands only when they come in writing. Another strategy is to give in to the demands, to join the practice of misuse and to remain as close and friendly to the top politicians as possible, in the hope that they will give protection when necessary. Both strategies are followed. Some managers opt more for the first, while others opt more for the second strategy. For the moment, it suffices to summarize the main point that lack of operational autonomy and political interference stand in the way of an entrepreneurial style of working.

6.5 CONCLUSION: CONTRADICTIONS IN STATE TRADING

This chapter started with a review of the activities and performance of the KaFCSC and KeSCSC. It was argued that both the impact on food availability and prices in the two States, and impact on the organization of private trade are probably limited, and that the financial situation of both Corporations is delicate. There have been years in which sizable profits were made, but both Corporations have also experienced years with substantial losses. The chapter then proceeded with a description of the various dilemmas that define the environment and the working of the Corporations. Following this, the contradictions implied in the different sets of objectives, in the relations established with private traders and in the practices around control and interference were discussed.

Although these contradictions do not perhaps fully explain why the Corporations function as they function and fail in as far as they fail, they certainly draw our attention to important issues. Among the important causes of substandard performance there are: multiplicity of objectives; lack of operational autonomy; constraining purchase procedures; unreasonable and short-sighted demands and illegitimate political interference.

On the other hand, we have to acknowledge that there are efforts to introduce new policies and measures to improve performance and increase the Corporations' activities. The *Maveli* initiative, described at the opening of this chapter, is perhaps the most far-reaching one. More generally, there are many managers and operational-level staff members who are very concerned with performance. Although some of the problematic features of the Corporations are, in part, produced and reproduced by the behaviour of this staff, it is also something many of them dislike and sometimes try to change. In short, the

Corporations are not homogeneous and static organizations. They have problems, but they are not fully spoiled or corrupted.

Another point suggested in this analysis is that it is not so much government ownership which is a problem with the Corporations, but rather the rigidity of some procedures and the private (mis)use of the Corporations, by some politicians. *Private* appropriation is much more a problem than the *public* character of the Corporations.

Both points mean that, in principle, there is scope for improvement, although this improvement would be no easy matter. As they operate now, the Corporations serve various functions. They contribute to state legitimacy. State food and/or civil supplies corporations offer a means to State governments to show how important food security is. As described in this chapter, especially in Kerala, the Corporation is used by the government or the ruling parties to establish and/or strengthen the legitimacy of their claim to state power. By promising—and actually opening—new *Maveli* stores and by keeping the *Maveli* prices low, the parties in power try to prove how seriously they take the food question. Moreover, the Corporations function as an additional arena and resource for politicians in charge to reproduce and reinforce their influence. Several politicians attempted—and often succeeded—to get their political followers a job, to use Corporation funds to have a banner made when the Prime Minister visited the State, or to purchase an air-conditioned car to be used by themselves, to influence/control transfer policy, or to give contracts to suppliers or subcontractors who paid them in exchange. As a former MD of the KeSCSC told me: 'The Corporation functions as a milch-cow for the Minister.'[31] Furthermore, the semi-autonomous status of the Corporations enables the government or responsible politicians to blame the Corporation when its performance falls short of expectations, even when the disappointing performance is due to political decisions primarily. For politicians, this is a safe arrangement but, as I indicated before, it means the top management is very vulnerable.

Nevertheless, despite the difficulties that one can expect, a reorganization of the Corporations would be worthwhile. The analysis presented in this chapter points at two key issues that need to be addressed: autonomy and accountability. The first refers to the close and dysfunctional relationship of the Corporations with the government. The government decides almost everything: purchase

[31] He himself did not mention that managers and staff members can also use the Corporation to further their own private interests.

procedures, prices, staffing, transfers, etc. This large say of the government in day-to-day operations prevents a more business-like style of working in the Corporations. Moreover, it facilitates illegitimate interference by politicians. It is absolutely crucial to reduce the role of government and to enlarge the powers of the Corporations themselves to make decisions regarding their mode of operation. A greater autonomy would, for instance, allow for the possibility of modifying the employment and recruitment policy somewhat: to reward people who perform well with promotion, and recruit specialists directly for specific tasks (instead of having promotions on the basis of seniority only, and appointing generalists to key positions).

Moreover, it could be considered that corporations be given a larger say in processes of policy making. As Austin and Fox (1987: 89) conclude on the basis of a study on food sector state-owned enterprises in Mexico: 'As key implementers, [state-owned enterprises], have a clearer understanding of the field, and these realities should be considered in policy formation to ensure that the proposed actions are feasible.' These authors further suggest that not only top managers of the state-owned enterprises should be consulted, 'but the operation-level staff as well. Participation [of this personnel] increases their commitment to the policy and thereby makes adherence more probable as well as more efficient' (ibid.: 89). These recommendations could also be considered in the case of the food and/or civil supplies corporations under review here. In both the Karnataka and Kerala Corporations there are some managers and other staff who are committed to the objectives of the Corporations, but frustrated by the day-to-day operation as well as their inability to change anything.

The second issue refers to the system of supervision, controls and checks. As illustrated in this chapter, the present system does not work very well. Political and ministerial control often results in interference that is detrimental to the organization. It makes a mess of administrative matters and obstructs proper decision-making. Interference should therefore be reduced to cases of clear mismanagement only. Unfortunately however, it is also obvious that this suggestion is more easily made than put into practice. It is a characteristic of Indian politics generally that holding office itself is used to build networks, increase dependencies and create obligations. Maybe it could be a first modest step to exclude ministers from membership (let alone appoint them as chair, as happens occasionally in Karnataka) of the Boards of the Corporations, and to appoint more professional outsiders to these positions, who can bring in a fresh look and who do not work directly under the minister (Ray, 1989: 85).

At the same time, while reducing the role of politicians, new mechanisms of control and accountability should be created. This would involve the creation of new forms of evaluation: the broad performance of the Corporations should be evaluated, rather than whether procedures are followed strictly enough and whether each rupee that is spent can be justified. In addition it is necessary to develop a much wider concept of accountability—that is not only towards superiors but also towards people working at similar and lower ranks within the organization as well as to the general public.

It is not easy to envisage how these kinds of changes could be brought about. They require political support and an active involvement and determination of all people concerned, including the operational-level staff and the public at large to fight for change. Political mobilization around the issue of food is necessary, as well as the general idea that public enterprises are, in principle, able to contribute positively to the organization of trade and distribution. Unfortunately, these conditions are not fulfilled. The present political climate stresses more the weaknesses and limitations of public enterprises than their potential to contribute to a better distribution of food.

7

Food Legislation
Enforcement of the Essential Commodities Act

Who wins in court loses, who loses in court dies

(expression in Kannada)

'The Essential Commodities Act is our bible,' said one of the highest placed police officials of the Food and Civil Supplies Enforcement Department in Bangalore. Earlier, he had argued that it is the duty of the government to ensure food to all citizens. 'For that, the government should have control over production and distribution. When traders can work as they like, society would be in trouble. The Essential Commodities Act is meant to prevent that.' He showed me the Compendium, an edition especially printed for enforcing officials in Karnataka, comprising the EC Act with (Central and Karnataka) control orders. 'These are our guidelines. It is our task to enforce these rules.'

The EC Act is meant to facilitate government regulation of trade and commerce. For officials enforcing the PDS, the Act is an important source of power. In each State, government orders, notifications and circulars are issued periodically describing the procedures to follow in public food distribution. The EC Act is the main statutory backing of these documents. In case traders or others do not comply with the stipulated regulations, they can be sued and penalized under the Act. Implementation of the PDS, hence, cannot be understood properly without an understanding of how the EC Act works in practice.

This chapter describes the relevance of the law for the Public Distribution System. In the first section, I describe the main characteristics of the Act and the struggle around its enactment: legislators in favour of strict legislation versus traders reacting and protesting against the special provisions. Section 2 presents some statistics regarding enforcement of the Act. What strikes one most is that, despite the explicit intention of legislators to deal harshly with traders, the conviction rate in EC crimes is relatively low as compared to crime cases generally. Sections 3 and 4 describe the use of the EC Act in various social processes. While the third section focuses on the interaction between traders, the police, the public and field staff of the Food and/or Civil Supplies Department, the fourth section deals with judges and public prosecutors. The sections show that actual regulation with the help of this law is a complicated social process. Indeed, traders and others do comply with the law to some extent, but this compliance is a result of various interactions and social struggles, some of which take place within, others outside the boundaries of the law. Not only traders, but also law enforcers, manipulate and reinterpret the law in ways that suit their interests. In the final section, I summarize the main functions and effects of the Essential Commodities Act in the implementation of the PDS.

7.1 THE ACT AND THE STRUGGLE AROUND ITS ENACTMENT

The purpose of the EC Act, according to its 1955 preamble, is to provide for control of production, distribution of and trade in certain—essential—commodities in the interest of the general public. The relevance of the EC Act goes, hence, far beyond the implementation of the PDS. The procedures described apply not only to ration dealers, but also to private traders, rice mill owners, transporters of essential commodities, and cooperative marketing societies. All these agents can be prosecuted when they are suspected of contravening certain provisions of the law. As far as the relevance for the PDS is concerned, in Karnataka the EC Act specifies the procedures for levy procurement, while in Kerala there is a special order laying down procedures for PDS rationing.[1]

The EC Act came into force in 1955, but some controls on trade and distribution already existed before that date. During World War II the British colonial government had implemented some control measures (under the Defence of India Rules), and since 1946 there has been legislation in the form of the Essential Supplies [Temporary Powers] Act, which was replaced in 1955 by the EC Act (see Jain,

[1] The Karnataka Rice Procurement (Levy) Order, 1966, and the Kerala Rationing Order, 1966, respectively. In 1991–2, there was no Karnataka Rationing Order, but I was told that the Karnataka government intended to enact a PDS Traders Licensing Order within the foreseeable future.

1964). Since 1955, the EC Act has undergone several amendments, always with the intention to increase the power of the government *vis-à-vis* traders. The number of commodities declared essential under the Act has multiplied over the year from 10 items in 1955 to over 60 in 1992.

Characteristics of the law

The printed version of the EC Act is only a few pages in length. There are, however, a large number of government orders issued under the Act. Section 3 stipulates that if the government is:

> ... of the opinion that it is necessary or expedient so to do for maintaining or increasing supplies of any essential commodity or for securing their equitable distribution and availability at fair prices..., it may, by order provide for regulating or prohibiting the production, supply and distribution thereof and trade and commerce therein.

The EC Act comes under the concurrent list, which implies that both Central and State governments can formulate orders under Section 3. In 1992, there were more that 70 Central control orders related to different commodities. Most State governments have also enacted several dozens of control orders.

There is a great deal of consensus among traders, lawyers and government officials that legislation regarding trade and distribution of essential commodities has not only become vast, but is also confusing and unimplementable, even when all the parties cooperate. Legislation is confusing because orders frequently change. In many States there is a great deal of litigation concerning (parts of) the various orders, and orders are sometimes reformulated after the High Court has nullified the previous one. The argument that the law and its orders are unimplementable refers to the detailed procedures laid down in some orders (for example in relation to how accounts should be kept).

The Act is a double-edged piece of legislation. Once a contravention is suspected, there are two possible procedures. The first is an administrative procedure, described under Sections 6A to 6C of the Act. These Sections provide for confiscation of the essential commodities with respect to which the owner/trader is alleged to have committed an offence. The power to confiscate rests with the District Collector, the highest official at the district level. The second procedure is prosecution for a criminal offence. Enforcing officials may file a charge-sheet in court and launch a criminal lawsuit against the trader.

Thus for the same offence, a trader may be involved in both an administrative case in the District Collector's office and a criminal case in a judicial court.[2]

Another important characteristic of the law is related to the burden of proof. Section 14 of the Act specifies that whenever a person is prosecuted for contravening any order issued under this Act, the burden of proof that he behaved according to the law lies on him, that is the accused. This characteristic is certainly not a common feature of Indian law.[3] Usually the burden of proof rests with the prosecution (see Chapter VII of the Indian Evidence Act).[4]

Since 1955, various amendments have been introduced. The 1967 amendment increased both the minimum and maximum punishments. The 1971 amendment further authorized the seizure of coverings, vehicles and animals used for transportion of offending goods. The 1974 amendment made EC crimes non-bailable, which means that

[2] The law itself does not prescribe under which conditions only an administrative or both procedures should be followed. The most logical view, and the one most in accordance with the spirit of the law, is either none or both. If there is no suspected offence, neither prosecution nor confiscation of goods is necessary, while in cases where a contravention is suspected, prosecution should follow. Because prosecution can only take place if there are commodities involved, there should be a confiscation case as well.

In reality, however, things are somewhat different. Since the EC Act came into force, State governments booked innumerable cases against erring traders and confiscated their goods (administrative cases), while the number of prosecutions was much less by comparison. This is an example of what Benda-Beckmann (1981) has called 'forum shopping': the involved actors search (shop) for the most suitable forum of decision-making. Generally traders try to prevent prosecution; they bribe or otherwise convince the officials not to start criminal prosecutions. On the other hand, government officials who aim to punish traders may also want to prevent criminal prosecution. As Section 6C(2) of the EC Act prescribes that the value of the property confiscated from the offender should be restored to the trader after acquittal by the criminal court (see also Koteswara Rao, 1986), and as most EC cases do indeed end in acquittal, confiscation without prosecution is often a safer way to punish a trader than to follow both procedures. See also Section 7.3 about this practice of 'forum shopping'.

[3] Other exceptions are related, for instance, to dowry deaths, bonded labour or child labour, where the burden of proof is with the husband (or his relatives), the employer accused of labour bondage, or the employer accused of employing children.

[4] In fact, in EC cases the primary burden of proof also lies with the public prosecutor. For instance the public prosecution has to assert that there was excess stock. Only then does the burden of proof shift to the accused, who has to show either that this was lawful, or that this fact cannot be asserted beyond reasonable doubt. Compared to most (but certainly not all) other pieces of law in India, in EC cases the burden of proof shifts easily from the prosecution to the accused.

bail can no longer be claimed as a matter of right and can be obtained only from judicial courts (and not from the police force or other officials). The 1981 amendment once again made it more difficult to obtain bail and introduced a mandatory minimum imprisonment of three months.[5] This amendment also changed the procedure for appeal after confiscation of commodities—from an appeal to the judiciary to an appeal to the government—and it established special courts to deal with EC cases in order to enhance efficiency.

Enactment, legislators and traders

Like many other pieces of law introduced in post-Independent India, the EC Act was meant to lay down the legal framework of a new type of development, based on equality and social justice. The idea behind the Act was that malpractices in trade could and should be prohibited and that a more equal distribution of essential commodities could and should be realized. A strict law,[6] it was thought, was an indispensable instrument to achieve this. To quote one of the advocates of the EC Act in 1955 when the Bill was discussed in the Lok Sabha, the Indian Parliament:

> If we are all agreed that a certain amount of control is necessary for the proper distribution of essential commodities in the country, then what is the use or what is the purpose in making the law so loose that the people who violate or the people who break these laws can escape under one or other of the legal quibbles? (Lok Sabha Debate, 21 Mar. 1955: 2777.)

Nevertheless, not all members of Parliament were in favour. It was argued that experiences with controls during World War II and afterwards were unsatisfactory, as the following quotes from some MPs make clear:

[5] But strangely enough this amendment reduced the maximum imprisonment. Section 7(1)(A)(ii) and Sub sections (2) and (2A) of Section 7 prescribe a maximum imprisonment of seven years. In 1981, however, the newly inserted Section 12A prescribes that all EC cases should be dealt with in a special court; Section 12AA(1)(f) says that all offences should be tried in a summary way and that a special court cannot pass a sentence of imprisonment exceeding two years as far as summary trials are concerned. In effect, the maximum sentence of imprisionment mentioned in Section 7 thus really amounts to an empty threat (see also Koteswara Rao, 1986, and Sengupta, 1984).

[6] The term 'strict' means that the law, according to its letter and spirit, does not allow much room for manoeuvre by the traders.

The moment you want to make any particular goods go out of public view in the market, you must bring them under control. If you bring them under control, the goods or materials suddenly disappear (LSD 5 Mar. 1955; 1302).

I oppose the Bill tooth and nail.... We have just got rid of controls and the country is feeling very much relieved after the control is taken away. Today, things are cheaper and the poor man can live.... If this Bill is passed, it would do a great injustice to the poor classes and the national income as a whole (LSD 21 Mar. 1955; 2783/4).

Still, there was no serious attempt to cancel the Bill and to withdraw controls on trade and distribution altogether. Most of the discussion did not concern approval or disapproval of the Bill, but the specific features of the law itself. A large part of the discussion focused on the question of whether it is legitimate to make the EC Act stricter than other pieces of law. The proposed Bill, which passed the Lok Sabha in 1955 without amendments, has certain provisions that are rare in Indian law generally.[7] Some MPs did not agree with this situation, arguing that usual norms of equity and jurisprudence should apply to people accused of EC crimes. Others argued that EC crimes should be dealt with in a more rigorous fashion, because theft of this kind not only robs an individual but the whole society of essential goods. As one advocate of the Bill put it:

What is it that we want? Do we want a strict enforcement of the control orders so that the distribution of controlled commodities may be equitable and in accordance with the law, or do you want to allow a certain amount of laxity in the administration? Do you want to allow, by a theoretical adherence or allegiance to the principle of jurisprudence, a practical injustice to be committed on the society? That is the fundamental question that has got to be answered (LSD 21 Mar. 1955; 2780).

Although this last argument is mainly rhetorical, it has been successful, not only in 1955 but also in all subsequent amendment discussions. The advocates of a stricter law have always succeeded in reducing the discussion to two opposing viewpoints: one which is against hoarding and black marketeering, and in favour of an equitable distribution of essential commodities and various exceptional measures to realize these; the other, opposed to these measures and in favour of a loose law, a lax administration, black marketeering and inflation.

[7] Among other things these are related to the already mentioned burden of proof, the fact that 'neglect' is sufficient reason for conviction, and the punishability of an attempt or abetment to contravene the law.

From the beginning, the EC Act was regarded as an instrument of punishment which thereby produces a deterrent effect. Traders are regarded as potential criminals, as people who can never be trusted and whose activities should be restricted in order to prevent much worse. The EC Act is clearly meant as a weapon in the fight against these 'hoarders [and] marketeers who are playing hell with the lives of millions of people', 'these maneaters [who] are too cunning and always escape through the lacunae in the law'.[8] The most controversial parts of the original law and most amendments are justified on the basis of this argument: hoarding and black marketeering are anti-social and anti-national activities in which many traders indulge, certainly in the absence of controls and sufficient punishment. The government should be armed with a tough instrument to deal with these problems.

The assumption that traders are always keen to break the law when it suits their interests goes together with an optimistic assumption regarding the behaviour of the enforcing officials. Although in all Lok Sabha discussions of the EC Act some have expressed their doubts about misuse of the law by officials, the advocates have always been able to convince the others that 'after all the officers and men and State Governments who will administer these things have some common sense' (LSD, 21 Mar 1955; 2825) or that 'extreme care will be taken to see that these powers are not misused' (LSD, 26 Aug. 1976; 265). Over the years the doubts expressed in the Lok Sabha about the usefulness of strict legislation in the absence of sufficient political and bureaucratic will-power to enforce these measures have grown. At the same time however, amendments have not only increased the force of the law as an instrument in the hands of enforcing officials, they have also effectively reduced the possibility of questioning the actions of these officials. The 1976 amendment removed the possibility of appeal against search and seizure. The 1981 amendment meant that appeal against confiscation of commodities was taken away from the judiciary and given to State governments, (i.e. top bureaucrats).

As could be expected, traders in essential commodities have been very much opposed to the EC Act and its various amendments and since 1981, their protests have focused on the 1981 EC (Special Provisions) Act in particular. Of all amendments to the original Act, this was one the most far-reaching. First implemented in 1982 for a period of five years, it was extended in 1987 and again in 1992. The traders deemed the law to be,

[8] From the preamble to the 1974 Amendment.

... not only unconstitutional, arbitrary and against all canons of Justice. It has done nothing except to encourage corruption in large scale and bringing the EC dealers to the level of second class citizens. (Text of postcards printed as part of traders' protests in 1992.)

In 1987, and especially in 1992, traders organized agitations and manifestations. Some went on hunger strike, or closed their shops in protest, and the traders' associations sent many petitions and memoranda to the State and Central governments. They attempted to convince members of Parliament and the concerned minister of the merits of their case, but all with limited success. In August 1992, it was decided to extend the EC (Special Provisions) Act by another five years.

So despite the fact that traders are generally moneyed people, that they were well-organized and that their protest had a very broad base—it was supported by almost all Central and State traders' associations—they were not able to influence the process of law making. In almost all discussions on the EC Act, the majority of politicians have been cautious not to side in public with traders. What this means is that there is a large discrepancy between the economic power of the trading class and its respectability in the political arena. After 1992, however, outside the official parliamentary arena, and backed by the general political climate favouring liberalization and deregulation, the continuing efforts of traders' associations have borne fruit. In 1992–3 a number of important provisions were dispensed with.[9] As observers put it, the Act was put in cold storage, even though the government did not dare to formally repeal it.[10] In other words, frontstage, the traders were unable to get what they wanted, but backstage, they were more successful in influencing policy making.

7.2 ENFORCEMENT IN STATISTICS

While the previous section was about the process of law formulation and enactment, this section deals with enforcement. It is based on aggregate figures on EC cases in Karnataka, Kerala and India. This section deals with criminal cases only and not with administrative cases because no aggregate figures are available on the latter. The

[9] For instance, the mandatory imprisonment, non-bailability of offences and summary trial ('Food Security—Victim of Economic Reform'. Editorial comment in *Economic and Political Weekly*, 16-23 January 1993).

[10] 'Prices: A Stalemate?' Editorial comment in *Economic and Political Weekly*, 18 November 1995.

questions addressed here are: how often has the Essential Commodities Act been put into use, and for which purposes? What do these figures suggest about the relevance of the law for 'dealing ... effectively with persons indulging in antisocial activities'?[11]

As compared to Karnataka, the total number of EC cases in Kerala is small. In Karnataka, there are relatively many more EC cases, as compared to India as a whole (see Table 7.1).

Table 7.1

Incidence and volume of EC crime cases (Karnataka, Kerala and India) (1988 and 1990)

	1988		1990	
	I	V	I	V
Karnataka	554	130	653	150
Kerala	76	30	85	30
All India	5704	70	6401	80

Notes: I = total number of EC cases; V = volume of crime per thousand of population

Source: Table 12, *Crime in India*, National Crime Records Bureau, Ministry of Home Affairs, Government of India (various volumes)

There is a clear difference between the two States regarding the type of cases that are brought before the special court. In Karnataka, the majority of cases involve either private foodgrain dealers (rice mill owners, foodgrain merchants), kerosene dealers or auto-rickshaw drivers who use kerosene as fuel, which is prohibited. In Kerala, hardly any private foodgrain dealer is brought before the special court.[12] The cases usually involve the sale or distribution of ration goods, coconut husk, kerosene, cement or edible oil. Table 7.2 gives an overview of

[11] From the Preamble to Amending Act 18 of 1981.

[12] This does not mean that private foodgrain dealers in Kerala are neglected by law enforcers. What struck me in the interviews I held with private traders in both States is that, while in Karnataka, the EC Act is the major bone of contention, in Kerala private traders are not bothered about the EC Act but complain bitterly about the irrational characteristics of the Food Adulteration Act, 1954 and the illegitimate behaviour of officials enforcing this Act. In Karnataka, private traders are hardly interested in the Food Adulteration Act. Unfortunately, the Food Adulteration Act is not included as a

the orders to which the cases in the Kerala special EC court pertain. It is clear that the Kerala Rationing Order is a relatively important order in this respect. It was impossible to collect similar data in Karnataka. While there is only one special court for EC cases in the whole of Kerala, in Karnataka each 'district and sessions' court is made special court for EC cases, which makes it more difficult to collect data about EC cases in the whole of Karnataka. In the Akkipura special court, by far the majority of cases are about foodgrains and involve violations of the Karnataka Essential Commodities Licensing Order, 1986 or the Karnataka Rice Procurement (Levy) Order, 1984. Other orders that are regularly violated in Karnataka are the Karnataka Kerosene Dealers Licensing Order, 1969 and the Kerosene (Fixation of Ceiling Prices) Order, 1970.[13]

Table 7.3 gives details about the disposal of cases in the area of fieldwork in Karnataka. The table shows that very few cases end in conviction of the accused. Table 7.4 gives details about verdicts of cases in Kerala. The conviction rate seems much higher than in Karnataka, but it is important to note that the two tables are incomparable. While Table 7.3 includes all cases initiated—also cases that are later withdrawn, have flawed charge sheets, or would never reach the final stage for other reasons—Table 7.4 takes into account only those cases in which a final verdict has been reached.

Table 7.3 further shows that it takes time for most cases to be disposed of. Of the cases initiated in 1986, 10 per cent were still pending in 1992, and less than 10 per cent of the cases begun in 1990 had been disposed of within two years. In Kerala also, the disposal of cases takes time. I collected forty-three judgements made between

---

separate crime head in the *Crime in India* records, so it is impossible to check whether indeed the volume of crime booked under this Act is much higher in Kerala than in Karnataka. But even without this statistical information, the difference as experienced by the traders in the two States is intriguing. It seems implausible that this difference between the two states can be fully explained by an excessive tendency of the Kerala trader to adulterate, while the Karnataka trader would be much more involved in violations of the EC Act. There must be other reasons as well, which, I guess, have to do with institutional arrangements: who are the enforcing officials; what is their authority; what is the division of tasks and responsibilities between various categories of enforcing officials. Unfortunately, I have not collected further material to corroborate or falsify this idea.

[13] Information from the Food and Civil Supplies Enforcement Department, Bangalore.

Table 7.2

Alleged violations of orders in special EC court in Kerala

	1987	1988	1989	1990
	n = 30 (100%)	n = 49 (100%)	n = 27 (100%)	n = 38 (100%)
Kerala Rationing Order, 1966	3 (10%)	24 (49%)	12 (44%)	16 (42%)
Kerala Coconut Husk (Procurement by Three Point Levy) Order, 1988 or Coir Retting (Licensing) Order, 1968	5 (17%)	1 (2%)	2 (7%)	4 (11%)
Kerala Kerosene Control Order, 1968	4 (13%)	6 (12%)	5 (19%)	5 (13%)
Kerala Cement Distribution (Licensing and Distribution) Order, 1974	10 (33%)	3 (6%)	3 (11%)	
Kerala Foodgrains Dealers' Licensing Order, 1967	3 (10%)	8 (16%)	1 (4%)	
Kerala Edible Oil Seeds, Edible Oils and Baby Food Dealers' Licensing Order, 1975	2 (7%)	7 (14%)	4 (15%)	6 (16%)
Other	3 (10%)	6 (12%)	1 (4%)	7 (18%)

Note: The column totals are sometimes more than n, the number of cases, as in some instances the charge was that more than one order was violated.

Source: Special court, Thrissur. The information in this table refers to a limited number of cases only, as the information available in the Thrissur court was incomplete.

Table 7.3

Disposal of EC cases initiated by the Food and Civil Supplies Enforcement Department, in five districts in Karnataka, including Akkipura

		1984	1986	1988	1990
No. of raids conducted		132	119	60	245
No. of cases booked		72 (100%)	40 (100%)	23 (100%)	74 (100%)
Percentages of cases	a) withdrawn	26	60	20	7
	b) conviction	0	5	0	1
	c) acquittal	74	25	32	0
Percentage of pending cases (as in 1992)		0	10	48	92

Source: Food and Civil Supplies Enforcement Department, Bangalore

1985 and 1992. The average time between the alleged violation of the EC Act and the sentence is 21 months, with a minimum of 4 months and a maximum of 7 years and 3 months.

Table 7.5 confirms these facts at the all-India level. The table shows that convictions are relatively rare in EC cases as compared to criminal cases generally.[14] The table also shows that the percentage of pending trials is much higher in EC crimes than in crime cases generally.

Table 7.4

Disposal of EC cases in special court Kerala 1985–1990

	Total (n = 212)
Percentages of cases	
a) acquitted	52
b) convicted	26
c) both	22

Source: Special court, Thrissur

The long duration of many EC crimes is unexpected, since from 1982 EC cases have been tried in special courts which are meant to guarantee quick disposal of such cases. Also the relatively low conviction rate is noteworthy, as it contrasts with the ideas and intentions of the legislator that traders are proto-criminals and should be dealt with firmly. Perhaps traders are acquitted because they are innocent and the assumptions of the legislator are mistaken. But it may also be that traders are often able to construct the cases and influence the verdicts in such a way that convictions become unlikely. The next two sections look at the interaction processes between traders and others, in order to get a better insight into what actually happens in the process of law implementation.

[14] According to Table 7.5, convictions as a percentage of total discharged cases (2b/[2a+2b+2c]) amount to about 50 per cent of EC cases (and 90 per cent of criminal cases generally). I have no insight into the way data are collected by the National Crime Records Bureau, whether flawed charge sheets, mistakes of law and refused investigations are included in the statistics or not. Again, it is important to emphasize that Tables 7.3, 7.4 and 7.5 are incomparable, although they are about similar issues and illustrate similar points.

Table 7.5

Disposal of crimes cases by courts (all-India)

	1988		1990	
	ECA	total crime cases	ECA	total crime cases
1. Total number of cases for trial (including pending trials)	16,343 (100%)	5,421,959 (100%)	21,723 (100%)	5,333,359 (100%)
2. Percentage of cases				
a) compounded or withdrawn	0.3	1.3	0.3	2.4
b) conviction	10.6	52.2	7.7	48.3
c) acquittal	9.4	5.1	7.1	6.3
3. Percentage of pending cases (at the end of the year)	79.8	41.3	85:0	43.0

Source: Tables 19 and 20, *Crime in India*, National Crime Records Bureau, Ministry of Home Affairs, Government of India (various volumes).

7.3 ABOUT TRADERS, THE POLICE, THE PUBLIC AND FIELD STAFF OF THE FOOD AND/OR CIVIL SUPPLIES DEPARTMENTS

In many interactions. and conflicts between traders, the police, the public and field staff of the Food and/or Civil Supplies Departments, the EC Act plays a role in one way or another. Whether the Act is directly referred to or not, it is often present at the back of the minds of the people involved. Government officials know they can use it as a threat, and traders know the Act can cause them great difficulties if the officials want. In this section, I will first explain the role of the law in levy procurement in Karnataka and then discuss the use of the EC Act in food distribution in Kerala.

The EC Act and levy procurement in Karnataka

Levy procurement in Akkipura district is a conflictual process, as I have already described in Chapter 4. Here I will start with a story that illustrates a number of important points regarding the use of the EC Act in levy procurement. The story is about a paddy/rice trader and mill owner in one of the *taluk* headquarters of Akkipura district. The trader, by the name of Anand, became involved in a criminal lawsuit. He won the case, but he lost his mill:[15]

In 1984, Anand's mill was raided by the Food and Civil Supplies Enforcement Department. In Anand's own words: 'I was not at home when the people of the Food Cell came. That is why they seized the mill. The Food Cell comes twice a year to collect money, (i.e. bribes). To satisfy their superiors they have to carry out one or two seizures as well. Naturally they select mills where the mill owner is not present to pay the money. If I was there I would have paid them.'

The officials seized all the commodities present in the mill, which was almost 400 quintal paddy and 100 quintal rice. This was subsequently confiscated and sold by the Deputy Commissioner. The money Anand received later in return for this was less than he would have got otherwise (namely procurement price rather than open market price).

Apart from this confiscation, Anand was also prosecuted. A few days after the seizure, a local police inspector made a phone call to Anand late at night, informing him that government lorries would soon arrive, not only to move the seized commodities but also to arrest Anand. However, the inspector said that a bribe would allow Anand to flee to the State capital. After some discussion and negotiation, a settlement was reached for Rs 25,000. While Anand was still handling this telephone call, police constables rang his doorbell to collect the money. Anand paid, and the same night he fled to Bangalore where he obtained bail. The manager of his rice mill was arrested, but later also released on bail.

Eight months after the seizure the local police filed a charge sheet in court, thereby launching a criminal case against Anand. The charge related to an alleged difference between book stock and physical stock: there was an excess of 10 tonnes of paddy, a shortage of 1 tonne of rice and an excess of 1 tonne of broken rice. Furthermore, it was alleged that Anand had not paid enough levy.

It took more than seven years to pass the judgement, and in the meantime Anand was called to court 166 times. During these years, several judges came and went, and most of them started afresh with hearing witnesses. As Anand did not live next door to the court building, each court appearance took up the whole day. Travelling back and forth to the court cost him a considerable amount of money. Usually, accused traders also arrange for a car to transport prosecution witnesses in order to guarantee that the witnesses will not give evidence against them. In 1988, Anand closed his mill and sold his plant. His own explanation was that he could not run the mill when he had to go to

[15] The story is based on interviews with Anand himself, with his brother and with the public prosecutor, and on the study of the court documents.

court so often, but his brother mentioned that Anand could not cope with the stress, humiliations and bribes.

In 1991, the judgement was passed and Anand was acquitted, but no compensation was given. The judgement stipulated that the court case should never have taken place. The charge sheet was filed in court eight months after the arrest took place, while the Code of Criminal Procedure prescribes that further investigation into the offence should cease after six months from the date of arrest. According to the judge: 'No application has been filed by the investigation officer for extension of time and the charge sheet has been submitted beyond the 6 months. Hence, even on the ground of not complying with the provision of sub-section 5 of section 167 Cr.P.C. the further proceedings should have been stopped against the accused persons.' (See n 18 of this chapter.)

The judgement continued that even on the basis of merits the case could not be won by the prosecution. The most important reason for this was that seizing officials of the Food and Civil Supplies Enforcement Department had not carried out any physical stock verification. They had looked at the heap of rice in the mill and assumed that the physical stock differed from the book stock. Furthermore, the accusation regarding levy could not be proved.

The story of Anand illustrates two important motives for invoking the EC Act: bribes and 'progress' in enforcement. Both are very common indeed. The EC Act is very useful for officials to collect bribes, as I have already indicated in Section 4.3. The Act is used as a threat. In the perception of most rice mill owners and traders in Akkipura, the threat can only be diverted by paying bribes and hardly by more law-abiding behaviour, as they think the law is so strict that they will always fail with respect to one minor detail or another. This aspect of the law as threat is recognized by the Indian and Karnataka governments, officially denounced, but nevertheless common practice.[16]

Although I have never found anything on paper indicating that enforcing officials generally, or the Food and Civil Supplies Department in particular, are pressurized to make more raids and

[16] There have been a number of letters from the Government of India, Ministry of Food and Civil Supplies to the State governments, saying that the Government of India has received 'a large number of representations from trade and industry alleging that the provisions of the [EC Special Provisions] Act were being misused at the field level by concerned officials ... to harass the traders' (from letter No. 26(12)86-ECR dated 9 Feb. 1988 of the Government of India, Ministry of Food and Civil Supplies to the Secretary, Food and Civil Supplies of all States and Union Territories). In 1988, special guidelines were formulated for the enforcement agencies, listing minor and technical lapses on the part of the trader 'for which it may not ordinarily be necessary to launch prosecutions'.

initiate more cases in order to show 'progress', this fact was mentioned several times to me, not only by traders and rice mill owners, but also by officials and lawyers.[17]

But apart from bribes and 'progress' in enforcement, there is a third important motive: the collection of levy rice. The EC Act is an important instrument to put pressure on traders and rice mill owners to pay levy, not only because the Rice Procurement (Levy) Order, 1984, prescribes levy procurement, but in particular because some of the other orders are suitable to threaten and harass the traders in order to make them comply with levy policy.

The story of Anand further suggests that officials lack interest that goes beyond adding to enforcement statistics and collecting bribes and levy. This is not uncommon. The efforts of enforcing officials often end when they have collected their bribe and/or levy or have made a contribution to the 'progress' reports. The result of this lack of interest is that the investigation is conducted very poorly, and that lawsuits are unsustainable by the prosecution, as in the case of Anand. Officials may not have carried out a proper stock verification; they may not have filed the charge sheet in time; they may have forgotten to include some essential information in the charge sheet, or they may not have taken all the relevant evidence into account during investigation. Moreover, some officials simply do not know the precise content of the EC Act and the concerned orders. A senior (defence) lawyer once commented that 'for us, it is impossible to win a case on the basis of merits. But we can always win on the basis of technical defects.'

Anand was not daring enough or he lacked the necessary contacts to avoid criminal prosecution. Many traders and rice mill owners in a similar position do try to influence the course of events. For instance, they bribe officials who conducted the raid not to hand over the case to the police force, or they bribe the policemen to wait for six months before filing the charge sheet in court. In some cases, they even bribe

[17] The annual reports of the Karnataka Food and Civil Supplies Department also confirm the idea that the performance of the Enforcement Department is primarily seen in terms of the number of activities undertaken. Under the heading 'Enforcement', these reports mention the number of raids and the total value and quantity of seized commodities. The end results of the cases initiated are not mentioned; neither is there any interpretation of the effects of these enforcement activities on the practices of hoarding, black marketeering and smuggling. In the administrative culture of the Food Department, 'progress' in enforcement means increasing the number of conflicts between traders and the Department in which the EC Act is invoked.

the public prosecutor to delay the case to a date six months after the arrest, in the hope that after that date the case will be regarded as unsustainable and will be dismissed.[18]

So, even though the prospect of losing the criminal lawsuit is small, accused traders and rice mill owners generally try to prevent prosecution. The real punishment, as they see it, is the fact that the case may drag on for years during which they have to appear regularly in court.[19] Apart from the fact that this costs them a considerable amount of money, they also find these innumerable court visits very humiliating. Outside the court, these traders are influential people who are treated with respect and submissiveness. In the court, however, they are seen as criminals, and—just as other accused persons—they are at the mercy of judges and other court personnel. The public prosecutor and judges are aware of the fact that for most traders this

[18] Whether or not a charge sheet can be submitted after six months from the date of arrest is a contested issue. The relevant section of the Code of Criminal Procedure, 1973, reads as follows: 'If in any case triable by a Magistrate as a summons-case, the investigation is not concluded within a period of six months from the date on which the accused was arrested, the Magistrate shall make an order stopping further investigation into the offence unless the officer making the investigation satisfies the Magistrate that for special reasons and in the interests of justice the continuation of the investigation beyond the period of six months is necessary' (Section 167, Subsection 5). In Anand's case, the judge has interpreted this section in the sense that no charge sheet can be filed after six months from the date of arrest, except if the investigating officer had applied for extension of time. Other judges have argued that this section means that charge sheets may be filed after six months, but no new material can be taken into account after this date. Another point of contestation is whether EC cases are indeed summons-cases. Section 167 (5) refers to summons-cases only. According to Section 2(w) of the Code of Criminal Procedure, a 'summons-case' is a case relating to an offence, and not being a 'warrant-case'. A 'warrant-case', according to Section 2(x) of the same Code is a case relating to an offence punishable with death, imprisonment for life or imprisonment for a term exceeding two years. This means that EC cases are warrant cases, because the maximum imprisonment is seven years. Hence Section 167 (5) would not be applicable. (I have to thank advocate K.B. Mohandas in Thrissur for pointing this out to me.) But as Section 12-AA(f) of the EC Act stipulates, all offences under the Act shall be tried in a summary way, with a maximum imprisionment of two years. In the case, *State of Karnataka versus Abdul Razak Mohammed Saheb and Others*, (1988(2) Kar.L.J. 453: ILJ 1988 Kar. 3175), the court decided that the special judge has the jurisdiction to stop investigation under Section 167(5) if the same is not completed within six months. A former public prosecutor in the Akkipura court told me in 1991 that at that time a High Court case was pending about the interpretation of Section 167, Subsection 5 of the Code of Criminal Procedure.

[19] One of the conditions of release on bail is that the accused should be available for interrogation and, hence, should appear at the court sessions.

is the real punishment. Judges I spoke to in Karnataka denied that this delay was created on purpose for this reason, but they admitted EC cases do not get any priority and are regarded as relatively unimportant, as compared to most other cases these 'district and session' judges have to deal with.

Not only accused traders and rice mill owners but also some of the enforcing officials consciously avoid criminal prosecution. It is well known that criminal prosecution usually leads to acquittal. Administrative cases, on the other hand, may easily lead to confiscation of commodities. Officially, this is not a punishment, but it is certainly a financial loss for traders and, hence, a kind of fine. Both the procedure to confiscate commodities—by the Deputy Commissioner—and criminal prosecution are subject to procedures prescribed in the Indian Evidence Act, 1872. Yet it is clear that the administration applies these procedures in a somewhat looser sense than the judiciary. To quote from an interview with a Deputy Commissioner:

> 'In the last one and a half year, I have had sixty-eight EC cases. Forty of these cases were useless; even the accused himself did not know why he had to appear before me. But there were twenty-eight real cases. Most of these cases ended in confiscation of the commodities involved. That is very easy for me; there is always something that is done wrong by the traders.' I was surprised because I knew that virtually all traders tried in the Akkipura court were acquitted, and I ventured my doubts. He continued: 'Really, it is true what I say. But as soon as the traders are tried by the judiciary, it is different. They can always show that the investigating officers made a mistake, and then they are acquitted. The difference is: the administration thinks about how it can best nail the accused. But the judiciary thinks about how it can best release the accused.'

So from the viewpoint of the administrator who wants to 'fine' the trader, it is often safer to go for confiscation only without criminal prosecution, especially because he knows there will probably be lapses in the charge sheet drawn up by investigating officers. (See also n 2 of this chapter). The interest of strict officials who want to teach traders a lesson and corrupt officials who have accepted money from accused traders, hence, coincides on this point. For different reasons, both may prefer to restrict the case to an administrative matter. Nevertheless, criminal prosecution cannot be avoided altogether. It is in the interest of all officials involved in enforcement that the threat emanating from criminal prosecution remains; moreover criminal prosecutions allow them to show they are dealing firmly with smuggling, hoarding and black marketeering.

The EC Act and food rationing in Kerala

There are two types of situations in which the Kerala Rationing Order, 1966, is invoked in an explicit way, namely, appointment of ration dealers and accusation of black marketing of ration commodities. The very threat of the latter situation—being accused of black marketeering and facing the possibility of a penalty under the EC Act—means the Act has a wider relevance. Fear of the Act is very widespread among ration dealers in Kerala, even in situations in which the Act is not explicitly referred to.

To start with the first situation, Sections 45 and 51 of the Kerala Rationing Order deal with the authorization of retail and wholesale ration dealers, respectively. These sections describe—among other things—criteria for appointment, and which categories of people may be given preference. Often there are several candidates, out of which the District Supply Officer (DSO)—in the case of a retail dealer—or the District Collector—in the case of a wholesale dealer—has to select one. In case one of the counter-candidates does not acquiesce in the decision, a long legal battle may develop. One such example I heard of is the following:

Thomas would like to become ARD. In 1984 he applied for a licence. The DSO decided, however, to appoint someone else, a rubber dealer, most probably because this person had bribed the DSO. Thomas found a lawyer, and the case came before the District Collector. The advocate argued that the rubber dealer had no previous experience with rationing, and succeeded in reversing the order: his client was appointed. Subsequently, the rubber dealer appealed to the Commissioner, who decided in Thomas' favour. Then the rubber dealer went to the government. The government ordered a fresh disposal by the DSO. In the meantime, there was a new DSO, who decided in Thomas' favour. Again the counter-candidate went to the District Collector, the Commissioner, and the government, who all decided in Thomas' favour. The last decision came in 1992, that is eight years after the legal battle had started. When I spoke to Thomas' lawyer, he was waiting to see whether the counter-candidate would go to the High Court for a last appeal. Somewhere in this eight-year battle, the counter-candidate had changed. The rubber dealer had lost interest, but someone else had taken his place, claiming that his financial position and experience were better than Thomas'. Thomas' lawyer had done his best to drag out the case, and during all these years Thomas had run the ration shop.

The case described is not exceptional. I collected several similar examples in which would-be ration dealers challenge the decision to appoint someone else as ARD or AWD (authorized wholesale dealer). The procedures laid down in the Kerala Rationing Order provide for many steps in this legal battle ('too much freedom to fight', according to some lawyer and officials), while one of the parties usually has an interest in prolonging the case as much as possible.

While appointment of ration dealers is the first category of cases in which the Kerala Rationing Order is invoked, alleged malpractices in trade is the second. Ration dealers can be accused of having violated certain parts of the Kerala Rationing Order, 1966. As a consequence, commodities may be confiscated, the concerned trader suspended and his licence cancelled. These decisions are taken by officers of the Civil Supplies Department, i.e. the administration. In addition, accused persons may be prosecuted and tried in the special court for EC cases.

The majority of such cases are initiated by 'the public'. I studied thirty-two cases[20] dealt with in the special court in which accused persons were alleged to have violated parts of the Kerala Rationing Order. Out of these, at least twenty-one were initiated by people who happened to have been eye-witnesses to a suspect event and who informed the police or officials of the Civil Supplies Department.

Sometimes the initial complaint made by eye-witnesses is informed by political motives, which is illustrated by the following quotation from a judgement (summary trial No.62/1990):

> According to the prosecution, the third accused [daughter of the ration shop licensee] ... with the knowledge and consent of the 2nd accused [her father] and without ration documents, ... has sold one gunny bag full of ration sugar to the first accused [a private trader conducting a provision store just adjacent to the ration shop]. At about 7.30 p.m. while the first accused was taking the sugar in the gunny bag through the corridor of the building, some of the youngsters of the locality intercepted and prohibited the first accused from removing the sugar bag to his shop. Keeping the sugar bag on the corridor, the police was informed.... ... [I]n cross examination [the youngster said] that actually he has not personally informed the matter to the police, but some DYFI [Marxist Youth Organization] workers have informed the matter to the police. In cross examination he would further state that the first accused is a known worker of Congress(I) political party (...).

The case described in this judgement is not exceptional. While in Karnataka EC cases concerning malpractices in trade are almost always initiated by enforcing officials, in Kerala the general public also plays an important role, motivated by a desire to improve food distribution,

[20] These cases were randomly selected from the office of the public prosecutor in the special court in Thrissur. These thirty-two cases come out of a total of 212 dealt with between 1985 and 1990 that I looked at (see Tables 7.4 and 7.7). Less than half of these 212 cases refer to violations of the Kerala Rationing Order, 1966 (see Table 7.2).

to take political revenge and/or to show active interest in the problems of the common man.

Only a minority of all the cases in which ARDs are alleged of malpractices become criminal cases tried in the special court. The majority of the cases are dealt with by the administration only. According to one of the senior officials in Civil Supplies Department in Thiruvananthapuram:

> There is no need to hand over cases to the police [who could start a lawsuit]. We can suspend the shops and cancel the licences, and that is sufficient punishment for the traders. Moreover, the police does not know about the Kerala Rationing Order, while we know everything about the ARDs and AWDs. If there are malpractices, we will detect them and take necessary action.

It seems that, as compared to the situation in Karnataka, the Civil Supplies administration in Kerala is even more reluctant to initiate criminal prosecution. This reluctance, I would hypothesize, is explained by the fact that criminal prosecution has several disadvantages for the officials concerned. They would have to appear in the special court in Thrissur to be heard as witnesses, and they would risk that ration dealers would also disclose some of the malpractices and misuse of power officials themselves are guilty of. As long as cases remain within the administration, officials are sure that their own behaviour will not be questioned.

In principle, this is the same in Karnataka. But the difference is that in Karnataka enforcing officials are faced with large wholesale traders and rice mill owners, influential and powerful people who are not easily impressed. For these kinds of traders a conflict with the Food and Civil Supplies administration is not really threatening, but criminal prosecution is. By contrast, in Kerala officers deal mainly with retail ration dealers who are less powerful and more easy to threaten. These traders are very afraid of accusations, since 'even an anonymous complaint may lead to a suspension', as they express themselves. Whether this is true or not does not really matter, but it illustrates their fear. As a consequence, these traders will tend to yield to requests for money from enforcing officials (which are relatively small requests anyway, as compared to demands made by their Karnataka colleagues). More drastic measures on the part of enforcing officials are not necessary. These would only introduce unnecessary tension into the relationship between supply officer and ration dealer.[21]

[21] Apart from retail ration dealers, enforcing officials also deal with AWDs. As far as wealth and political influence are concerned, these AWDs are probably comparable to the Karnataka wholesale traders and rice mill owners. It may well be that in their

What the descriptions in this section show is that the EC Act—including the various orders issued under the Act—functions as a resource in the struggles and interactions between several categories of actors. Sometimes, for some of these actors, it is the proper implementation of official policy that is at stake in these interactions. This is, for instance, the case for some government officials in Karnataka who aspire to reach the target set for procurement, or for some representatives of 'the public' in Kerala whose interventions may help to guarantee proper food distribution. For others, the Act has an additional function: they use it as a resource to collect bribes, contribute to the department's 'progress' reports, increase their status as active local politicians or social workers, or fight government decisions that have turned out to their disadvantage.

7.4 ABOUT JUDGES AND PUBLIC PROSECUTORS

As described in Section 7.1, the debate on the EC Act focuses on the special characteristics of the Act: mandatory imprisonment, non-bailability, summary trial, unfavourable burden of proof conditions, etc. All these provisions are related to the procedures of criminal prosecution. Thus a relevant question is: what happens in and around the court-room, and how is this perceived by the various actors involved?

I have already discussed the perceptions of traders. Generally, they feel humiliated by lawyers and court personnel. Even when they would admit to have contravened some orders, they feel they owe more respect than they get in court. They hate to go there for a hearing and then to be informed at the end of the day that the hearing is postponed. They are used to being treated with respect, but in court they are at the mercy of others.

Traders' prime opponents are public prosecutors. Usually, their role starts only in court, as most public prosecutors are not involved in the construction of cases before they are launched in court. They depend fully on investigating officers (i.e. policemen) and the work they deliver. Occasionally, however, they take an active interest themselves in constructing sustainable and genuine cases. A former public prosecutor in Thrissur, Kerala, for instance, said that:

---

case criminal prosecution is a more effective threat than an administrative case. However, I have the impression—but further investigation is necessary to substantiate this idea—that this category of traders is more or less neglected anyway by enforcing officials.

... before the police filed a charge sheet, they used to come to my office, so that I could approve of the charge sheet or reject it. Sometimes the police construct charge sheets in which only drivers, headload workers and cleaners are accused, while the real black marketeers remain outside the charge sheet. I have never accepted that.

During court hearings the influence of the public prosecutor is considerable. He can prepare the case well or very badly, call strong witnesses or relatively weak ones, even decide whether to turn up in court or not! Although a weak public prosecutor is in the interest of the defence lawyer, many advocates I talked to complained about the lack of expertise and poor work ethic of public prosecutors, claiming that they were corruptible, not interested in the final result or appointed for political reasons only. In a district adjacent to Akkipura, I once attended a session in the office of the Deputy Commissioner, where several EC cases were heard and where, indeed, the public prosecutor was very badly prepared. Although this was an administrative case rather than a judicial one, I will quote a fragment from my research diary as an illustration of the way in which the various actors in the hearing can influence the final outcome:

Shenoy, a lawyer specializing in EC cases, had invited me that afternoon to join him at the Deputy Commissioner's office to attend a hearing. At exactly 15.00 p.m. we were invited into the room of the Deputy Commissioner. The Deputy Commissioner was sitting behind his desk. There is a portrait of Mahatma Gandhi on the wall behind his desk. In front of his desk, there is a large table, with a length of more than 10m and a width of approximately 2m. Shenoy takes a chair close to the Deputy Commissioner. The public prosecutor sits on the other side of the table, opposite to Shenoy. There are several other advocates sitting around the table. On one side of the room, there is a second and a third row of chairs, on which I sit, together with a few concerned clients whose cases are dealt with this afternoon....

The second case this afternoon is an EC case, to be defended by a young lawyer. The case is as follows. The police force has seized a lorry transporting paddy within the district. The public prosecutor states that an offence was committed by the owner of the paddy, and demands confiscation of the lorry as well as of the paddy. I think the lawyer wants to argue that there is nothing illegal about paddy transport within the district, but he is very unclear and badly prepared. Also the Deputy Commissioner does not understand what he wants to argue. Then the lawyer consults Shenoy. Shenoy requests the Deputy Commissioner to allow him to clarify the matter on behalf of the other advocate, to which the Deputy Commissioner agrees. Shenoy argues that there is only one order under the EC Act that says anything about paddy transport, namely the Rice Procurement (Levy) Order, 1984. But according to Shenoy, the section that restricted paddy transport has been struck down by a High Court Order. Then in 1989, the government published a Food Policy, in which paddy transport within the district was restricted. That order was also struck down by the High Court in the same year. 'So, my question to the public prosecutor is, hence,' Shenoy said, 'in which law or legal order is it said that paddy transport is not free, or that specific documents are required?' The public prosecutor is unpleasantly surprised by this direct question. He gives several inadequate answers. He refers to a section of the law that refers to rice, and not to paddy. He also refers to an order that has been struck down. It is clear that the Deputy Commissioner also is not knowledgeable about the various details of the relevant laws. Moreover, the Deputy Commissioner seems convinced that Shenoy is actually the only one present in the room who knows about these things and he asks for several clarifications. He is even making faces each time the public prosecutor wants to say something.

In this case, both the defence lawyer and the public prosecutor were hardly able to argue their case, while the Deputy Commissioner was not aware of all the intricacies of the law. In such situations, a lot depends on the inclination and sympathies of the people making the final verdict: in this case the Deputy Commissioner.

As indicated earlier, as compared to administrative cases, in criminal prosecution more weight is given to procedures followed by investigating officers and the quality of evidence produced before the court. Yet the inclinations of judges matter. Table 7.6 shows that there is considerable variation among judges in the conviction rate. The table refers to Kerala, but the same is probably true in Karnataka, where some judges have the reputation of looking more at the merits of a case, while others are said to give more weight to the technicalities of a case.

Table 7.6

Disposal of EC Cases in special court Kerala by judges 1985–1990

	Total n = 212	Judge 1 n = 10	Judge 2 n = 3	Judge 3 n = 42	Judge 4 n = 68	Judge 5 n = 18	Judge 6 n = 71
Percentage of cases							
a) acquitted	52	100	100	81	47	39	34
b) convicted	26	0	0	12	29	6	42
c) both	22	0	0	7	24	55	24

Source: Special court, Thrissur.

Several judges I talked to seem to have difficulties in balancing their anti-trader sentiments with the necessity to follow proper procedures.

As a result, they have developed two different and almost unrelated ways of talking about EC crimes. To quote from an interview with the Akkipura special judge:

'Economic crimes are worse than other types of crimes, as not only individuals but the whole society is robbed. The culprits should be dealt with with an iron hand. Everybody has a right to essential commodities, and the Act has to guarantee that distribution of essential commodities functions smoothly. The business class and merchants are exploiting others. How else is it possible that they are multimillionaires within a few years? It is their ambition to deprive others. We really have to teach them a lesson; only that will frighten others. We have to punish black marketeers and hoarders severely, not only with fines but also with imprisonment. Only that will work and deter others.'

When I remarked that, still, the conviction rate is very low, he changed his stance and said: 'You are right. There are no independent witnesses. We cannot rely on the policemen only, and the other witnesses are purchased by the accused. So, the offence cannot be proved. One of the principles of our criminal law is that it is better to acquit ninety-five criminals than to convict one innocent person.'

This principle, that an accused can only be convicted if his guilt can be proved beyond reasonable doubt, is the argument behind many acquittals. The defence lawyer is often able to highlight some weak points in the accusation that may create doubt in the mind of the judge or force him to order an acquittal even in cases where he himself is convinced the accused is guilty.

As the judge quoted above indicates, prosecution witnesses are often unreliable. They have either forgotten exactly what happened or have changed their minds. Even villagers in Kerala who themselves take the initiative to inform the police about malpractices regularly 'turn hostile'. During the first investigation they make statements which they contradict later during court examination. As first statements made to the police are never signed (Code of Criminal Procedure, 1973, Section 162), there is no authentic document proving that the witnesses may be giving false evidence. The reasons for this change can be many. Often prosecution witnesses belong to the same locality as the accused, are won over, or do not want to risk any negative repercussions.

The fact that some of the cases drag on for several years also adds to the chance that witnesses decide to give evidence against the prosecution. Political alliances may change in the course of time or become less important, so that even in politically motivated cases the witnesses sometimes 'turn hostile'.

The reasons for a long period of duration before a final verdict is reached are many. First, the courts are overburdened. This is especially so in Karnataka, where EC cases compete with murder cases and other severe crimes. The latter cases are usually given a higher priority, especially when the accused persons are kept in custody. But apart from this, second is that defence lawyers also sometimes have an interest in prolonging cases, in particular when they are paid by clients per hearing/appearance, rather than in a lump sum. This is a thorn in the flesh of some of the clients/traders, who feel, however, too dependent upon their lawyers to antagonize them.[22]

That the investigation is often poor, that witnesses turn hostile and that public prosecutors do their work badly, are among the reasons that few judges take pride in EC cases, But also apart from this, many judges do regard EC cases as unchallenging and uninteresting. Those dealing with EC cases are always senior judges.[23] For them especially, EC cases are relatively small and simple as compared to other cases they (could) deal with. As mentioned before, in Karnataka, EC cases are tried by the 'district and session' judges, who have been appointed special judges for EC cases. These are the highest judges at the district level, who preside over all other courts in the district and subdistrict. In their own perception, they have more important things to deal with than EC crimes. In Kerala, there is one special judge who deals with EC cases and motor accidents only. Between 1984 and 1992, the average tenure of this post was just over one year. I spoke to two who had served in the Kerala EC court. Both of them had tried to get transfers within a few months after their appointment. They complained about the routine character of the EC cases. 'It is boring,' one of them said.[24]

Thus, what we observe is a large discrepancy between the concern of the legislator and that of judges and public prosecutors. In general, they seem to agree that it is a task of the government to contribute to a more equitable distribution of essential commodities, and that people

[22] See also Kidder (1974) about ambivalences in the lawyer-client relationship in south India.

[23] According to the EC Amendment Act, 1981, only judges that are qualified for appointment as High Court judge, or judges that have been session judges, or additional session judges for a period of at least one year, can be appointed as judges of a special court.

[24] Besides they complained about the relatively unattractive working conditions. Special judges get fewer holidays than other judges, because nobody can replace them when they are away.

committing offences in this respect deserve severe penalties. But while the legislator attributes much weight to the procedures of criminal prosecution—finding expression in the establishment of special courts, appointing only senior judges as special judges for EC cases, introduction of mandatory imprisonment, unfavourable burden of proof conditions, etc.—judges and public prosecutors who are responsible for executing these procedures lack interest and often think they have more important things to do. Although these two attitudes seem conflicting at first glance, they go well together. The special provisions of the EC Act are important for the working and effectiveness of the Act. They contribute to fear and, to some extent, compliance. This effect is established in the court room, but as a by-product of the official hearing. It is due to being regarded a criminal and being at the mercy of an advocate. The sheer indifference of some of the judges towards the cause of traders only adds to the humiliation and the deterrent effect of the law.

7.5 CONCLUSION: THE FUNCTIONS AND EFFECTS OF THE EC ACT

Like many other pieces of legislation introduced in post-Independence India, the EC Act was seen—at least by some of its advocates—as a contribution to a more equitable society.[25] The objective was to prohibit profit making in food at the expense of 'the poor man', which was seen as a step towards a more just distribution of food. The discussions in the Lok Sabha and the various preambles to the law and its amendments express clear anti-trader sentiments and a concern with 'the lives of millions of people'. This spirit has certainly found its reflection in the letter of the law. As I have indicated in this chapter, the law is exceptionally strict, which is, indeed, resented by traders in essential commodities.

So it is not the interest of the trading class that is represented in this Act. But then, whose interest is?

First of all, the Act is in the interest of the administration. The underlying idea is that the administration needs a tough instrument in order to deal with traders in the interest of society at large. But apart from that, the law also enables individual civil servants to pursue their own interests by extracting money from the trading class, without running too much risk themselves. In addition, the law enables populist

[25] See Dhagamwar (1992) about law framing in this period.

politicians and policy makers to present themselves in a favourable light to the public. Thus while the Act is troublesome for the trader and a resource (a weapon to use as threat or a kind of holy writ point of reference) for the administrator, it is a showpiece for the populist policy maker or politician.[26]

But has the law contributed to a reduction of the economic power of traders and a more equitable distribution of food? This question is difficult to answer as we do not know what would have happened in the absence of the EC Act. Moreover, compliance with the law is, in itself, no guarantee of the realization of the more remote objectives. There is no simple correspondence between rules and procedures laid down in the various orders of the law and the far-reaching goals pertaining to a more equitable distribution of food. On the basis of the material presented in this and previous chapters we can only evaluate the contribution of the EC Act to the implementation of the PDS.

.One obvious conclusion that can be drawn is that there is a wide gap between the various dos and don'ts as laid down in government orders issued under the Act, and actual behaviour of rice mill owners, traders, and wholesale and retail ration dealers. The Act certainly does not simply structure behaviour, although the existence of the Act does influence human conduct because people make use of it and others are confronted with that.[27] This and previous chapters have described instances of interactions and conflicts in which the involved actors abide obediently, manipulate, by-pass or neglect the EC Act. Yet, despite these various kinds of manipulations, we can also conclude that in the end the result is that procurement and distribution take place, not fully as intended by some policy makers and politicians, but nevertheless within the limits of what is deemed acceptable. Despite, or rather in and through all the described interactions and manipulations of the law, the PDS is implemented. In fact, *this* is implementation: the social practices in which legal structures and material resources provided by the government are put into use by, and redistributed among, the various actors involved.

Although, as already said, the EC Act does not itself structure behaviour directly, it helps force traders to comply with food policy.

[26] Similar metaphors have been used by others in relation to other pieces of legislation. For instance Turk (1976) also analyses law as a weapon in social conflict, while Benda-Beckmann (1989) speaks of law as 'scapegoat' or 'magic charm'.

[27] See Abel (1980), Benda-Beckmann (1983), Nelken (1981; 1985) about the general point that normative structures cannot be conflated with real practices.

An important mechanism is fear. Many traders are afraid of being sued for contravention or being suspended. This fear erodes their 'being in command' and makes them more vulnerable, even *vis-à-vis* lower level officials. But the fear and the threat are not the same for all traders. They can be reduced by bringing in social relations and influence, money and favours. So the more moneyed the traders and the better their connections, the more counterweight there is and the less effective the threat.

The threat does not necessarily come only from law-enforcing officials; it may also be caused by the active participation and interference of the general public or its representatives, as happens in Kerala. This interference adds to the activities undertaken by the government officials responsible and, hence, to controls and checks on traders. But apart from that, it also has a effect on ration dealers, directly as it makes them aware that they cannot afford to poke fun at their clients. Ration dealers know they are watched with keen interest and that they have to behave (somewhat) accordingly.

Besides compliance, there is also a great deal of non-compliance on the part of traders and ration dealers. They manipulate or neglect certain provisions of the law, bribe enforcing officials, or mobilize political or other pressure when their interests are threatened. Often this happens with the full connivance of enforcing officials. If the discussion so far has suggested that a struggle between traders and law enforcers is the most important characteristic of their relationship, I have given the wrong impression. The interaction between these two parties is characterized by mutual understanding as much as by conflict. As indicated above, the process of law enforcement is a process of bargaining and negotiation into which *all* parties bring their various demands. So it would be misleading to think that it is mainly the interests of traders which constrain the process of enforcement. Enforcing civil servants, and also some of the judges and public prosecutors, are equally important in the creation of non-compliance.

The role of politicians is of particular interest, as it varies from context to context, even more than in the case of the other actors involved. As far as politicians take part in the framing of the law, they are usually in favour of strict legislation. In the process of law enforcement in Karnataka, however, they often represent the interests of traders, through whom they have been drawn into the cases in the first place. In Kerala, local politicians more often represent the interests of consumers. So the role of politicians in food policy implementation is very diverse. In certain cases, it obstructs compliance and cooperation with official policies. But if political activity results from grass roots mobilization, it may enhance an active interest of the bureaucracy in proper implementation, compliance with the law, and perhaps also a more equitable distribution of food in the long run.

8

Food Policy and Politics
Summary and conclusions

Fifty years have passed since India acquired Independence. In this period many things have changed. To mention just a few, there has been economic growth and development, the Indian government has undertaken major social development efforts, the democratic system has involved large parts of the population in the political process. If we look at matters of food, India has become self-sufficient in foodgrains, and the role of the government in stimulating production and organizing redistribution has increased enormously.

In this book I have analysed the PDS. On a very limited scale food distribution existed already before Independence, but especially after 1947 it became an increasingly important intervention in the food economy. I looked both at its history and the day-to-day practices around this system. In particular, I focused on the relationship between food policy and politics: the political projects supported by the scheme, the struggles around its implementation, the use of food and food policy in various types of contestations.

In this last chapter, I come back to the central research questions posed in the first chapter. Section 1 discusses the first question—the effects of food distribution policy on consumption, economic redistribution and power—while Section 2 discusses the historical shaping and day-to-day reproduction of the system. Section 3 is on the third question: what are the implications of the experiences with PDS for a conceptualization of the Indian state? In the last section, I discuss the future of the PDS. In the mid-1990s, it is argued by several people that the PDS has 'landed in a severe crisis and faces an uncertain future'. What are the options for reform and how feasible are they?

8.1 THE EFFECTS OF FOOD DISTRIBUTION POLICY

Food, as stated earlier, is a commodity with many dimensions. In this study of the public distribution system in India three dimensions were considered particularly relevant: food as nutritional commodity, food as economic commodity and food as political commodity. It is along these three lines that I will evaluate food distribution policy. The question, hence, is: what is the impact of food distribution policy on consumption, economic redistribution and power? As will be clear from the following discussion, there is some overlap between the three categories. In particular, the impact of food distribution on prices (discussed under economic redistribution) has immediate implications for consumption.

The answer that I can provide to the question of impact is not a quantitative one. As explained earlier, the fieldwork methodology does not allow for an evaluation of the effects in terms of numbers, percentages and averages. The type of answer I can give is concerned with mechanisms: the ways in which food distribution policy affects (or may affect) consumption; prices, incomes, and profits; and power.

Consumption

If we leave aside the long-term effects of the PDS on foodgrain production, the important question is: does food subsidy reach the poor? The material collected in my research does not allow for a detailed estimate, but the answer is probably in the affirmative to some extent, although richer households may profit more on average than poorer households.[1] The two case studies in Naguraj (Karnataka) and Pattambi (Kerala) give no reason to think that food subsidy reaches the poorest people particularly (and, hence, that food distribution implies a substantial net shift in consumption), but they do indicate that the poorest households were interested, and purchased rationed commodities whenever they were in a position to do so. Their access to food was, however, somewhat restricted, as I analysed in Chapter 5, as a result of poverty (no money to buy rationed commodities; cards mortgaged), the specific conditions under which foodgrains are distributed (no possibility to buy on credit, limited opening of the shop) and the fact that a substantial amount of subsidized foodgrains never reaches the card holders.[2]

[1] See also Jha (1992), who calculates on the basis of NSS data that the highest income groups receive more PDS food and a larger part of the subsidy than the lower income groups.

[2] For similar points, see also Vyas and Bhargava (1995: 2567–8), who concluded nevertheless that 'even with the existing limitations, the availability of essential food items through PDS has ensured equity in access to food to a significant extent' (P. 2568). What the basis of that conclusion is, is not quite clear.

Apart from redistribution between categories of people within States, food distribution also implies a net physical shift of foodgrains between States. Kerala receives approximately 2 million tonnes of foodgrains per year, which I estimated as about a third of the foodgrain requirement in the State. Other States, notably Punjab, Haryana and Uttar Pradesh, are net suppliers of foodgrains. We could expect that in the absence of food distribution policy some redistribution of food between States would take place. In the case of Kerala it is, however, plausible that the PDS does contribute to overall foodgrain availability, specially because the PDS foodgrains are much cheaper than other imported foodgrains.[3]

Economic redistribution

In order to evaluate the impact of food distribution policy on economic redistribution, we have to look at prices, incomes and profits. In order to study the impact of the policy on prices, one needs to have a long-term perspective, which was beyond the scope of my project. Other researchers have argued that the PDS has contributed significantly to price stabilization and, hence, stabilization and protection of entitlements (Drèze and Sen, 1989). In periods of severe drought the government releases additional amounts of foodgrains through the PDS. The result has been stabilization of supply, prices and quantities consumed. Balakrishnan and Ramaswami (1992) make a similar point. Stocks held by the government smooth out intra- and inter-year foodgrain price differences. Others are less positive about the buffer stock policy of the FCI. Radhakrishna and Hanumantha Rao (1994: 27) conclude that 'the stock policy does not seem to have met with much success in influencing market expectations and thereby regulating the speculative behaviour of traders'. Also Bhalla (1994: 153–4) asserts that the FCI enters only rarely into open market operations. Its role as a price stabilizer is marginal. Nevertheless, all these authors acknowledge that the Indian food management system has helped to prevent the occurrence of famines and to organize scarcity and/or drought relief.

At the same time, many economists agree that food procurement has an upward effect on the open market price level of rice and wheat.

[3] In the long run there PDS imports may, however have had a negative impact on foodgrain availability in the state. It might well be that the large-scale imports of subsidized foodgrains have contributed to the decline in rice production in Kerala.

A study carried out by the Indian Statistical Institute, for instance, concludes that 'whenever there is procurement by the Government the open market price goes up steeply to enable the farmer to receive the weighted average price for his total sales which is not less than what he would have received in the absence of procurement.'[4] This observation is supported by information I got from rice millers and traders in Karnataka who are liable to pay a rice levy to the government. Many of them told me that they compensate the losses they incur as a result of compulsory procurement by demanding higher prices in their open market sales.

Thus it seems likely that PDS causes foodgrain prices to remain relatively stable but—in areas where procurement takes place—at a higher level than they would have been otherwise.[5] A higher level of open market rice and wheat prices means that the most vulnerable people who do not produce their own food have less access to food, unless this higher price is outweighed by enough subsidized food. It goes far beyond the scope of this study to estimate who is a net profiter or who a net loser, but it is likely that for those who are poor and who are excluded from public food distribution and who do not produce their own food, the system has a negative impact on the average quantities consumed (although there may be less fluctuation in consumption over time).

As far as incomes and profits are concerned, five different mechanisms can be discerned. Consumers who buy subsidized foodgrains instead of open market food, experience a financial benefit. On average this benefit amounts to Rs 12–25 per month per household in Karnataka and approximately Rs 75 per month per household in Kerala (Section 5.1), provided that all the foodgrains meant for public food distribution indeed reach the card holder. Second, in as far as the PDS contributes to price stabilization, it reduces the profitability of hoarding and speculation. Withholding food from the market in the hope that prices may rise is indeed a strategy I never came across. Many wholesale rice traders did admit that they make large profits, but not through speculation. The third impact is that levy policy means a direct tax on traders and rice mill owners and, hence, a transfer of income from these traders to the state. This is compensated by a fourth

[4] Data from Indian Statistical Institute (1985) quoted in Tyagi (1990: 96–7). See also Dantwala (1993), De Janvry and Subbarao (1986), Mundle (1981), Radhakrishna and Hanumantha Rao (1994).

[5] An implication of this is that the regional distribution of prices may change as a result of the regional character of procurement.

impact: food procurement influences the market structure. As I suggested in chapter 4, arbitrary implementation of procurement policy contributes to a market with oligopolistic characteristics, in which the maintenance of extra-economic and extra-administrative relationships is of crucial strategic importance. Competition between firms takes place primarily along these lines, while competition through prices seems somewhat secondary. Traders can work with relatively large margins and relatively high selling prices. As a rice mill owner in Akkipura explained:

> Before the introduction of mill point levy there was free trade. We could sell as many loads to Kerala as we wanted. There was a lot of competition, so we could only charge a nominal margin. Compared to those days, the margin is much better now. There are also less traders at present, but due to all the controls it is less easy to export rice to Kerala. So the volume of our trade (excluding levy rice) has come down, but the margin has increased.

A part of the profits made by rice traders is shared with government employees and politicians. A fifth way in which food distribution affects incomes and profits is through opening up the possibility of illegal sales of subsidized food. Illegal sales happen at almost all levels. A substantial amount of PDS foodgrains is black marketed by ration dealers, warehouse managers, transporters of foodgrains and others. I estimated that during my fieldwork about 10 per cent of the rice and 40 per cent of the wheat were sold illegally (Section 5.4). In the literature even higher percentages are mentioned (Ahluwalia, 1993). Here also the profits are shared with others: superior officers and/or politicians.

Power

The effects of the PDS on relationships and balances of power are diverse. As far as food distribution contributes to food security of the poorest people, it may add to their bargaining power in their interactions with moneylenders, landlords and employers. Because food is so essential for human survival, food insecurity makes people willing to accept loans, tenancy arrangements or work under unfavourable conditions, only to acquire some food. A well-functioning food distribution scheme that reaches the underprivileged would strengthen their position, that is reduce their dependency on others. In my fieldwork, I have never directly observed improvements in bargaining power of the poorest people as a result of food distribution, but it seems quite likely that the well-functioning PDS in Kerala is not only the result of political mobilization and public action, but that the reverse is also true: that a reliable food supply through the PDS contributes to bargaining power and functions as a condition of mobilization and public action. This, clearly, is a hypothesis that needs further investigation.

Thus if PDS foodgrains reach the weakest party, it is likely that they add to its bargaining power. If they are appropriated by the stronger party, food becomes a resource in relations of power and patronage. Ration dealers, members of local vigilance committees and others who succeed in gaining command over food can derive additional power from it. They are able to turn food distribution into a distribution of favours, through which they reinforce patron-client relationships.

It may be worthwhile to recall here the differences observed between Karnataka and Kerala. The nexus between food distribution and patronage was more evident in rural Karnataka than in rural Kerala. In Karnataka, fair price shops were often run by locally influential people, who seem to have succeeded in getting hold of an additional source of power in this way. In many places there is no effective political opposition. This means that for poor people the safest strategy to optimize food entitlements is to adjust to the local power structure, that is to act as clients. In Kerala, where organized political opposition exists at all levels of society, it is less easy for ration dealers to use food as a resource in patron-client relationships, as they soon would attract attention and be punished.

Another way in which the PDS affects power relations is connected to the administrative organization of the system. Those who are in a position to grant licences or permits, to force private traders to comply with levy policy, or to authorize others to distribute food, derive discretionary powers from food distribution policy. The PDS gives them a large number of rules and regulations which they can use in their interactions with others. As analysed in Chapters 4, 5 and 7, these resources can be used to harrass, as a threat or as a source of legitimacy. The institutions set up for the sake of food distribution, such as the food and/or civil supplies corporations, also function as an additional resource for those in charge to reproduce or reinforce their influence (Chapter 6).

Yet another interconnection between the PDS and the power structure is the following. At the level of the State, food distribution policy is used by State politicians to buy political support. This has happened both in Karnataka and Kerala, as well as in other States. State politicians seek to acquire political legitimacy. They promise to launch, revive or intensify food distribution schemes, and hope to catch votes and support. Such promises may, indeed, be instrumental in winning State assembly elections. The most prominent example of a politician pursuing this strategy was N.T. Rama Rao in Andhra Pradesh. In the run-up to the 1983 elections he promised cheap food for the poor, which he indeed introduced when he came to power. In the course of time, the programme slackened. During his election campaign in 1994 he promised to revive the scheme, and again he was elected.[6] In Karnataka and Kerala, the promises are less extravagant, but it is unmistakable in these two States also, that the legitimacy of ruling the State is linked to food programmes and prices.

8.2 THE POLITICAL SHAPING OF FOOD DISTRIBUTION

While the first question phrased at the beginning of this book was about the impact of food distribution, the second one was about the social construction of food distribution policy. In and through which political processes is food distribution shaped historically and reproduced on a day-to-day basis?

Historical shaping

The historical shaping was discussed in Chapter 3, in which I analysed the emergence and evolution of the PDS. Food distribution policy is a result of domestic, as well as international politics, neither of these remaining constant over the years. Here I will summarize the most important trends.

In the first quarter of a century of its existence (1939–65), the PDS served mainly the interests of industrial capital. Particularly between 1955 and 1965, during the Second and Third Plans, food distribution functioned as a means to contain price rises and inflation. With the help of cheap imported foodgrains, the Indian government was able to pursue a low wage policy and to maintain a stable political climate. In this period, the type of economic development pursued by the state was primarily industrial development.

From 1965 onwards, the situation changed. A class of capitalist farmers was developing. Increasingly, food policy began to serve the interests of rural capitalists as well. The foodgrain price policy adopted

[6] See Pai (1996) for an analysis of the 1994 State elections in Andhra Pradesh.

after 1965, especially the wheat price policy, was favourable to the (mainly capitalist) wheat farmers in north India.

This shift in policy is, of course, no autonomous process. It is brought about by the conscious efforts of planners, policy makers, politicians and farmers' movements. From the 1960s onwards, farmers became increasingly represented in various state structures and state organizations, not only at the level of State but also at the Central level. Farmers were able to redirect foodgrain price policy in a direction favourable to them.

Although the direct impact of the underprivileged classes on the content of policies is small, their importance as voters has increased over time. While for a long time the usual pattern was that ruling governments were re-elected, this trend changed from the 1960s and 1970s onwards. At the moment, fifty years after Independence, national and State elections generally lead to a change of government. It is an exception when ruling parties are allowed to continue their government. This means the legitimacy of ruling governments is no longer a natural phenomenon, but it has to be established and defended. One of the ways in which politicians and political parties try to establish this legitimacy is through populist programmes that appeal to large parts of the population. Food distribution has obviously become one of them.

Apart from its role in political legitimacy at the national level, food policy is also part of a project to establish political legitimacy in the international arena. In the 1960s, advisors of the World Bank and the Ford Foundation were very critical of India's food and agricultural policy. Together with American experts they argued that the food problem could be solved through the application of modern technology, supported by large investments in modern inputs and price incentives to farmers. According to Frankel (1978: 275), foreign experts enjoyed a 'maximum influence on the thinking of the agriculture minister' in these years. Subsidies to individual farmers were introduced, and a new price policy took shape. Thirty years later, in the 1990s, again the influence of international pressure is clearly felt. Ironically, however, the same agencies now favour a reduction of government expenditure, subsidy and direct involvement in production and trade. Although this advice has been followed only partly, it has had—and is having—an impact on PDS prices and food distribution generally.

Day-to-day reproduction

The day-to-day reproduction of the system takes place in innumerable interactions between the various actors involved: ration dealers, card holders, private traders, warehouse managers, transporters, senior civil servants, politicians and others. In the preceding chapters many of these interactions were described and analysed. Here I will summarize the most relevant ones under four broad headings: issuing of ration cards, issuing and suspending licences of ration dealers, procurement of foodgrains, and political interference in the administration.

The *procedure of issuing ration cards* is of crucial importance for those who would like to become beneficiaries of the PDS. The ration card is the entry ticket to the system. Those without a ration card are excluded, and those possessing a ration card have a right to subsidized food. In addition, the ration card functions as an identity card. Hence it is no surprise that those who issue ration cards can exercise power over others who would like to have one. They can make them wait, they can humiliate them in other ways, and they can ask for bribes. In Chapter 5, I described various ways in which cards are issued. In Madhyapura, it appeared, the procedure for getting a ration card was transparent. People had to wait for hours, but in the end almost everyone succeeded in getting a ration card. The only exceptions I came across were ultra-poor people in remote areas who could not afford the necessary bus fares to go to *taluk* headquarters and who were illegal squatters without a permanent address. In Akkipura, many people had paid a small bribe of Rs 10–25 to get a ration card. Green cards were issued only during a restricted period after the introduction of the scheme in 1985 and during a re-survey in 1992. Migrant labourers who worked elsewhere at the time cards were issued were often unsuccessful in getting a green card, but most others succeeded. As compared to Madhyapura and Akkipura, access was more restricted in Bangalore. I analysed the situation as a 'complex queue' because the procedures were unclear, ambiguous and dependent on the discretion of officials. There were several 'gates' and gate-keepers, and bribes were often required.

Issuing of licences to wholesale and retail ration dealers is done by officers from the food and/or civil supplies departments. In both States there are official criteria regarding the selection of candidates, but often these criteria do not give definite answers as to who should be authorized, or are overruled by other considerations. In both States, I have heard of several examples of people willing to pay large bribes to become licensees. In Kerala, where the selection criteria are laid down in the Kerala Rationing Order, 1966, aspiring ration dealers can even make an official appeal if they do not agree with the decision taken by the administration. In Karnataka, appeals have a more informal character: 'convincing' senior officers or politicians that the wrong decision has been taken and that someone else should be appointed.

The local *taluk*, or district administration, decides also on suspension or cancellation of licences. In Karnataka, suspensions are rare, but in Kerala they happen more often. They usually result from complaints made by alert villagers who are dissatisfied with the services of the ration dealer. After hearing the complaints, local officials often order an immediate temporary suspension pending investigation. It is only in rare cases that suspensions end in licence cancellations. Nevertheless, the system works. For ration dealers the possibility of immediate suspension, even before any guilt has been proved, functions as a threat. For card holders, on the other hand, it means that they have an instrument to keep ration dealers on their toes. In some cases, as I explained in Section 7.3, the complaints of the card holders are informed by political motives. The case may be genuine, but the desire to cause trouble to the ration dealer is prompted by political rivalry.

Procurement of foodgrains is analysed in the fourth chapter. I discussed various types of interactions between rice mill owners, traders, government officials and politicians. One of the major findings is the importance of threats in the collection of levy. Officials who want to realize procurement threaten rice mill owners and/or traders who do not cooperate, with raids on their premises, seizure or confiscation of their stocks and criminal prosecution. Their main instrument is the EC Act, 1955, a piece of law that defines many dos and don'ts of trade in essential commodities. Several orders issued under this Act apply to rice mill owners and/or rice traders. These orders prescribe trading procedures in such detail that it is almost impossible to act fully in accordance with them. The result is that traders and/or rice mill owners are almost always to blame for some smaller or larger mistakes. Hence, they are vulnerable to threats and harassment (see Chapter 7).

Threats and harassment induce traders and/or rice mill owners to surrender not only levy, but also bribes. For government officials the EC Act is also a valuable instrument in the process of bribe collection.

Bribes are a very regular phenomenon in interactions between rice mill owners and/or traders and government officials. In fact, it seems virtually impossible to run a large trading business without paying bribes now and then. Bribes are not only meant to avert threats. They can also be used to please officials and to cement social relationships. The interactions around procurement are not always conflictual; in many instances both parties profit from the deals made. From the perspective of the administration, bribes have an additional function. They help to shift the balance of power between those liable to pay levy and those responsible for implementing this policy in favour of the latter, and thereby help create compliance.

Political interference happens at almost all levels of food policy implementation: selection of ration dealers, effecting contracts with third parties, appointment of personnel, transfers in the department or corporation, procurement, etc. Political interference can be of three types. The first type is primarily in the interest of the politician himself, and happens on his own initiative. Some examples of this type are given in Chapter 6 on food and/or civil supplies corporations. Both in Karnataka and Kerala ministers try to interfere in administrative matters, just for their own or their party's sake. They claim money for an air-conditioned car or for a banner to welcome the Prime Minister. They exercise pressure to appoint certain people (e.g. workers in *Maveli* shops) or to give contracts to specific contractors or trading companies. This first type of interference is clearly illegal.

The second type of interference is political brokerage, mediation in conflicts between law-or policy enforcers and others. Often this brokerage happens at the instigation of one of the parties in the conflict, usually not the civil servants but the other party. For instance rice mill owners call upon the MLA to solve a conflict with the Deputy Commissioner who insists upon levy. This type of interference is what many people would consider as the actual job of State politicians (MLAs). In the eyes of many people, successful MLAs are 'fixers' (Potter, 1986: 152). They mediate in conflicts, smooth policy implementation and defend the interests of their constituents. Whether this type of interference is legal or illegal depends on the deal that is reached. There is nothing wrong with mediation *per se*, but when the outcome involves a bribe for the MLA and an order for the government officer to stop doing what he is supposed to do, it is clear that this type of interference is not according to law.

The third type of political interference is watch-dog behaviour: protesting against mischief. This 'barking' can be on the initiative of the politician himself, but it may also be that others have directed his attention to the matter. Politicians may either raise the issue in the appropriate political body, or address the administration directly. An example of the former is an MLA raising the issue of unlawful procedures of procurement in the Karnataka Assembly. An example of the latter is that DYFI (Marxist youth organization) workers in Kerala complain to the police about malpractices of a ration dealer. This third type of interference is usually not referred to as political interference but as public action. I mention it here to stress that not all interference by politicians in administrative matters is illegal or detrimental to policy implementation. Politics in India has a bad reputation; it is often regarded as an obstruction to policy implementation or an impediment to reform (e.g. World Bank, 1995). The point I want to emphasize is that this is not necessarily true. Some forms of political interference may contribute positively to policy implementation.

8.3 FOOD POLICY AND THEORIES OF THE INDIAN STATE

In the second chapter, I described four different perspectives on the Indian state. These are recent interpretations of the role of the Indian state in economic development and the nature of the Indian democratic system. Three of these approaches are very critical of the state. Together they support the dominant view that there is something fundamentally wrong with the Indian state. These three currents of thought are (*a*) the neoclassical political-economic conceptualization of the Indian state as rent-seeking, (*b*) the political science interpretation of the 'erosion' of the political system, and (*c*) the idea that state professionals form a dominant proprietary or political class. The fourth interpretation holds on to the concept of the developmental state. Although it is acknowledged that the Indian state contributed to developmental failures, the idea that the state may be an important vehicle in economic and social development is not renounced. As outlined in Section 2.4 all the four interpretations give rise to specific sets of expectations regarding the social evolution of food policy and day-to-day practices of implementation. The question here is to what extent the data and analysis presented in this book support or undercut the plausibility of the four interpretations.

The history of the PDS and plausibility of theoretical perspectives

Let me start with the history of public food distribution. The first perspective does not give many clues for a historical interpretation, but the second, third and fourth perspectives do. Reasoning on the basis of the second perspective, we would expect that the political function of food distribution changed when the dominant party system broke down and the erosion of Indian politics started. Food policy has always had a political function. Till the mid-1960s, we can assume, this function had to do with strategic long-term projects, while from 1967 onwards, political opportunism and vote catching became more important. We can also expect a shift in foodgrain price policy around the same date as a result of the increasing political influence of the rural bourgeoisie.

The third perspective focuses less exclusively on the political system and the role of politicians. State professionals are considered as an important class influencing the shape of policies, but so are agrarian capitalists and the industrial bourgeoisie (Bardhan) or labour (Rudolph and Rudolph). Food policy, we can expect, will be the result of a compromise between these contending categories of people in society. The interests of these three categories of people in food distribution policy are different: respectively state resources and discretionary powers, high procurement prices, and low consumer prices. All these interests have to be accommodated to some extent. Because they conflict with one another we can expect an in-built structural difficulty in food policy.

The fourth perspective puts more emphasis on development planning and strategies to overcome poverty and inequality. Reasoning from this perspective, we would expect that food distribution policy will be part of a conscious effort of the state to develop the Indian economy. Food distribution would be consistent with a larger developmental strategy. In addition, we can also expect that food policy itself has its own secular rationale: to improve food security at the micro and macro levels.

The interpretation of the history of food distribution presented in Chapter 3 corroborates some of these expectations, while others are not supported. According to my interpretation, there was indeed a shift somewhere in the mid-1960s. Food policy took a first definite form in 1957, marked by the publication of the Ashok Mehta report. From 1957 to 1965 there was a consistent foodgrain price policy that aimed to keep equilibrium prices low. This type of foodgrain price policy was advantageous to the industrial sector, but unfavourable for foodgrain-producing farmers. In the mid-1960s, a new price regime took shape, this time aiming to increase the equilibrium level of foodgrain prices (Mundle, 1981). This new price policy supported the income of foodgrain producers. Such a shift (see Section 3.1 for more details) fits in with the second interpretation of the Indian state. The political impact of the rural bourgeoisie increased, as Vanaik (1990) and Frankel (1978) assert, and henceforward also its influence on foodgrain prices. The fourth interpretation of the Indian state is also supported. Food policy remained consistent with long-term development planning, but the content of the plans changed in the course of time. During the first three Five-Year Plans (1950–65) industrial development was given full priority, but from 1965 onwards development of the agrarian sector got more prominence.

The other shift predicted on the basis of the 'erosion thesis', (i.e. from food policy as a means to realize long-term political projects to food policy as an instrument in short-term opportunistic politics) has taken place indeed, but much later than one would expect on the basis of this thesis. In the 1960s and 1970s, food policy supported industrial development and agrarian production. It was only in the 1980s that food and food programmes became an obvious element of political opportunism. In the 1970s, populist slogans meant to catch votes had to do with poverty, not with food directly. The introduction of food in populist politics dates only from the 1980s (and then it is mainly employed by some politicians in some south Indian States).

Yet, despite the evocation of food in populist vote-catching practices, the development trajectory of food distribution policy has not become fully subordinate to political opportunism. In fact, food policy is still closely linked to wider issues of development and planned state intervention. In that respect the fourth approach, stressing the embeddedness of policies and state activities in a larger developmental strategy, is right. Although this perspective does not pay sufficient attention to the role of politics, it provides a necessary supplement to the 'erosion thesis'. The development of food policy in the 1980s and 1990s cannot be understood through reference to populist politics alone. There is also the connection with structural adjustment policies. I recall that PDS issue prices have been increased in compliance with these economic policies and that there is discussion about a reduction of the subsidy and restructuring of the whole system. In short, it is not only opportunistic politics that forms the wider context in which food policy is shaped, but also economic policy.

What is noteworthy here is that these two contexts belong, by and large to two different levels of the Indian state: economic policy to the Centre state and political opportunism to federal States. Structural adjustment is initiated by the Centre state. No doubt, there are implications for federal States, but these are imposed rather than self-determined by politicians of the federal States. On the other hand, food-related populist politics is a phenomenon especially prevalent at the level of the States; it hardly exists at the level of the Centre. Hence, we can conclude that the 'erosion thesis' is particularly relevant for understanding the evolution of food policy at the level of federal States, while the idea of a developmental state is more relevant in order to understand the social shaping of food distribution as far as this happens at the Central level.

These two tendencies in the development of food policy—compliance with economic policy and adjustment to populist politics—do not necessarily work in the same direction. In the 1990s, there is indeed growing discord between the two. The logic of structural adjustment dictates a reduction of food subsidy and dwindling of the system. The logic of populist politics, on the other hand, implies further enlargement of the system, the inclusion of hitherto excluded categories of people and a continuing burden on the exchequer.

On the basis of the third perspective on the Indian state, one would expect that three social classes are particularly relevant in the emergence and evolution of the PDS: industrial capitalists or labour (both are interested in low foodgrain prices), the agrarian bourgeoisie (striving for high procurement prices) and state professionals (who are interested in an enlargement of the system and an expansion of their discretionary powers). It will be clear by now that in my view such an interpretation underrates the influence of State politicians. This influence is distinct from that of state professionals. While the former have to think about their re-election and popularity, the latter may be concerned with slightly longer-term worries: how to devise a scheme that will last for some time. To give an example of the distinct influence of politicians and officials on policy making, the Green Card scheme in Karnataka was initiated by the Chief Minister (and political leader) Ramakrishna Hegde. He and other politicians were in favour of a large impressive scheme, while several senior officers of the department held a more moderate view. The latter argued that only a restricted number of people should be included in the scheme, that each included household should receive less foodgrains than the politicians proposed (10 kg rather than 25), and that the additional subsidy given by the Karnataka state should be limited.

This example illustrates that politicians and state professionals held different opinions about the policy to be devised. Moreover, it shows that politicians cannot be regarded as more or less neutral arbiters, negotiating the diverging demands made by the three proprietary classes (what Bardhan suggests), but that they have their own distinct interests and demands. The example further illustrates that state professionals do not simply behave in line with their ascribed interests. Their behaviour cannot be understood as an attempt to increase their ownership or control of state property, resources and authority. In fact, they were bothered by considerations of manageability and financial viability. In other words, good governance. Thus the example illustrates that the state bureaucracy, does not always behave as a proprietary or third class, seeking to enlarge or consolidate its resource base. It may also act in line with the ideal of the developmental state.

Despite these limitations, the third perspective, with its emphasis on conflicts between the dominant classes, offers a helpful interpretation of the present crisis in the PDS system. Several conflicting interests (of foodgrain producers, industrialists, populist politicians, voters/consumers) have to be met in one way or another. The result has been an increasingly expensive system. PDS issue prices have been raised in the 1990s in order to reduce the amount of subsidy, but due to further increases of the procurement prices, the system has only become more costly. Moreover, the increase of the issue price impelled some State politicians to grant additional amounts of subsidy for special schemes for the poor. The incompatibility of interests and the desire to serve them all to some extent by the same policy has created an increasingly expensive programme.

Policy implementation and plausibility of theoretical perspectives

At far as policy implementation is concerned, it is undeniable that several of the expectations formulated on the basis of the rent-seeking perspective have been confirmed in the preceding chapters. The rent-seeking perspective draws our attention to the way individual civil servants and politicians make use of distribution policy. Indeed, as I described, some government employees appropriate and sell subsidized foodgrains (e.g. warehouse managers, Chapter 5), several civil servants use laws and policies as instruments to collect bribes (e.g. officials responsible for procurement, Chapters, 4 and 7), some politicians divert institutional funds for their own purposes (e.g. ministers, Chapter 6), some political leaders use food policy to buy popularity and political support (see Chapters 3 and 6), many officials compete for jobs in which large additional incomes can be earned (e.g. jobs in procurement, as food inspectors or food assistants). The potential usefulness and actual usage of food and food policy for individual enrichment and aggrandizement is indeed significant.

However, while this perspective is correct in pointing out a number of important practices, it is less helpful in offering an explanation. The theoretical starting point that politicians and civil servants—in fact, all people—are individual optimizers is an assumption. This assumption may be valid in certain circumstances, but there is no reason to think that it is a universal truth. In fact, in many situations people do not behave as rational egoists.[7] I have already given the example of the senior officers in Karnataka who were responsible for the framing of the Green Card scheme and who were led by considerations of good governance. Another example is the labour union of the KaFCSC, which regularly protests against mismanagement and misuse of Corporation resources, (see e.g. Section 6.4). To put it more generally, in addition to individual enrichment people may act out of compassion or solidarity with others; they may be committed to certain political or religious values; they may identify with certain groups; they may strive for honesty, decency, even impartiality.[8] The implication of this is not that the approach is always absolutely wrong in describing people as optimizing individuals. Indeed, in certain situations people behave as such. But the point is that if they do, an explanation is required. There is nothing particularly natural about individual optimization. So when Indian civil servants and politicians do behave as individual optimizers the intriguing question is why and under what conditions, in which circumstances, this is so. And if they do not why not? Contextualizing behaviour is necessary. Neoclassical political economy is not very helpful in this respect.

For many officials, professional life is much more complex than the individual optimization theorem suggests. As I described in Chapters 4 and 6, the position of many civil servants is very contradictory. They are responsible for policy implementation, but their work is seriously constrained by frequent political interference and the 'need' to collect money for their next transfer. Officials have to deal with double standards and commitments. On the one hand, the developmental role of the state is partly internalized. Many officials

[7] See Sen (1977) for a critique of the conceptualization of human agency in economic science.

[8] This is almost a literal translation of de Beus' description of Sen's conceptualization of human agency (de Beus, 1995: 19).

do feel some sort of commitment to the job they have to perform. Their first response to a question posed by a researcher about food policy is always in terms of official objectives and procedures. This is not just an effort to misguide the researcher. It also shows their own perception of what the state is, does, should be, or should do. They partly identify with these official objectives. On the other hand, they realize that there are also illegal sales of foodgrains, misuse of power and bribery. They observe that others are involved in these practices, and there is pressure on them to do the same. This pressure comes both from outside the state (the bribe-giving party, private traders), as well as from superior officers and politicians who want a share of the money. The various conflicting objectives and commitments have to be negotiated somehow. The result is not uncompromised rent seeking, but a mixture of individual enrichment and working towards the developmental goals of the state.[9]

It would be too simple to regard the drive towards individual enrichment and rent seeking as an illustration of individual optimization. In fact, it is not. This kind of behaviour also is rule - governed and part of a larger social structure. To my knowledge Wade's work (1982, 1985) is the most elaborate treatment of this. In his description, rent- seeking is an institutionalized practice with its own rules, norms, relations of hierarchy and redistribution of collected spoils. This system is known to the participants, and its norms are at least partially shared. My own data confirm this interpretation. In the food department there are also institutionalized practices and routines regarding job transfers. Ministers who try to change these routines, who ask too much money or who transfer too often are considered unreliable and *too* corrupt. There are implicit and explicit ideas about how much money should be given to whom, for which favours. In the eyes of bribe givers (i.e. rice mill owners and traders) an official is considered honest and reliable when he does not overcharge and does (or does not) what he is paid for, even when this payment and the (non)activity that follow are illegal. In other words, rent, seeking is not just optimizing behaviour of rational individuals. It is a social

[9] Sometimes it was possible to discuss these conflicts with government officials. In fact, referring to this pluralist loyalty proved quite a useful strategy to make them more forthcoming. I used to say such things as: 'Your position seems to me so difficult. There are so many contrasting demands. One day the minister insists on procurement; the next day he orders not to harass the rice mill owners. That must be difficult for you.' Very often this was confirmed, and sometimes this remark initiated rather more openness in the discussion.

activity that is bound and structured by collectively shared norms, ideas and ideals.

What this implies is that the Indian state is characterized by normative pluralism, as there are two different sets of norms, rules of conduct or laws governing behaviour of bureaucrats and politicians. On the one hand, the behaviour of these actors is based upon official government laws and policies. They are committed to the realization of official policy objectives and act accordingly. On the other, their behaviour is based upon the rules of conduct as developed within this corrupt bureaucracy—rules concerning the collection and redistribution of rents, rules concerning competition for jobs, etc. Different sets of rules thus exist within the same state institutions (Mooij, 1992).

Thus although the rent-seeking perspective is correct in the sense that it directs our attention to a number of important phenomena and characteristics of the Indian state, it is faulty in two respects. It mistakes rent seeking for a form of atomistic behaviour, while it is, in fact, characteristic of a social structure. It is rule governed. There are sanctions and punishments. Rent-seeking behaviour is shaped in and through interactions with others. Second, the perspective overlooks the fact that for many civil servants and politicians there is not just only one ultimate commitment or objective (individual enrichment, aggrandizement, optimization). To a certain extent, many of them also feel responsible for their officially assigned or self-proclaimed tasks and duties: working towards economic development, redistribution and social equality. In short, the Indian state is not only rent seeking, but also developmental.

8.4 THE FUTURE OF PUBLIC FOOD DISTRIBUTION

An implication of this conclusion—that the state is not only rent seeking but also developmental—is that the state is not only a problem, but also part of the solution (Evans, 1992). To be more concrete, and applying this insight to the field of food insecurity, food policy is not doomed to be futile and a mere means of power and income in the hands of policy makers and politicians. State food policy can have a positive impact on access to food of the most vulnerable consumers and on overall food security. This means it is worthwhile to think about the role the Indian state can play in improving food security. In this section, I will first discuss the likelihood of the present proposals for reform of the PDS. In the concluding section, I will come back very briefly to the more general point: how to devise policies that support the developmental features of the state and undercut the rent-seeking ones.

Critiques and proposals

In the mid-1990s, the public distribution system is under serious discussion and severe critique. In this respect, the analysis presented in the preceding chapters is not new or special. Critical opinions are voiced by many other interpreters. To mention the most important points, it is argued that the PDS is too expensive. The budgeted estimate of food subsidy for 1995–6 is Rs 5250 crore, which is more than the total estimated budget deficit of the Centre state in the same year (Rs 5000 crore) (Suryanarayana, 1995b). Such an amount of subsidy is considered unsupportable (e.g. Bhagwati and Srinivasan, 1993; Randhawa, 1994). The fixed cost component, in particular the operational cost of the FCI, is considered too high (Vyas, 1994). Another point of critique is related to the considerable leakages. Food that is meant to be sold at fair prices in ration shops sometimes never reaches the card holders because it is lost or sold illegally to others (Ahluwalia, 1993).

A more fundamental point of critique is related to the persistence of malnutrition. Despite the huge subsidy and the large scale of this intervention (around 10 per cent of foodgrains produced in India are purchased for the PDS), the food security of many vulnerable households is still marginal or insufficient. Distribution to the States has not been proportionate to the number of poor people in each State (see Appendix 1, Table 3). In addition, as Tyagi (1990: 92) argues, the supplies available within particular States have not gravitated in favour of the poor. Tyagi's data relate to the 1980s. It may be that the Revamped PDS, introduced in 1991–2, has changed this pattern somewhat, but (case) studies as undertaken by Swaminathan (1995) and Geetha and Suryanarayana (1993) warn against too much optimism. Apart from the various mechanisms that restrict access, it seems that the specific form of food distribution does not suit the needs of the most vulnerable consumers. The PDS is supposed to increase household food security by stabilizing and reducing foodgrain prices. But for the most vulnerable households, food security depends not only on the prices of foodgrains but also on a variety of access relations and entitlements. In general, the more (exchange) entitlement relations, the more secure the food situation. People whose income depends on only one source are more vulnerable than people who rely on several income sources. The PDS changes the existing exchange relations, but it does not contribute to a diversification of exchange entitlements, which a dole or a public work employment contract does.

Several of these points could have been voiced ten or fifteen years ago, and indeed were.[10] Yet, it is undeniable that in the 1990s, the critique of the PDS has become more outspoken and widely shared. The system is now said to be 'in crisis'. It should be 'revamped', 'streamlined', 'pruned' or 'made viable', to mention a few of the terms that figure in newspaper articles and policy discussions. The reasons behind the acuteness of the issue are multiple. The subsidy has doubled in the relatively short time span of three–four years. This has happened in the same period in which the off–take of the PDS has declined from 16.64 million tonnes in 1991–2 to 12.57 million tonnes in 1994–5 (Gopalan, 1995: A136). Procurement has continued at high price levels. Between 1990–1 and 1994–5 the procurement price increased by 60 per cent for rice and 66 per cent for wheat. As a result, the stocks held by the FCI reached unprecedented high levels. By May 1995, the food stocks had touched 37.5 million tonnes (EPW editorial, 18 Nov. 1995), while an amount between 16.5 and 21.4 million tonnes has been assessed to be sufficient as buffer stock and operational stock for the PDS.[11] In 1995–6 part of the stocks have even been exported.[12]

The decline in PDS off-take is not surprising. PDS issue prices have increased several times since 1991–2, with the result that the price difference between PDS foodgrains and open market foodgrains has come down. Foodgrains that were distributed through the Revamped PDS were subsidized additionally. These foodgrains are cheaper by about 10 per cent. Just over a quarter of the total PDS foodgrain in 1994–5 was distributed through the revamped PDS scheme (Gopalan, 1995: Fig. 1). But despite this additional subsidy, even the off-take of the Revamped PDS was much less than the allotted quantity (*Economic Times*, 23 Oct. 1993).

Apart from this particular 'crisis' the whole political-economic climate adds to the urgency of the feeling that something should be done. On the one hand, the structural adjustment reforms introduced in 1991 are at odds with large-scale interventions in the food economy. Bhagwati and Srinivasan, two leading advocates of the economic

[10] See, for instance, Harriss (1983).

[11] This was recommended by a technical group constituted by the Government of India in 1984 (Radhakrishna and Hanumantha Rao, 1994).

[12] In this way, food policy acquired an additional function. It became a means of

reforms and advisors to the Government of India, formulate this as follows.[13] In their view, India is 'at crossroads'. Economic reforms are necessary in many fields, also with regard to food. There is a 'macro-economic necessity' to rein in subsidies. Hence the PDS requires 'immediate reform'. On the other hand, international trade agreements prescribe a general deregulation. The provisions laid down in the General Agreement on Tariffs and Trade reduce the possibilities for individual governments to subsidize food and agriculture and undertake state trading activities (Bhalla, 1994). So from various sides there is a push towards reducing subsidies and curtailing the role of the state as an active economic agent. The PDS too is viewed from this perspective.

The suggestions made are basically two-fold: (*a*) to reform the PDS from a universal to a targeted scheme, and (*b*) to abolish the PDS and introduce another scheme in its place, for instance food stamps. These two suggestions do not necessarily exclude each other, although they are often presented as alternatives. Apart from these two options, there is a third suggestion I encountered during my fieldwork and which is also made implicitly in the literature. To put it blunty, the suggestion is to regard Kerala as a model, since the PDS in Kerala reaches almost everybody and adds to food security at macro and micro levels. So why not try to reform the PDS in the rest of India along the same lines?

Kerala as a model?

The argument behind this third option as it is made in the literature is rather more subtle and implicit than as formulated above. It runs as follows (see, e.g. Drèze and Sen, 1989; Franke and Chasin, 1992; Kannan, 1995). Kerala's achievements in the fields of health, nutrition and poverty alleviation are impressive. A crucial role is played by the PDS. The system has added substantially to food security in the State. Poverty alleviation and increasing food security have occurred even while the economy was stagnant. Thus it is concluded that well-designed and well-implemented programmes, among which the PDS deserves a prominent place, can help to reduce hunger and deprivation.

---

dealing with the trade deficit that is increasing as a result of the enhanced import bill in the liberalized trading environment (Ghosh, Sen and Chandrashekar, 1996: 1236).

[13] See Pinstrup-Andersen (1987) for a general discussion of the relationship between macroeconomic reforms and interventions in the food economy.

This is considered a 'lesson' to be learnt from the Kerala experience. To quote Drèze and Sen:

> The success of Kerala in achieving support-led security adds force to the plausibility of following this route even when the economy is very poor. The fact that Kerala has achieved such success through careful and wide-coverage public support shows how much can be achieved even at a low level of income, if public action is aimed at promoting people's basic entitlements and capabilities (1989: 225).

Of course, the authors are cautious enough to mention the various conditions on the basis of which Kerala could achieve its high levels of health and nutritional well-being. Apart from Kerala's history, these have to do with public action in the last four decades: there has been mass literacy, agrarian relations have been transformed, caste oppression has diminished, there is a relative absence of gender bias in education and health, and the Kerala state has contributed positively with public policy interventions (Drèze and Sen, 1989; Ramachandran, 1995).

Although it is not easy to reproduce these conditions elsewhere, an attempt in that direction is not doomed to be futile either. there is no reason to assume that these conditions are restricted to Kerala, that they can never occur (together) in other States. Besides, all the conditions are positive achievements in themselves, so there is every reason to stimulate developments in these directions.

Yet, what is rarely mentioned in positive evaluations of the PDS in Kerala is the simple fact that Kerala receives a relatively large share of total PDS foodgrains without having to worry about the subsidy burden. Kerala receives approximately 10 per cent of the total amount of distributed foodgrains in India, while its share in the population is about 3.5 per cent. This means that if the whole of India had to be covered by the PDS to the same level as Kerala is at present, the total amount of food to be distributed would have to triple. The required food subsidy would also rise, perhaps not in the same proportion but still considerably. For Kerala, PDS foodgrains are cheap as the required subsidy is provided by the Central state. If Kerala were to bear a subsidy burden relative to its off-take, it would have to incur an amount of approximately Rs 500 crore, which is 15–20 per cent of the total development expenditure in Kerala. This would be a substantial addition to the budget deficit there already is. So if we take the costs of the system into consideration, it is very unlikely that the PDS in Kerala will or could ever serve as an example for the rest of India.

Targeting of the PDS

But how realistic and sensible are the other two options? Let us first take targeting. Targeting of the PDS implies that (a certain part of) controlled commodities are meant exclusively for a specifically defined target group. The idea of targeting of the PDS is not new; in fact to some extent the PDS has been targeted already for some time. For instance the Green Card scheme in Karnataka, meant for the rural poor, is an example of a targeted programme. Also the revamped PDS, which existed only in a number of selected blocks (selected because they are tribal, hilly or otherwise 'backward') was a targeted scheme. These targeted programmes exist alongside universal distribution, and are, in fact, complementary programmes.

Targeting which excludes the richer sections of the population has been proposed by Bhagwati and Srinivasan (1993). It was also advocated by the World Bank (World Bank, 1991). The latest proposal from 1996–7 involved the introduction of a dual pricing system within the PDS. Households below the poverty line would receive 10 kg of rice per month through the PDS at half the normal price, while for others the PDS prices would go up. This proposal was introduced in 1997.

The rationale behind targeting is that it would be a mechanism by which the costs of the PDS can be contained—as only individuals who are deserving or needy are included—while the effectiveness of the intervention would increase. In other words, both E-mistakes (excessive coverage—those who do not deserve are nevertheless included) as well as F-mistakes (failure to include those who deserve to be included) would be reduced (Cornia and Stewart, 1993).

It is noteworthy that the discussion about targeting narrows down the objectives of the PDS to only one: to help the most vulnerable people. The other two objectives, that is price stabilization and remunerative prices for foodgrain producers (see Chapter 3), are no longer taken into account, not to mention the unofficial objectives such as buying political support or supporting particular political projects.

There are various ways of targeting. Gopalakrishna Kumar and Stewart (1992: 271) distinguish seven types. Schemes may be targeted by:

1. Income, where access is confined to those below a certain income;
2. Nutritional needs, as identified by diet surveys or anthropometric measures;

3. Commodity, subsidizing certain types of food, (e.g. basic or 'inferior' commodities);
4. Geography, locating subsidized food in certain areas;
5. Age, providing subsidies for all those of a certain age or status, (e.g. under-fives, school-age children pregnant and lactating women);
6. Employment, through food-for-work schemes;
7. Season, providing free or subsidized foods at certain times of the year.

Targeting on the basis of geography, age- and status-related needs, and employment exists already for some time as complementary to the universal PDS. The first two of these, however, have the disadvantage that non-deserving individuals (e.g. rich people who happen to live in so-called backward areas or upper class children) are also included. Seasonal distribution has the same disadvantage. Targeting on the basis of nutritional needs is extremely complicated. Imagine organizing diet surveys or anthropometric investigations in a country with 844 million inhabitants. The discussion and proposals in India, and hence also here, focus mostly on income-and commodity-based targeting.

At first sight, commodity-wise targeting seems the easiest option. No administrative effort is required to select who is poor and deserving and who is not, as it is based on self-targeting. The idea behind this type of targeting is that coarse cereals (such as sorghum and millet) are consumed largely by the poorer sections of the population, while rice and wheat are eaten more by the rich. The PDS should, hence, be confined to coarse cereals and exclude sugar and edible oil (Ahluwalia, 1993; Bhagwati and Srinivasan, 1993).

On further consideration, however, it can be expected that this type of targeting is very difficult to implement. The FCI is unfit for the procurement and distribution of coarse cereals. Rice and wheat are relatively easy to procure. They are purchased from commercial farmers or traders who deal with large quantities. There is expertise within the FCI about how to preserve these foodgrains for very long periods of time, and there is a standardized set of criteria that procured foodgrains have to fulfil (including moisture content, foreign matter, damaged or discoloured grains, admixture of lower varieties). Procurement and distribution of coarse cereals would produce difficulties in all these respects. They are produced by relatively small producers and the market is less developed. For a Centre-State organization that is used to buying in bulk according to standardized procedures, procurement of coarse cereals would be difficult to manage. Storage would require different technologies and expertise than are available within the FCI at present. So, it can be expected that commodity-based targeting would require a major effort, reorganization and retraining of/within the key procurement institution.

Moreover, the main premise underlying commodity-based targeting is doubtful. A recent study has come to the conclusion that the scope of commodity-based targeting is limited. According to Suryanarayana:

> It is no longer valid that coarse cereals constitute a major consumption item of the poor and are consumed largely only by them. The consumption patterns of the poorest decile groups, in rural and urban India, have undergone a change against coarse cereals and in favour of superior cereals in response to both relative price and taste changes. Now coarse cereals are equiproportionately consumed by all decile groups in rural India but disproportionately more by the poorest three decile groups in urban India. Thus the scope for commodity-based targeting and limiting leakages by reorienting it in favour of coarse cereals seems to be very limited particularly in rural India. As regards to urban India, even though coarse foodgrains are consumed disproportionately largely by the poorer decile groups, scope for PDS delivering these grains seems to be limited since their absolute consumption itself is limited (1995a: 695).

So commodity-wise targeting is not only difficult to implement, most probably it will also not produce the desired results, i.e. effectively exclude the middle and richer income groups from the PDS.

The alternative is income-wise targeting. This can be achieved through a means test, or by entrusting the task of identifying the poor to local bodies, possibly even social action groups (Bhagwati and Srinivasan, 1993). Targeting has always been resisted, but in 1997 the Government of India decided to restructure the PDS into a Targeted PDS (TPDS). This new scheme involved the introduction of differential prices for the poor and the non-poor. The difficult process of how to select the beneficiaries was left to the state governments.

When the benefits of inclusion are substantial, implementation of income-wise targeting is problematic. Both E-mistakes and F-mistakes can be expected. Poor people are often also relatively powerless and dependent on more well-to-do landlords, moneylenders or patrons. In many areas of India, they will not easily come forward to claim that they are entitled to subsidized food rather than their more wealthy neighbours, employers or patrons. Income-wise targeting requires independent local officials who are committed to their task or it requires public action and participation of the poorest people in the procedure of selecting the beneficiaries. In many areas in India these preconditions do not exist or are not easily generated. In fact, we can expect that in all areas in which the PDS functions well—because of an accountable government and/or a vigilant population—the selection of beneficiaries will happen reasonably well, while it will be problematic in other areas.

The new PDS will not mean a reduction of the overall subsidy expenditure. Food for the people below the poverty line has only became cheaper, which means that more subsidy is required. Moreover, procurement (price) policy has not changed. Thus the overall volume of the commodities purchased by the FCI is not likely to come down. All this means targeting is not only difficult to implement, it also does not solve the problem it is meant to solve.

Food stamps

The abolishment of the present PDS and the introduction of a system of food stamps in its place is considered as an alternative to targeting of the PDS (Suryanarayana, 1995b: A151), although, in principle, the two may well go together. The situation in Sri Lanka is often referred to as an example. In 1979, following economic liberalization, the Sri Lankan government replaced a general food subsidies programme by a new targeted food stamp scheme. By doing so, the share of food subsidies in total government expenditure decreased from 15 per cent in the mid-1970s to about 3 per cent in 1984 (Edirisinghe, 1987).

The principle of a food stamp scheme is that households having incomes below a specified level receive food coupons worth a certain amount of money which they can use to buy certain commodities in shops that are authorized to accept food coupons. In contrast to the present PDS, food stamps do not involve a dual marketing system. The government does not need to procure, store, transport and distribute foodgrains. Food stamps are used to buy food on the open market. The advantage of this scheme is, hence, that the entire network of the FCI and ration shops can be dismantled. This makes the administrative costs of a food stamp scheme relatively small which reduces the amount of subsidy required.

As with PDS targeting, a food stamps scheme also narrows down the objective of food policy to only one. Food stamps are meant to increase food security of the poorest people, not to stabilize prices or to support farmers' incomes.[14] Thus as compared to the present distribution system, the objectives are more limited.

Leakages, in the sense of illegal sales of controlled commodities, will not occur in a food stamp system, because there is no physical difference between subsidized food and non-subsidized food. It is only because the buyer, disposes over food stamps or not, that subsidy is involved or not. In fact, food subsidy in a food stamp scheme is an income subsidy. Food coupons are a kind of money.

The abolition of the present PDS and the introduction of a food stamp scheme will, I expect, raise considerable opposition, both from segments of society that benefit from the present PDS but would be excluded in a targeted food stamp scheme, and by vested interests within the present system. The dismantling of the FCI would be a major operation and would require great resoluteness. The FCI is one of the biggest enterprises in India and employs approximately 70,000 people (Bhalla, 1994). These people would probably protest if their jobs disappeared. Apart from the FCI, the food and/or civil supplies corporations and departments in the various States would also lose some of their responsibilities. Of course, a food stamp scheme also requires some administration, but it is likely that the total amount of labour that is necessary to run a food stamp scheme is less than in the present set-up. Also private wholesale dealers, retail ration dealers and cooperative societies would lose a source of income.

Thus a varied chorus of protests can be expected. Yet, I do not think that this opposition from within the bureaucracy will be so strong and powerful that we can altogether rule out the introduction of a food stamp scheme as a replacement of the present PDS. Those who would take the decision to dismantle the PDS are not themselves immediately threatened. It is, in principle, possible that this decision will be taken by Centre state politicians and their financial advisors and imposed on the bureaucracy (as has happened with policy measures introduced as part of structural adjustment).

The selection of beneficiaries would be a major problem. Again, it is especially those sections of society that have the least political clout that have to be included. There is ample scope for corruption and patronage. People who do not belong to the target group will make an effort to be included while others are left out. In other words it will be difficult to avoid E-, and specially, F-mistakes.

[14]Although, in principle, it is possible to combine a food stamp system with buffer stocking policy.

By way of conclusion

To conclude, the introduction of neither of the two options, tight targeting of the PDS (i.e. excluding richer sections of the population) or a new food stamp scheme, seems very likely and attractive. What seems more likely is a continuation of the present trend: targeting alongside universal distribution. For the poor an additional subsidy is introduced; for the others the issue prices are raised somewhat, but they are not excluded altogether. Procurement prices will increase, in order not to antagonize the farmers, and as a result the subsidy will increase further. In some States, political leaders will cash in on this failure of the Centre state to tackle the 'food question' (Bernstein et al., 1990). They will introduce or intensify state-wise distribution programmes and perhaps win elections for this reason. To some extent, this last development would mean, in fact, a transfer of the subsidy burden from the Centre state to the federal States.

On the other hand, one can never be completely sure about future developments. It has to be realized that policy changes after 1991 have shown that the Indian government is able to take measures that go against the interests of categories of people that are powerful or large in number. Although I do not think it is very likely, I also do not fully rule out the possibility of a policy change towards tight targeting. Most probably, if it is done, it will not happen shortly before elections, but perhaps somewhere in the first half of a government term.

But would tight targeting of food distribution be desirable? And is a food subsidy of Rs 50 billion indeed too much? To compare, Rs 50 billion is about 3 per cent of total government expenditure of the Central state, and about 0.6 per cent of the gross domestic product. Defence expenditure accounts for about 13 per cent of Central state expenditure and economic services for 13.5 per cent, while education and health expenses are around 1.5 and 2 per cent respectively (Gupta, 1994: Table 25). I think a food subsidy of 3% of total government expenditure is high but would be justifiable if it worked.[15] If food security of the landless, indebted, semi- or unemployed and other vulnerable people, i.e. between 150 and 300 million people, improved substantially, the money would be worth it. This means the issue is not how to reduce the subsidy burden, but how to make food policy more effective in reaching the most underprivileged classes.

[15] Nadkarni made a similar argument in 1993, when food subsidy was (estimated) as 2–2.5 per cent of total government expenditure (p. 42).

Targeting is not necessarily the right way. It neglects that since the mid 1960's the PDS has been a multi-purpose policy, and that is one of the reasons why it could count on broad support. There are many people who potentially benefit from the PDS: net foodgrain buyers (rich and poor), foodgrain producers, industrialists, politicians. Policies that address only one constituency are more vulnerable. There are no broad political coalitions to support them, so in times of fiscal stress they may be easily reduced (Echeverri-Gent, 1993: 197; see also Skocpol, 1995).

Thus the real challenge is to frame a food policy that is effective and politically viable. Effective means that it should help to increase food security and reduce dependency relations of the have-nots on the haves for their food supply. Ideally, such a policy should provide for an additional food entitlement relation for the underclasses, so that their economic base is broadened and their subordination to employers, landlords, moneylenders and patrons reduced. But, of course, stabilization and strengthening of already existing food entitlement—through low food prices and price stabilization—is also very important.

Political viability means that there should be sufficient social and political support. The more expensive a particular policy the more necessary that it is popular among, and regarded as important by, large parts of the population. It should have a widespread appeal and satisfy various social interests. An example of such a policy is the Employment Guarantee Scheme (EGS) in Maharashtra, which is attractive to everybody:

> The rural poor get jobs, urban residents get less overcrowding, cultivators profit from the creation of agricultural infrastructure and freedom from traditional obligations [to feed the poor also during the lean season], and politicians benefit from a progressive image not to mention an abundant source of patronage. The result is widespread support that makes the EGS one of the state's most popular programs (Echeverri-Gent, 1988: 1296).

Similarly, the PDS includes various interests, as I argued above. But in contrast to the EGS, in the case of the PDS not only the long-term interests of those involved vary markedly, but also the immediate short-term interests. High procurement prices are incompatible with low consumer's prices, except when the government bridges the financial gap. This makes the in-built contradiction more urgent and problematic than in the case of the EGS (see also Vyas, 1996).

Of course, it is impossible for policies to suit all classes in society equally. India is a polarized society; there are fundamental conflicts of interest that can never be overcome by cleverly formulated policies. Yet coalitions in support of policies—as broad as possible—are necessary to attract sufficient funds and to make people work for them. I do realize that some people might react to these suggestions by arguing that policies that try to cater to various interests are not radical enough, and that farther reaching redistribution is necessary, such as, for instance, land reform. I do agree with this critique, but unfortunately in the mid-1990s such policies do not figure on the political agenda. Radical redistributive policies are not considered a serious policy alternative. Instead, what seems within limits of what is possible, and what should be tried, is to frame policies that appeal to many people, but trigger a dynamics towards political awareness and mobilization of the underprivileged classes. In the long run, we may hope, this increased awareness and political mobilization could help to place more radical redistributive policies on the political agenda.

The present food distribution system largely fails in this respect. It has not contributed to political awareness and mobilization. Certainly, it has increased the feeling that all citizens have a right to fair-priced food and that the government has a duty to provide it. But voting for politicians who promise cheap food is not sufficient.

Or, to put it differently, the public distribution system has contributed to formal entitlements: households holding ration cards are entitled to a certain amount of fair priced food. Apart from this, the last fifty years have witnessed important increases in enfranchisement.[16] In some States, people have used this enfranchisement to demand cheap food through the ballot box. Yet as foregoing chapters illustrate, formal entitlements and enfranchisement are not enough. This is why Agarwal has suggested that the concept of empowerment be added, defined in this context as 'the ability of an individual or group to legitimately ensure that decisions relating to entitlements are taken in its favour' (1990: 395). In the case of food policy this would require active involvement of consumers/clients in policy making and implementation.

As I have argued in the foregoing pages, the Indian state is both developmental and rent seeking. It is unlikely that the push towards strengthening the first characteristic and weakening the second will come from within the state itself. It has to be forced upon it by vigilant

[16] See Appadurai (1984) about enfranchisement in relation to entitlements. Appadurai defines enfranchisement as 'the degree to which an individual or group can legitimately participate in decisions of a given society about entitlements' (p. 481).

and organized citizens. If there is one lesson to be learned from the Kerala experience with food policy, it is that public action and popular participation in policy implementation makes the state more accountable and active in the fields in which it has assumed responsibility. In the long run, these daily struggles around implementation may contribute to a more politically organized and empowered population, which is a prerequisite for more radical reform directed at a more equitable distribution of income, property and power.

Even policies that accommodate various interests and can count on broad support can and should have the potential to lay a basis for more empowerment and progressive reform in the future. Food distribution as it is organized at present is not likely to have this effect. It has to be reframed in such a way that participation is enhanced and may lead to pressures for accountability in policy implementation. We can think of village councils or other locally elected bodies checking distribution processes and the role of the local bureaucracy therein, or groups of card holders running fair price shops, but much more thinking is necessary. I do realize that it is likely that especially in circumstances where there is a powerful elite, these forms of participation may easily lead to new forms of control (see also Section 5.3). Yet there are historical examples of cases where institutional reform created possibilities for participation and collective action 'from below', with the result that food policy became more effective, even undermined the power of regional elites, and contributed to rural reform.[17]

Furthermore, in order to increase the potential effectiveness of popular participation, it is important not to isolate food policy from other policy fields (as is usually done in the present discussion about the future of the PDS), but to link it to other capability-enhancing terrains of public policy,[18] such as education (school feeding programmes) and employment (food-for-work, employment programmes). Also in these programmes popular participation can be built in by involving the parents of the children in the organization of child-feeding programmes and making representatives of the workers responsible for the distribution of the food in employment programmes. We need to think about these kinds of arrangements. After all, as food is a political commodity, we had better confront the issue explicitly and work towards another politics of public food distribution.

[17] See Fox (1992) for a very interesting example of food distribution in Mexico.

[18] See Drèze and Sen (1989) about nutrition and capabilities.

Appendix 1

PDS in Tables

Table 1

Growth of the PDS in India 1950–1996

	Distribution of foodgrains (million tonnes)	Number of Fair Price Shops (thousands)	Total subsidy on foodgrains (millions)
1950–1	7.6	N.A.	—
1951–2	7.9	N.A.	—
1952–3	6.7	N.A.	—
1953–4	4.6	N.A.	—
1954–5	2.2	N.A.	—
1955–6	1.6	N.A.	—
1956–7	2.1	18	—
1957–8	3.1	38	—
1958–9	4.0	46	—
1959–60	5.2	52	—
1960–1	4.9	51	—
1961–2	4.0	48	—
1962–3	4.4	51	—
1963–4	5.2	60	—
1964–5	8.7	102	—
1965–6	10.1	110	—
1966–7	14.1	136	—
1967–8	13.2	143	—
1968–9	10.2	140	—
1969–70	9.4	139	—
1970–1	8.8	122	100
1971–2	7.8	121	—
1972–3	11.4	165	1700[c)]
1973–4	11.4	201	2500[c)]
1974–5	10.8	222	2700[c)]
1975–6	11.3	240	2861[d)]
1976–7	9.2	236	4410[d)]
1977–8	11.7	239	5340[d)]
1978–9	10.2	239	5570[d)]
1979–80	11.6	244	

	Distribution of foodgrains (million tonnes)	Number of Fair Price Shops (thousands)	Total subsidy on foodgrains (millions)
1980–1	15.0	284	—
1981–2	13.0	283	—
1982–3	14.8	278	9440[d)]
1983–4	16.2	284	10910[d)]
1984–5	13.3	302	13530[d)]
1985–6	15.8	315	18910[d)]
1986–7	17.3	325	20000[e)]
1987–8	18.7	333	20000[e)]
1988–9	18.6	345	22000[e)]
1989–90	16.4	352	24760[e)]
1990–1	16.0	358	24500[e)]
1991–2	16.6[a)]	399[f)]	28500[e)]
1992–3	16.6[a)]	409[f)]	28000[c)]
1993–4	14.5[a)]	424[f)]	55370[c)]
1994–5	12.6[a)]	433[f)]	51000 (RB)[c)]
1995–6	10.7[b)]		55000 (RB)[g)]

Note: RB = Revised Budget estimate

Sources: Unless otherwise indicated: *Bulletin of Food Statistics*; Directory of Economics and Statistics, Ministry of Agriculture, GoI (various issues); [a)] Gopalan (1995: Figure 1); [b)] Ghosh, Sen and Chandrashekar (1996: 1235); [c)] Bapna (1990: 144); [d)] FCI (quoted in Tyagi, 1990: 131); [e)] EPW Research Foundation (1995: table 3); [f)] Government of India, *Economic Survey* (various years); [g)] Gulati (1996: 930)

With the exception of Tyagi ([d)]), the original source of the data is not mentioned in these sources.

Table 2

Procurement and distribution of some selected States 1983–1988

	Wheat procurement		Rice procurement		Distribution	
	thousand tonnes per year	%	thousand tonnes per year	%	thousand tonnes per year	kg per capita per year
Andhra Pradesh			1566.4	18.0	1427.2	23.3
Bihar	13.6	0.1	18.0	0.2	792.4	10.0
Gujarat			13.8	0.2	645.2	21.8
Haryana	1943.4	21.0	728.6	8.4	154.2	10.0
Karnataka			103.0	1.2	914.2	23.2
Kerala					1664.2	61.9
Madhya Pradesh	32.6	0.4	396.0	4.5	506.6	9.2
Maharashtra			0.4	0.0	1524.2	22.7
Orissa			111.8	1.3	367.0	13.3
Punjab	5444.6	58.8	3895.4	44.7	228.4	9.5
Rajasthan	119.6	1.3	33.8	0.4	518.0	18.6
Tamil Nadu			787.6	9.0	1750.0	31.1
Uttar Pradesh	1704.2	18.4	923.8	10.6	843.0	7.2
West Bengal	0.4	0.0	71.6	0.8	2186.6	32.7
Others	8.4	0.1	65.0	0.7	2806.0	
						All–India average:
Total	9267	(100%)	8715.0	(100%)	16327.0	21.7

Source: Bulletin of Food Statistics; Directory of Economics and Statistics, Ministry of Agriculture, GoI (various issues) (quoted in Tyagi, 1990: 34, 35, 41, 90).

Table 3

Per capita distribution of foodgrains through the PDS and poverty of some selected States

State	Per capita distribution 1986–7 (kg per year)[a]	Per capita net State domestic product 1991–2 (Rs/year)[b]	Population below poverty line 1987–8[d] (1994–5)[e]
Andhra Pradesh	22.8	5,570	27.2 (22.0)
Bihar	6.5	2,904	53.4 (55.0)
Gujarat	24.5	6,425	32.3 (24.0)
Haryana	6.2	8,690	16.6 (25.0)
Karnataka	19.9	5,555	38.1 (33.0)
Kerala	60.2	4,618	32.1 (25.0)
Madhya Pradesh	7.4	4,077	43.4 (42.5)
Maharashtra	22.4	8,180	40.1 (37.0)
Orissa	7.1	4,068	55.6 (48.6)
Punjab	4.7	9,643	12.7 (11.7)
Rajasthan	17.4	4,361	34.6 (27.4)
Tamil Nadu	25.4	5,078	45.1 (35.0)
Uttar Pradesh	2.9	4,012	42.0 (40.1)
West Bengal	26.1	5,383	44.0 (N.A.)
All-India	18.1	5,583[c]	39.3 (36.0)

Sources: [a] Based on NSS 42nd round, calculated by Jha (1994) (quoted in Drèze and Sen, 1995: Table A3); [b] Government of India (1994), *Economic Review 1993–94* (quoted in Drèze and Sen, 1995: Table A3); [c] Per capita net national product [d] Government of India, Perspective Planning Division, Planning Commission (1993) *Report of the Expert Group on Estimation of Proportion and Number of Poor* (quoted in Alagh, 1995); [e] Lakdawala Committee's estimates (quoted in Parthasarathy and Nirmala, 1997).

Appendix 2

Excerpts of Letters sent by Karnataka Rice Mill Owners Associations Concerning Levy Policy and the Essential Commodities Act

–: BRIEF NOTE :–

I. Request for total abolition of Mill Point Rice Levy because of the following sufferings of the Rice Millers of Karnataka.

(a) Only Rice Millers are singled out for a hostile discrimination, inspite of their incessant prayers for relief.

(b) The Purchase price at which the Rice Millers are paid towards the value of Rice supplied by them under Levy referred to is considerably lower than the actual cost price incurred by the Miller. Hence, the Millers are put under jeopardy of suffering capital loss cumulatively year after year—as indicated in the accompanying statement.

(c) Since the government have not fixed control rate for paddy, and since the paddy movement throughout the State is made free, the Rice Millers are made to purchase, their required stocks of paddy in open market at exhorbitant rate—Karnataka being itself a deficit state adjoined by similarly situated states such as Kerala and Tamil Nadu which are also rice consuming states, the rate of paddy are always high.

(d) The State A.P.M.C. has made it compulsory to purchase paddy as a notified agricultural produce at the market yard only at the price fixed by the Committee, on pain of penalty. The rates of paddy fixed at A.P.M.C. are high and the Government have not been paying heed to this serious price factor to reduce the injury.

(e) The government by imposing ceiling on holding on stocks of paddy and rice by Millers caused them irrepairable predicament. Paddy can not be imported from other States and it being a seasonal crop the Rice Miller has to stock to his minimum requirement at the harvest season.

II If the Government still feel that Rice Levy System need continue, the Millers pray for the following reliefs:

(a) Remove the ceiling imposed on holding of Stocks of paddy and rice as Mill Point Levy and imposition of Ceiling on stocks do not go hand in hand.

(b) Make movement of rice as well as paddy throughout the State free so that equal treatment is given to Rice and paddy as a matter of common policy and in the public and common man's interest.

(c) Pay the Millers at the A.P.M.C. rate for the stocks of Rice the Millers deliver under levy and also maintain a marginal rate difference of not less than Rs. 50/- between coarse, fine and superfine. Make the F.C.I. pay market cess at 1% as purchasers or in the alternative include this in the purchase price.

(d) Instead of Mill Point Levy introduce levy on those who trade outside the State by way of export levy by reducing the levy percentage to 20% instead of prevailing rate at 33 1/3rd percent, so that principle of "Less Percentage ensures higher collection" is maintained.

(e) Reduce the State Levy Target to a reasonable achievable minimum based on comparative figures of levy targets and achievements recorded during the last years.

(f) Raise the Milling charges, due to day to day rate of inflation to Rs. 25/- per quintal of paddy as also handling charges such as transport at the same rate at which the F.C.I. pay to their regular contractors. Likewise make proportionate increase in transport charges where distance exceeds more than 8 Kms.

(g) Make relaxation in assessing broken rice by increasing the present 22% to 35% because of unfavourable weather condition as procurement starts only at the commencement of the harvest season when crop has moisture.

(h) Supply of Gunny Bags by F.C.I. and arrangements are made to lift the Levy rice from Mill premises as it is a Mill Point Levy. In case the F.C.I. desires the Millers to supply new Gunny Bags, then they be paid at fair market price and stitching charges are paid instead of prevailing rate 95 paise per bag to Rs. 1–50 per bag and due to allowance made for the weight of empty gunny bags reasonably.

(i) The varieties of paddy locally and popularly known by name "ROSE KAR", "JYOTHI", "GIDDA" and "RASSI" etc., may also be included in the list of recognised varieties for being appropriately treated under fine and superfine quality as case may be.

STATEMENT SHOWING THE ACTUAL COST PRICE OF ONE QUINTAL OF RICE INCURRED BY A RICE MILLER—DURING THE CURRENT SEASON—1992 IN RESPECT OF COMMON VARIETY OF RICE FOR EXAMPLE:

Items of expenses	Actual rate of paddy per Quintal	Converted to 1 quintal of rice	Purchase Rate by F.C.I.
1. Value at market rate (A.P.M.C.) of per quintal of paddy	Rs. 356–00	534–00	
Broker's commission @ 2%	7–12	10–68	
R.M.C. fee @ 1%	3–56	5–34	
	366–68	550–02	
2. Cost of Milling charges per quintal of rice or 1.5 quintal of paddy	37–50	37–50	
3. Transport charges, etc., from Market Yard to Mill premises per quintal of Rice or 1.5 quintal of paddy	3–00	4–50	
TOTAL	Rs. 407–18	592–02	Rs. 369–00

Please note: 1.5 quintal of paddy is equivalent to 1 quintal rice.

Hence, the difference between the Actual cost incurred by the Miller and the Purchase price at which he is paid	592–02 369–00
Difference Rs.	**223–02**

Hence, the capital loss per quintal of rice of common variety incurred by the Miller is Rs. 223. 02 or about 40 %

Appendix 3

Data on the Karnataka Food and Civil Supplies Corporation and the Kerala State Civil Supplies Corporation

Table 1

Some financial details of KaFCSC and KeSCSC (in Rs millions)

	KaFCSC		KeSCSC	
	Turnover	Profit/loss	Turnover	Profit/loss
1973–4	69.337	0.131	—	—
1974–5	259.833	1.710	57.523	4.4
1975–6	271.610	1.565	127.546	2.2
1976–7	261.338	1.371	202.941	–0.2
1977–8	322.985	–1.392	71.267	–13.4
1978–9	237.167	–2.218	105.417	–3.6
1979–80	488.401	–3.438	231.367	–1.2
1980–1	692.306	3.695	845.734	7.3
1981–2	989.706	2.849	1035.313	–19.4
1982–3	1208.346	–29.607	1192.783	–41.5
1983–4	1502.055	4.717	1623.447	–119.9
1984–5	1698.492	6.739	1745.622	56.4
1985–6	2097.489	7.757	1583.242	12.1
1986–7	2442.115	13.718	1678.450	43.8
1987–8	3100.609	14.495	2199.469	101.8
1988–9	1935.969	2.710	2502.888	–29.4
1989–90	2513.115	–8.706	2354.003	–1.3
1990–1	2767.961	–14.275	2244.686	–1.0
1991–2	2827.007	– 2.172	2143.012	–2.3
1992–3	3511.930	35.539	2749.898	–1.7

Source: Kerala State Civil Supplies Corporation; Economic Review, Planning Board, Government of Kerala, (various years); KaFCSC.

Table 2

Sale of foodgrains and other commodities by the KaFCSC (in Rs)

	Rice		Wheat		Sugar		Palmolein oil	
	tonnes	million	tonnes	million	tonnes	million	tonnes	million
1981–2	—	440.6	—	19.0	—	248.0	—	125.2
1982–3	—	562.4	—	28.0	—	298.8	—	159.9
1983–4	—	608.8	—	76.0	—	408.3	—	243.8
1984–5	—	—	—	67.8	—	—	—	—
1985–6	334799	734.0	49182	86.5	—	570.4	35230	414.2
1986–7	328520	753.4	74722	122.8	126423	600.8	54218	621.0
1987–8	384806	968.1	100820	175.6	135596	660.6	78819	982.6
1988–9	217733	585.8	67204	106.0	103123	520.2	25902	412.8
1989–90	274383	813.6	133364	221.6	139718	720.4	22150	388.2
1990–1	284075	807.6	184371	334.5	141139	668.5	85572	591.3
1991–2	342429	1124.2	282306	575.4	153042	833.3	17339	155.3
1992–3	388847	1724.4	158239	400.1	161194	1019.6	16144	176.2

Source: KaFCSC.

Table 3

Essential commodities distributed by the Kerala State Civil Supplies Corporation

	Rice		Other foodgrains*)		Edible oil		Sugar**)		Vegetables
	MT	million Rs	MT	million Rs	MT	million Rs	MT	million Rs	million Rs
1974–5	4554	12.724	25059	44.793					
1975–6	9240	25.979	86246	96.911	143	1.206	8	0.35	
1976–7	49577	114.206	62098	55.110	518	4.504	456	22.23	0.756
1977–8	20989	39.461	3761	5.591	73	0.817	133	4.94	1.060
1978–9	14865	25.435	1959	3.408	119	1.312	119	3.48	0.874
1979–80	2350	4.749	2079	6.491	397	4.658	28688	828.62	5.857***
1980–1	31855	64.092		19.902	16798	144.697	136220	4250.65	6.868***)
1981–2	42966	111.353		71.092	23024	211.534	125501	4451.97	3.681
1982–3	42397	120.130		87.166	28310	266.958	132725	4887.99	2.734
1983–4	156592	492.288		62.602	30227	302.268	133841	5055.97	—
1984–5	69587	198.042		34.858	61685	739.115	134025	5317.67	—
1985–6	45393	132.123		39.388	41004	505.099	144144	6569.58	—
1986–7	64998	215.069		59.138	23958	375.706	168533	8125.52	—
1987–8	51223	178.830	12043	89.058	58997	956.889	157945	7727.79	3.004
1988–9	91731	338.503	32394	254.389	44576	893.315	150380	7673.85	8.145
1989–90	136623	528.393	25762	177.264	30237	590.468	147824	7740.13	7.678
1990–1	81528	335.780	18513	169.708	32660	625.092	143986	7519.54	7.884
1991–2	75783	328.228	19589	202.889	11826	334.868	131754	6697.12	13.276
1992–3	48577	299.340	24324	289.037	15822	477.601	157216	11019.64	7.315

Note: *)Other foodgrain means wheat, wheat products and pulses; in 1991–2 and 1992–3 only pulses; **) Sugar includes levy sugar and free sale sugar; ***) including lubricants (1979–80) or pulses (1980–1) and other items.

Source: KeSCSC.

References

Newspapers, popular (bi)weeklies, editorial comments from the *Economic and Political Weekly*, letters, court judgements, etc. are not included in this list. Their references can be found in footnotes or in the text itself.

ABEL, R.L. (1980). 'Redirecting Social Studies of Law'. *Law and Society Review*, 14, no. 3, pp. 805–29.

ACHARYA, K.C.S. (1983). *Food Security System of India. Evolution of the Bufferstocking Policy and Its Evaluation.* Concept Publishing House, Delhi.

AGARWAL, BINA (1990). 'Social Security and the Family: Coping with Seasonality and Calamity in Rural India'. *Journal of Peasant Studies*, 17, no. 3, pp. 341–413.

AHLUWALIA, DEEPAK (1993). 'Public Distribution of Food in India: Coverage, Targeting and Leakages'. *Food Policy*, 18, no. 1, pp. 33–54.

ALAGH, YOGINDER K. (1995). 'Poverty and Food Security: Toward a Policy System for Food Security'. *Economic and Political Weekly*, 30, no. 52, pp. A 142–50.

ALAVI, HAMZA (1972). 'The State in Post-colonial Societies: Pakistan and Bangladesh'. *New Left Review*, no. 74, pp. 59–81.

—— (1982). 'State and Class under Peripheral Capitalism', in Hamza Alavi and Teodor Shanin (eds.), *Introduction to the Sociology of Developing Societies*. Macmillan, London, pp. 289–307.

ALEXANDER, K.C. (1989). 'Caste Mobilization and Class Consciousness: The Emergence of Agrarian Movements in Kerala and Tamil Nadu', in Francine R. Frankel and M.S.A. Rao (eds.), *Dominance and State Power in Modern India: Decline of a Social Order*, vol. 1. Oxford University Press, Delhi, pp. 362–413.

APPADURAI, ARJUN (1984). 'How Moral is South Asia's Economy? A Review Article'. *Journal of Asian Studies*, 43, no. 3, pp. 481–97.

ASHOK RAO, K. (1987). 'Issues Regarding the Public Sector that Need Public Debate'. *Social Scientist*, 15, no. 6, pp. 55–66.

AUSTIN, JAMES E. and JONATHAN FOX (1987). 'State-owned Enterprises : Food Policy Implementers', in James E. Austin and Gustavo Esteva (eds.), *Food Policy in Mexico: The Search for Self-sufficiency.* Cornell University Press, Ithaca and London, pp. 61–91.

BAGCHI, AMIYA KUMAR (1993). '"Rent-seeking", New Political Economy and Negation of Politics'. *Economic and Political Weekly*, 28, no. 34, pp. 1729–36.

BAGCHI, AMIYA KUMAR (1994). 'Public Sector Industry and the Political Economy of Indian Development', in T.J. Byres (ed.), *The State and Development Planning in India.* Oxford University Press, Delhi, pp. 391–432.

BAILEY, F.G. (1962). 'Parliamentary Government in Orissa, 1947–1959'. *Journal of Commonwealth Studies*, 1 (May).

BALAKRISHNAN, PULAPRE and BHARAT RAMASWAMI (1992). 'Public Storage and Private Speculation. The Competition for Supplies in the Indian Wheat Market'. Paper prepared for presentation at the Far East and South Asia Econometrics Society Meeting in Bombay, December 1992.

BAPNA, S.L. (1990). 'Food Security through PDS: the Indian Experience', in D.S. Tyagi and Vijay Shankar Vyas (eds.), *Increasing Access to Food. The Asian Experience.* Sage Publications, New Delhi etc., pp. 99–144.

BARDHAN, PRANAB (1984). *The Political Economy of Development in India.* Oxford University Press, Delhi and Blackwell, Oxford.

—— (1988) 'Dominant Proprietary Classes and India's Democracy', in Atul Kohli (ed.) *India's Democracy. An Analysis of Changing State-Society Relations.* Princeton University Press, Princeton, pp. 214–23.

—— (1989). 'The Third Dominant Class'. *Economic and Political Weekly*, January 21, pp. 155–6.

BARDHAN, P.K. (1991). 'State versus Society; Discourse in Social Science'. Paper presented at Queen Elizabeth House, 15.1.1991.

BARU, SANJAYA (1994). 'Conference Summary and Report', in T.J. Byres (ed.) *The State and Development Planning in India.* Oxford University Press, Delhi etc., pp. 528–45.

BASU, KAUSHIK (1993). 'Structural Reform in India, 1991–93. Experience and Agenda'. *Economic and Political Weekly*, November 27, pp. 2599–605.

BENDA-BECKMANN, FRANZ VON (1983). 'Why Law does not Behave — Critical and Constructive Reflection on the Social Scientific Perception of the Social Significance of Law'. Paper presented to the Symposium on Folk Law and Legal Pluralism, Canada.

—— (1989) 'Scape-goat and Magic Charm. Law in Development Theory and Practice'. *Journal of Legal Pluralism*, no. 28, pp. 129–48.

BENDA-BECKMANN, K. VON (1981). 'Forum Shopping and Shopping Forums: Dispute Settlement in a Minangkabau Village in West Sumatra'. *Journal of Legal Pluralism*, no. 19, pp. 117–59.

BERNSTEIN, HENRY (1979). 'African Peasantries: A Theoretical Framework'. *Journal of Peasant Studies*, 6, no. 4, pp. 421–43.

BERNSTEIN, HENRY, BEN CROW, MAUREEN MACKINTOSH and C. MARTIN (eds.) (1990). *The Food Question. Profits versus People.* Earthscan Publications, London.

BÉTEILLE, ANDRÉ (1989). 'Are the Intelligentsia a Ruling Class?' *Economic and Political Weekly*, January 21, pp. 151–5.

BETTELHEIM, CHARLES (1968). *India Independent*. London.

BEUS, JOS DE (1995). 'Inleiding. Naar een politieke economie van het pluralisme', in Amartya Sen, *Welzijn, vrijheid en maatschappelijke keuze. Opstellen over de politieke economie van het pluralisme*. Selected and introduced by Jos de Beus. Van Gennep, Amsterdam, pp. 7–37.

BHADURI, AMIT (1985). 'Class Relations and Commercialization in Indian Agriculture: A Study in the Post-Independence Agrarian Reforms of Uttar Pradesh', in K.N. Raj, N. Bhattacharya, S. Guha and S. Padni (eds.), *Essays on the Commercialization of Indian Agriculture*. Oxford University Press, Delhi etc., pp. 306–18.

BHAGWATI, JAGDISH (1982). 'Directly Unproductive Profit-seeking (DUP) Activities'. *Journal of Political Economy*, 90, no. 5, pp. 988–1002.

—— (1993). *India in Transition. Freeing the Economy*. Clarendon Press, Oxford.

BHAGWATI, JAGDISH and T.N. SRINIVASAN (1993). *India's Economic Reforms*. Ministry of Finance, G.o.I., New Delhi.

BHALLA, G.S. (1994). 'Policy for Food Security in India', in G.S. Bhalla (ed.), *Economic Liberalization and Indian Agriculture*. Institute for Studies in Industrial Development, New Delhi, pp. 133–70.

BHARADWAJ, KRISHNA (1985). 'A View on Commercialisation of Indian Agriculture and the Development of Capitalism'. *Journal of Peasant Studies*, 12, no. 4, pp. 7–25.

—— (1994). 'Agricultural Price Policy for Growth: the Emerging Contradictions', in T.J. Byres (ed.), *The State and Development Planning in India*. Oxford University Press, Delhi etc., pp. 291–346.

BHATIA, B.M. (1991). *Famines in India*. Konark Publishers, Delhi.

BINSWANGER, HANS P. and JAIME B. QUIZON (1988). 'Distributional Consequences of Alternative Food Policies in India', in Per Pinstrup-Andersen (ed.), *Food Subsidies in Developing Countries. Costs, Benefits and Policy Options*. John Hopkins University Press, Baltimore and London, pp. 301–19.

BOSE, ASHISH (1991). *Demographic Diversity in India. 1991 Census. State and District Level. A Reference Book*. B.R. Publishing Corporation, Delhi.

BOWBRICK, P. (1986). 'The Causes of Famine. A Refutation of Professor Sen's Theory'. *Food Policy*, 11, no. 2, pp. 105–24.

BRASS, PAUL R. (1990). *The Politics of India since Independence*. The New Cambridge History of India, IV.1, Cambridge University Press, Cambridge.

BRASS, TOM (ed.) (1995). *New Farmers' Movements in India.* Frank Cass, Essex and Portland.

BREMAN, J. (1993). *Beyond Patronage and Exploitation: Changing Agrarian Relations in South Gujarat.* Oxford University Press, Delhi.

BUCHANAN, J.M., R. TOLLISON and G. TULLOCK (eds.) (1980). *Toward a Theory of the Rent-Seeking Society.* Texas A&M University Press.

BYRES, T.J. (1979). 'Of Neo-Populist Pipe Dreams: Daedalus in the Third World and the Myth of Urban Bias'. *Journal of Peasant Studies*, 6, no. 2, pp. 210–44.

—— (1988). 'A Chicago View of the Indian State: An Oriental Grin without an Oriental Cat and Political Economy without Classes'. *The Journal of Commonwealth and Comparative Politics*, 26, no. 3, pp. 246–69.

—— (ed.) (1994). *The State and Development Planning in India.* Oxford University Press, Delhi etc.

BYRES, T.J. and B. CROW, with MAE WAN HO (1983). *The Green Revolution in India. Case Study 5.* The Open University Press, Walton Hall, Milton Keynes.

CALDWELL, JOHN C. (1986). 'Routes to Low Mortality in Poor Countries'. *Population and Development Review*, 12, no. 2, pp. 171–220.

CASSEN, ROBERT and VIJAY JOSHI (eds.) (1995). *India: The Future of Economic Reform.* Oxford University Press, Oxford.

Centre for Development Studies (1977). *Poverty, Unemployment and Development Policy: A Case Study of Selected Issues with Reference to Kerala.* Orient Longman, Madras.

CHAKRAVARTY, SUKHAMOY (1985). 'Book Review of "The Political Economy of Development in India", by Pranab Bardhan'. *Journal of Peasant Studies*, 13, no. 1, pp. 134–6.

—— (1987). *Development Planning. The Indian Experience.* Oxford University Press, Delhi etc.

CHANDRASEKARA, NAIDU V. (1983). 'National Sample Surveys Data on Household Consumer Expenditure – A Critique'. *Working Paper* no. 43, Madras Institute of Development Studies.

CHANDRASHEKAR, B.K. (1984). 'Panchayati Raj Law in Karnataka. Janata Initiative in Decentralization'. *Economic and Political Weekly*, 19, no. 16, pp. 683–92.

CHATTERJEE, PARTHA (1994). 'Development Planning and the Indian State', in T.J. Byres (ed.) *The State and Development Planning in India.* Oxford University Press, Delhi etc., pp. 51–72.

CHAUDHURI, SUDIP (1994). 'Public Enterprises and Private Purposes'. *Economic and Political Weekly*, 29, no. 22, pp. 1338–47.

CHOPRA, R.N. (1988). *Food Policy in India. A Survey.* Intellectual Publishing House, New Delhi.

CLAY, E.J., B. HARRISS, C. BENSON and S. GILLESPIE (1988). *Food Strategy in India. Approaches to Food Strategy in the Natural Resources Sector.* Relief and Development Institute, London.

COLANDER, DAVID C. (ed.) (1984). *Neoclassical Political Economy.* Ballinger Publishing Company, Cambridge, Massachusetts.

CORNIA, GIOVANNI ANDREA, R. JOLLY AND F. STEWART (eds.) (1987). *Adjustment with a Human Face.* Clarendon Press, Oxford.

CORNIA, GIOVANNI ANDREA and FRANCES STEWART (1993). 'Two Errors of Targeting'. *Journal of International Development*, 5, no. 5, pp. 459–96.

CROW, BEN (1990). 'Moving the Lever: a New Food Aid Imperialism?', in Henry Bernstein et al. (eds.) *The Food Question. Profits versus People.* Earthscan Publications, London, pp. 32–42.

CROW, BEN and K.A.S. MURSHID (1994). 'Economic Returns to Social Power: Merchants' Finance and Interlinkage in the Grain Markets of Bangladesh'. *World Development*, 22, no. 7, pp. 1011.

DANDEKAR, V.M. (1981). 'On Measurement of Poverty'. *Economic and Political Weekly*, July 25, pp. 1241–50.

—— (1994). *The Indian Economy 1947–92. vol.I: Agriculture.* Sage Publications, New Delhi etc.

DANTWALA, M.L. (1993). 'Agricultural Policy: Prices and Public Distribution System: A Review'. *Indian Journal of Agricultural Economics*, 48, no. 2.

DE JANVRY, ALAIN, and K. SUBBARAO (1986). *Agricultural Price Policy and Income Distribution in India.* Oxford University Press, Delhi etc.

DEV, S. MAHENDRA and M.H. SURYANARAYANA (1991). 'Is PDS Urban Biased and Pro-rich: An Evaluation'. *Economic and Political Weekly*, 26, no. 4, pp. 2357–66.

DE WAAL, ALEX (1990). 'A Re-Assessment of Entitlement Theory in the Light of the Recent Famines in Africa'. *Development and Change*, 21, no. 3, pp. 469–90.

DE ZWART, FRANK (1992). 'Mobiele Bureaucratie. Manipulaties met Overplaatsingen van Ambtenaren in India'. Dissertation, University of Amsterdam.

DHAGAMWAR, VASUDHA (1992). 'The Disadvantaged and the Law', in Barbara Harriss, S. Guhan and R.H. Cassen (eds.), *Poverty in India. Research and Policy.* Oxford University Press, Bombay, etc., pp. 433–48.

DIRKS, NICHOLAS B. (1994). 'From Reel to Reel: Cinema and Politics in Tamil Nadu'. Paper presented at the Centre for Asian Studies, Amsterdam, 3.5.1994.

DRÈZE, JEAN and AMARTYA SEN (1989). *Hunger and Public Action*, Clarendon Press, Oxford.

DRÈZE, JEAN and AMARTYA SEN (1995). *India. Economic Development and Social Opportunity*. Oxford University Press, Delhi etc.

ECHEVERRI-GENT, JOHN (1988). 'Guaranteed Employment in an Indian State'. *Asian Survey*, 28, no. 12, pp. 1294–310.

—— (1993). *The State and the Poor. Public Policy and Political Development in India and the United States*. University of California Press, Berkeley.

EDIRISINGHE, NEVILLE (1987). *The Food Stamp Scheme in Sri Lanka: Costs, Benefits and Options for Modification*. Research Report no. 58, International Food Policy Research Institute, Washington, D.C.

EPW Research Foundation (1994). 'Social Indicators of Development for India'. *Economic and Political Weekly*, May 21, pp. 1300–8.

—— (1995). 'Finances of Government of India'. *Economic and Political Weekly*, 30, no. 18–19, pp. 1125–32.

EVANS, PETER B. (1989). *Predatory, Developmental and other Apparatuses. A Comparative Political Economy Perspective on the Third World State. Working paper* 11, Dept. of Sociology, University of New Mexico.

EVANS, PETER (1992). 'The State as Problem and Solution: Predation, Embedded Economy and Structural Change', in Stephen Haggard and Robert R. Kaufman (eds.), *The Politics of Economic Adjustment. International Constraints, Distributive Conflicts, and the State*. Princeton University Press, Princeton, New Jersey, pp. 139–81.

FENELON, K.G. (1952). *Britain's Food Supplies*. Methuen, London.

FOX, JONATHAN (1992). *The Politics of Food in Mexico. State Power and Social Mobilization*. Cornell University Press, Ithaca and London.

FRANKE, RICHARD W. and BARBARA H. CHASIN (1992). *Kerala. Development through Radical Reform*. Promilla & Co Publishers, New Delhi in collaboration with The Institute for Food and Development Policy, San Francisco.

FRANKEL, FRANCINE (1978). *India's Political Economy. The Gradual Revolution*. Princeton University Press, Princeton, NJ.

FRANKEL, FRANCINE R. and M.S.A. RAO (eds.) (1989, 1990). *Dominance and State Power in Modern India*. Vol. I–II, Oxford University Press, Delhi.

FRIEDMANN, HARRIET (1982). 'The Political Economy of Food: the Rise and Fall of the Postwar International Food Order', in M. Burawoy and T. Skocpol (eds.), *Marxist Inquiries. Studies in Labor, Class and States*. University of Chicago Press, London and Chicago, pp. S248–86.

GALANTER, M. (1974). 'Why the Haves come out Ahead: Speculations on the Limits of Legal Change'. *Law and Society Review*, 9, pp. 95–160.

GEETHA, S. and M.H. SURYANARAYANA (1993). 'Revamping PDS: Some Issues and Implications'. *Economic and Political Weekly*, 28, no. 41, pp. 2207–13.

GEORGE, P.S. (1979). *Public Distribution of Foodgrains in Kerala: Income Distribution Implications and Effectiveness.* International Food Policy Research Institute, Research Report no. 7, Washington D.C.

GHOSH, ARUN (1994). 'Ideologues and Ideology. Privatisation of Public Enterprises'. *Economic and Political Weekly*, 29, no. 30, pp. 1929–31.

GHOSH, JAYATI, ABHIJIT SEN and C.P. CHANDRASHEKAR (1996). 'Using Foodstocks Productively'. *Economic and Political Weekly*, 31, no. 21, pp. 1235–7.

GIBBON, D. and A. PAIN (1985). *Crops of the Drier Regions of the Tropics.* Longman, London and New York.

GIDDENS, ANTHONY (1984). *The Constitution of Society. Outline of the Theory of Structuration.* Polity Press, Cambridge.

GOPALAN, C. (1995). 'Towards Food and Nutrition Security'. *Economic and Political Weekly*, 30, no. 52, pp. A 134–41.

GOPALAKRISHNA KUMAR and FRANCES STEWART (1992). 'Tackling Malnutrition: What can Targeted Nutritional Interventions Achieve?', in Barbara Harriss, S. Guhan and R.H. Cassen (eds.), *Poverty in India. Research and Policy.* Oxford University Press, Bombay etc., pp. 259–81.

Government of India (1956). *Second Five Year Plan.* Planning Commission.

—— (1957). *Report of the Foodgrains Enquiry Committee, 1957.* Ministry of Food and Agriculture (Department of Food).

—— (1965). *Report of the Foodgrain Prices Committee.* Ministry of Food and Agriculture.

—— (1991). *Indian Economic Statistics, Public Finance 1991.* Ministry of Finance, Department of Economic Affairs, Economic Division.

—— (1993). *Economic Reforms. Two Years After and the Tasks Ahead. Discussion Paper.* Ministry of Finance, Department of Economic Affairs.

—— (various years). *Bulletin of Food Statistics.* Directory of Economics and Statistics, Ministry of Agriculture.

—— (various years). *Crime in India.* National Crime Records Bureau, Ministry of Home Affairs.

—— (various years). *Economic Survey.* Ministry of Finance, Economic Division.

—— (various years). *Lok Sabha Debates.*

Government of Karnataka (various years). *Annual Reports.* Food and Civil Supplies Department.

—— (various years). *Economic Survey.* Planning Department.

Government of Kerala (1989). *Where There is a Will...* Department of Public Relations.

—— (various years). *Economic Review.* State Planning Board.

GOVINDAN KUTTY, K. (1990). *Vararuchi's Children. Aspects of Kerala.* Macmillan India Limited, Madras etc.

GRAMSCI, ANTONIO (1971). *Selection from the Prison Notebook.* International Publishers, New York.

GREENOUGH, PAUL R. (1982). *Prosperity and Misery in Modern Bengal: the Famine of 1943–1944.* Oxford University Press, New York.

GULATI, ASHOK (1996). 'Harvesting the Crop. Interim Budget 1996–97'. *Economic and Political Weekly*, 31, no. 15, pp. 929–30.

GULATI, ASHOK and S.R. HASHIM (1994). 'Discussant's Comments on a Paper 'Liberalisation and Implications for Agricultural Policy—An Overview Paper', by N.S. Randhawa', in G.S. Bhalla (ed.), *Economic Liberalization and Indian Agriculture.* Institute for Studies in Industrial Development, New Delhi, pp. 379–80.

GULATI, LEELA (1977). 'Rationing in a Peri-Urban Community. Case Study of a Squatter Habitat'. *Economic and Political Weekly*, March 19, pp. 501–6.

GUPTA, S.P. (1994). 'Recent Economic Reforms and their Impact on the Poor and Vulnerable Sections of the Society'. Paper in: '*Structural Adjustment and Poverty in India: Policy and Research Issues*', Papers and Proceedings of an IDPAD Seminar, 29–30 Nov. 1994.

HAMMERSLEY, MARTYN, and PAUL ATKINSON (1983). *Ethnography. Principles in Practice.* Routledge, London and New York.

HANSON, A.H. (1966). *The Process of Planning: A Study of India's Five Year Plans 1950–1964.* London.

HANUMANTHA RAO, C.H. and ROHINI NAYYAR (1994). 'New Initiatives for Rural Poverty Alleviation'. Paper presented at IDPAD seminar '*Structural Adjustment and Poverty in India: Policy and Research Issues*', 29–30 November 1994, The Hague.

HARRISS, BARBARA (1981). *Transitional Trade and Rural Development.* Vikas, New Delhi.

—— (1983). 'Implementation of Food Distribution Policies. A Case Study in South India'. *Food Policy*, May 1983, pp. 121–30.

—— (1984a). *State and Market.* Concept, New Delhi.

—— (1984b). 'Agrarian Change and the Merchant State in Tamil Nadu', in Tim P. Bayliss-Smith and Sudhir Wanmali (eds.), *Understanding Green Revolutions. Agrarian Change and Development Planning in South Asia. Essays in Honour of B.H. Farmer.* Cambridge University Press, Cambridge etc., pp. 53–83.

—— (1988). 'Policy is What it Does: State Trading in Rural South India'. *Public Administration and Development*, 8 no. 2, pp. 151–60.

HARRISS, BARBARA (1989). 'Organised Power of Grain Merchants in Dhaka Region of Bangladesh. Comparison with Indian Cases'. *Economic and Political Weekly*, 24, 25.3.89, pp. A39–44.

—— (1991). 'The Give and Take of Calories: Tamil Nadu's Food and Nutrition Policies and Village Food Energy Economy during Drought in the Early Eighties', in C.T. Kurien, E.R. Prabhakar and S. Gopal (eds.), *Economy, Society and Development. Essays and Reflections in Honour of Malcolm S. Adiseshiah*. Sage Publications, Delhi etc., pp. 107–24.

HARRISS-WHITE, BARBARA (1993). 'Collective Politics of Foodgrains Markets in South Asia'. *IDS Bulletin*, 24, no. 3, pp. 54–62.

—— (1995). 'Introduction', in Barbara Harriss-White and Sir Raymond Hoffenberg (eds.), *Food. Multi-disciplinary Perspectives*. Basil Blackwell, Oxford, pp. 1–26.

HARRISS, BARBARA and CLAIRE KELLY (1982). 'Food Processing: Policy for Rice and Oil Technology in South Asia'. *IDS Bulletin*, 13, no. 3, pp. 32–44.

HARRISS, JOHN (ed.) (1982). *Rural Development. Theories of Peasant Economy and Agrarian Change*. Hutchinson, London etc.

HELD, DAVID (1991). 'Editor's Introduction', in David Held (ed.), *Political Theory Today*. Polity Press, Cambridge, pp. 1–21.

HERRING, RONALD (1980). 'Abolition of Landlordism in Kerala: A Redistribution of Privilege'. *Economic and Political Weekly*, 15, no. 26, pp. A59–A69.

HILL, POLLY (1984). 'The Poor Quality of Official Socio-Economic Statistics relating to the Rural Tropical World: With Special Reference to South India'. *Modern Asian Studies*, 18, no. 3, pp. 491–514.

—— (1986). 'Kerala is Different'. *Modern Asian Studies*, 20, no. 4, pp. 779–92.

HOWES, STEPHEN and SHIKHA JHA (1992). 'Urban Bias in Indian Public Distribution System'. *Economic and Political Weekly*, 27, no. 19, pp. 1022–30.

ILO-ARTEP (1993). Employment, Poverty and Economic Policies. International Labour Organisation (ILO) and Asian Regional Team for Employment Promotion (ARTEP), December 1993.

IYER, RAMASWAMY R. (1994). 'Public Enterprises and Private Purposes'. *Economic and Political Weekly*, 29, no. 34, pp. 2246–8.

JAIN, P.M. (1964). *Administrative Process Under the Essential Commodities Act, 1955*. The Indian Law Institute Studies. United India Press, New Delhi.

JEFFREY, ROBIN (1992). *Politics, Women and Well-being: How Kerala became a 'Model'*. Macmillan, London.

JESSOP, BOB (1984). *The Capitalist State. Marxist Theories and Methods.* Basil Blackwell, Oxford.

—— (1990). *State Theory. Putting Capitalist States in their Place.* The Pennsylvania State University Press, Pennsylvania.

JHA, PREM SHANKAR (1980). *India: A Political Economy of Stagnation.* Oxford University Press, Bombay etc.

JHA, SHIKHA (1992). 'Consumer Subsidies in India: Is Targeting Effective?'. *Development and Change*, 23, no. 4, pp. 101–28.

—— (1994). 'Foodgrain Price and Distribution Policies in India: Performance, Problems and Prospects'. Reprint no. 134–1994, Indira Gandhi Institute of Development Research, Bombay; forthcoming in *Asia-Pacific Development Journal.*

JOSHI, VIJAY and I.M.D. LITTLE (eds.), (1994). *India: Macroeconomics and Political Economy, 1964–1991.* The World Bank, Washington D.C., pp. 342–351.

KAHLON, A.S. and D.S. TYAGI (1980). 'Intersectoral Terms of Trade'. *Economic and Political Weekly*, 15, no. 52, pp. A173–184.

KANNAN, K.P. (1995). 'Declining Incidence of Rural Poverty in Kerala'. *Economic and Political Weekly*, 30, no. 41–2, pp. 2651–62.

KANNAN, K.P., K.R. THANKAPPAN, V. RAMANKUTTY and K.P. ARAVINDAN (1991). *Health and Development in Kerala. A Study of the Linkages Between Socioeconomic Status and Health Status.* Integrated Rural Technology Centre of the Kerala Sastra Sahitya Parishad, Trivandrum.

Karnataka Food and Civil Supplies Department (not dated). *A Decade of Dedication to the Consumer.*

KAVIRAJ, SUDIPTA (1986). 'Indira Gandhi and Indian Politics'. *Economic and Political Weekly*, 21, no. 38 and 39, pp. 1697–1708.

KIDDER, ROBERT L. (1974). 'Formal Litigation and Professional Insecurity: Legal Entrepreneurship in South India'. *Law and Society*, 9, no. 1, pp. 11–37.

KOHLI, ATUL (1980). 'Democracy, Economic Growth and Inequality in India's Development'. *World Politics*, 32, no. 4 July, pp. 623–38.

—— (1987). *The State and Poverty in India. The Politics of Reform.* Cambridge University Press, Cambridge etc.

—— (ed.) (1988). *India's Democracy. An Analysis of Changing State-Society Relations.* Princeton University Press, Princeton.

KOSHY, ABRAHAM (1989). 'Managing Public Sector Undertakings: A Case Study of a Government Trading Corporation in Kerala', in Abdul Aziz (ed.), *Management Problems of State Public Undertakings.* Printwell Publishers, Jaipur, pp. 196–208.

Koteswararao (1986). 'What ails the Enforcement of the Essential Commodities Act, 1955 and the Functioning of the Public Distribution System?' *Criminal Law Journal*, 92, pp. 65–72.

Kothari, Rajni (1964). 'The Congress "system" in India'. *Asian Survey*, December, pp 1161–73.

—— (1988). *State Against Democracy. In Search of Humane Governance.* Ajanta Publications, Delhi.

Krishnaji, N. (1981). 'On Measuring the Incidence of Undernutrition. A Note of Sukhatme's Procedure'. *Economic and Political Weekly*, May 30, pp. 989–92.

Krishnan, T.N. (1989). 'Kerala Economy: Performance, Problems and Prospects', in Malcolm S. Adiseshiah (ed.), *The Economics of the States in the Indian Union*. Lancer International, pp. 411–17.

—— (1994). *Foreign Remittances, Consumption and Income*. AKG Centre for Research and Studies, Thiruvananthapuram.

Krishnaswamy, K.S. (1980). 'What Ails the Public Sector?' *The Fourth Ajit Bhagat Memorial Lecture*. Ajit Bhagat Memorial Trust, Ahmedabad.

Krueger, A. (1974). 'The Political Economy of the Rent-seeking Society'. *American Economic Review*, 64, no. 3, pp. 291–303.

Kumar, Gopalakrishna and Frances Stewart (1992). 'Tackling Malnutrition: What can Targeted Nutritional Interventions Achieve?', in Barbara Harriss, S. Guhan and R.H. Cassen (eds.), *Poverty in India: Research and Policy*. Oxford University Press, Bombay etc., pp. 259–81.

Kurian, Matthew K. (ed.) (1975). *India: State and Society*. Madras.

Laclau, Ernest (1975). 'The Specificity of the Political: The Poulantzas-Miliband Debate'. *Economy and Society*, 4, no. 1, pp. 87–110.

Lal, Deepak (1988). *The Hindu Equilibrium: Cultural Stability and Economic Stagnation, India c.1500BC–AD1980*. Vol.1, Clarendon Press, Oxford.

Levi, Margaret (1988). *Of Rule and Revenue*. University of California Press, Berkeley.

Lipton, Michael (1977). *Why Poor People Stay Poor. A Study of Urban Bias in World Development*. Temple-Smith, London.

—— (1991). 'Agriculture, Rural People, the State and the Surplus in some Asian Countries: Thoughts on some Implications of Three Recent Approaches in Social Science'. in Jan Breman and Sudipto Mundle (eds.), *Rural Transformation in Asia*. Oxford University Press, Delhi etc., pp. 93–124.

Long, N. (ed.) (1989). *Encounters at the interface: A Perspective on Structural Discontinuity in Rural Development*. Pudoc Wageningen.

LONG, NORMAN, JANDOUWE VAN DER PLOEG, CHRIS CURTIN and LOUK BOX (1986). *The Commoditization Debate: Labour Process, Strategy and Social Network*. Papers of the Department of Sociology 17, Agricultural University Wageningen.

LONG, NORMAN and JANDOUWE VAN DER PLOEG (1989). 'Demythologizing Planned Intervention: an Actor Perspective'. *Sociologia Ruralis*, 29, no. 3/4, pp. 226–49.

MACKINTOSH, MAUREEN (1990). 'Abstract Markets and Real Needs' in Henry Bernstein *et al.* (eds.), *The Food Question. Profits versus People?* Earthscan Publications, London, pp. 43–53.

—— (1992). 'Introduction', in Marc Wuyts, Maureen Mackintosh and Tom Hewitt (eds.), *Development Policy and Public Action*. Oxford University Press, in association with the Open University, Oxford, pp. 1–9.

MANOR, JAMES (1978). 'Where Congress Survived: Five States in the Indian General Election of 1977'. *Asian Survey*, 18, no. 8, pp. 785–803.

—— (1984). 'Blurring the Lines between Parties and Social Bases. Gundu Rao and Emergence of a Janata Government in Karnataka'. *Economic and Political Weekly*, 19, no. 37, pp. 1623–32.

—— (1988). 'Parties and the Party System', in Atul Kohli (ed.), *India's Democracy. An Analysis of Changing State-Society Relations*. Princeton University Press, Princeton, pp. 62–98.

—— (1989). 'Karnataka: Caste, Class, Dominance and Politics in a Cohesive Society', in Francine R. Frankel and M.S.A. Rao (eds.), *Dominance and State Power in Modern India. Decline of a Social Order*. vol. 1. Oxford University Press, Delhi etc., pp. 322–61.

MARX, KARL (1954). *Capital. A Critique of Political Economy*. Vol. 1. Progress Publishers, Moscow.

MATHEW, GEORGE (1989). *Communal Road to a Secular Kerala*. Concept Publishing Company, New Delhi.

MENCHER, JOAN (1978). 'Agrarian Relations in Two Regions in Kerala'. *Economic and Political Weekly*, 13, no. 6–7, pp. 349–66.

—— (1980). 'The Lessons and non-Lessons of Kerala: Agricultural Labourers and Poverty'. *Economic and Political Weekly*, special number, 29, no. 41–3, pp 1781–1802.

MILIBAND, RALPH (1973). 'Poulantzas and the Capitalist State'. *New Left Review*, no. 82, pp. 83–92.

MITRA, ASHOK (1977) *Terms of Trade and Class Relations*. Frank Cass, London.

MOOIJ, JOS E. (1992). 'Private Pockets and Public Policies. Rethinking the Concept of Corruption', in F. von Benda-Beckmann and M. van der Velde (eds.), *Law as a Resource in Agrarian Struggles*. Wageningse Sociologische Studies No 33, Agricultural University Wageningen.

—— (1995). 'The Social Construction of Food Distribution Policy in India, 1939–90', in Paul Baak (ed.), *CASA Nova Aspects of Asian Societies 1*. Centre for Asian Studies Amsterdam, pp. 107–32.

—— (forthcoming). 'Public Food Distribution and the Black Box of the State. Studying the Politics of Food Distribution', in B. Harris-White (ed.), *The Visible Hand*. Macmillan (in press).

MORRIS-JONES, W.H. (1971). *The Government and Politics of India*. Hutchinson University Library, London.

MOZOOMDAR, AJIT (1994). 'The Rise and Decline of Development Planning in India', in T.J. Byres (ed.) *The State and Development Planning in India*. Oxford University Press, Delhi etc., pp. 73–108.

MUKHERJEE, AMITAVA (1994). *Structural Adjustment Programme and Food Security*. Avebury, Aldershot etc.

MUNDLE, SUDIPTO (1981). *Surplus Flows and Growth Imbalances. The Inter-sectoral Flow of Real Resources in India, 1951–71*. Allied Publishers, Bombay etc.

—— (1994). *Deprivation and Public Policy. Redefining the Developmental State*. The Wertheim lecture 5. Centre for Asian Studies Amsterdam, Amsterdam.

MUNDLE, SUDIPTO and M. GOVINDA RAO (1991). 'Volume and Composition of Government Subsidies in India, 1987–88'. *Economic and Political Weekly*, 26, no. 18, pp. 1157–1172.

MYRDAL, G. (1968). *Asian Drama: An Enquiry into the Poverty of Nations*. Pelican, London.

NADKARNI, M.V. (1987). *Farmers' Movements in India*. Allied Publishers, New Delhi etc.

—— (1993). *Agricultural Policy in India. Context, Issues and Instruments*. Development Research Group, Study 5, Department of Economic Analysis and Policy, Reserve Bank of India, Bombay.

NAG, MONI (1989). 'Political Awareness as a Factor in Accessibility of Health Services. A Case Study of Rural Kerala'. *Economic and Political Weekly*, 24, no. 8, pp. 417–26.

National Sample Survey Organisation (1989). *Utilisation of PDS*. NSS 42nd Round, no. 362. Department of Statistics, New Delhi.

——(1990). *Tables with Notes on Consumer Expenditure*. NSS 44th Round, no. 370/2. Department of Statistics, New Delhi.

NELKEN, DAVID (1981). 'The "Gap Problem" in the Sociology of Law: a Theoretical Review', in *Windsor Yearbook of Access to Justice*, pp. 35–61.

—— (1985). 'Legislation and its Constraints: A Case Study of the 1965 British Rent Act', in Adam Podgorechi, Christopher J. Whelan and Dinesh

Khosla (eds.) *Social Systems and Legal Systems*. Croom Helm, London etc.

NOLAN, PETER (1993). 'The Causation and Prevention of Famines. A Critique of A.K. Sen'. *Journal of Peasant Studies*, 21, no. 1, pp. 1–28.

OLSEN, W.K. (1989). 'Eat Now, Pay Later. Impact of Rs. 2/kg. Scheme'. *Economic and Political Weekly*, 24.

OOMMEN, T.K. (1975). 'Agrarian Legislation and Movements as Sources of Change. The Case of Kerala'. *Economic and Political Weekly*, 10, no. 40, pp. 1571–84.

—— (1985) *From Mobilization to Institutionalization. The Dynamics of Agrarian Reform in 20th Century Kerala*. Popular Prakashan, Bombay.

PACEY, ARNOLD and PHILIP PAYNE (eds.) (1985). *Agricultural Development and Nutrition*. Hutchinson, London etc.

PAI, SUDHA (1996). 'Andhra Pradesh: Elections and Fiscal Reform'. *Economic and Political Weekly*, 31, no. 2–3, pp. 142–8.

PAL, SURESH, D.K. BAHL and MRUTHYUNJAYA (1993). 'Government Interventions in Foodgrain Markets. The Case of India'. *Food Policy*, 18, pp. 414–27.

PANIKKAR, K.N. (1989). *Against Lord and State. Religion and Peasant Uprisings in Malabar 1836–1921*. Oxford University Press, Delhi etc.

PANIKULANGARA, VINCENT (1976). 'Paddy Procurement through Producer Levy: A Case Study of Kerala'. *Social Scientist*, 4, no. 8, pp. 44–55.

PARTHASARATHY, G. and K.A. NIRMALA (1997). 'Lakdawala Estimate of Poverty and Targeted PDS. Injustice to Andhra Pradesh'. *Economic and Political Weekly*, 32, no. 16, pp. 815–16.

PATNAIK, PRABHAT and C.P. CHANDRASEKHAR (1995). 'Indian Economy Under "Structural Adjustment"'. *Economic and Political Weekly*, 30, no. 47, pp. 3001–13.

PATNAIK, UTSA (1991). 'Food Availability and Famine: A Longer View'. *Journal of Peasant Studies*, 19, no. 1, pp. 1–25.

—— (1994). 'India's Agricultural Development in the Light of Historical Experience', in T.J. Byres (ed.), *The State and Development Planning in India*. Oxford University Press, Delhi etc., pp. 265–90.

—— (1995). 'Food Security, Class Structure and Export Oriented Agriculture in Developing Countries and in India', in *Proceedings of the Congress 'Agrarian Questions. The Politics of Farming Anno 1995'*. May 1995, Wageningen.

PAUL, SAMUEL (1993). 'Bangalore's Public Services. A Report Card'. *Economic and Political Weekly*, 33, no. 52, pp. 2901–9.

PEDERSON, JORGEN DIGE (1992). 'State, Bureaucracy and Change in India'. *Journal of Development Studies*, 28, no. 4, pp. 616–39.

PINSTRUP-ANDERSEN, Per (1987). 'Macroeconomic Adjustment Policies and Human Nutrition: Available Evidence and Research Needs'. *Food and Nutrition Bulletin*, 9, no. 1, pp. 69–86.

PINTO, AMBROSE (1992). 'Karnataka: Institutionalized Corruption'. *Economic and Political Weekly*, 27, no. 35, pp. 1837–8.

POTTER, DAVID C. (1986). *India's Political Administrators 1919–1983*. Clarendon Press, Oxford.

—— (1987) 'IAS Mobility Patterns'. *Indian Journal of Public Administration*, 33, No. 4, pp. 845–56.

—— (1988). 'Mobility Patterns in State Government Departments in India', *Indian Journal of Public Administration*, 34, no. 4, pp. 907–32.

POULANTZAS, NICOS (1973). *Political Power and Social Classes*. New Left Books, London.

—— (1976). 'The Capitalist State: A Reply to Miliband and Laclau'. *New Left Review*, no. 95, pp. 63–83.

PURSELL, G. and ASHOK GULATI (1993). 'Liberating Indian Agriculture: An Agenda for Reform'. *Policy Research Working Papers*, September, World Bank, Washington D.C.

RADHAKRISHNA, R. and K. HANUMANTHA RAO (1994). *Food Security, Public Distribution and Price Policy*. Centre for Economic and Social Studies, *Working Paper* 26, Hyderabad.

RADHAKRISHNA, R. and S. INDRAKANT (1991). 'Foodgrain Sector: Growth, Equity and Market Intervention', in M.V. Nadkarni, A.S. Seetharamu and Abdul Aziz (eds.), *India: The Emerging Challenges*. Sage Publications, New Delhi etc., pp. 175–96.

RADHAKRISHNAN, V., E.K. THOMAS and K. JESSY THOMAS (1994). 'Performance of Rice Crop in Kerala', in B.A. Prakash (eds.), *Kerala's Economy. Performance, Problems, Prospects*. Sage Publications, New Delhi etc., pp. 160–78.

RAM, R. (1986). 'Government Size and Economic Growth'. *American Economic Review*, 76, no. 1.

RAMACHANDRAN, V.K. (1995). *Kerala's Development Achievements: A Review*. Indira Gandhi Institute of Development Research, Bombay.

RANDHAWA, N.S. (1994). 'Liberalization and Implications for Agricultural Policy: An Overview,' in G.S. Bhalla (ed.), *Economic Liberalization and Indian Agriculture*. Institute for Studies in Industrial Development, New Delhi, pp. 353–78.

RAO, V.M. (1995). 'Beyond "Surpluses". Food Security in Changing Context'. *Economic and Political Weekly*, 30, no. 4, pp. 215–19.

RAY, AMAL (1989). 'Public Enterprises in India. Their Managerial Aspects', in Abdul Aziz (ed.), *Management Problems of State Public Undertakings*. Printwell Publishers, Jaipur, pp. 78–87.

ROY, S. (1984). *Pricing, Planning and Politics: A Study of Economic Distortions in India*. Institute of Economic Affairs, London.

RUDOLPH, LLOYD I. and SUSANNE HOEBER RUDOLPH (1987). *In Pursuit of Lakshmi. The Political Economy of the Indian State*. University of Chicago Press, Chicago and London.

—— (1988). 'Lakshmi Defended'. *The Journal of Commonwealth and Comparative Politics*, 26, no. 3, pp. 270–95.

RUDRA, ASHOK (1989) 'Emergence of the Intelligentsia as a Ruling Class in India'. *Economic and Political Weekly*, January 21, pp. 142–50.

SARAP KAILAS (1991). *Interlinked Agrarian Markets in Rural India*. Sage Publications, New Delhi etc.

SATHYAMURTHY, T.V. (1985). *India Since Independence. Studies in the Development of the Power of the State. Vol. 1: Centre-state Relations; the Case of Kerala*. Ajanta Publications, Delhi.

SAYER, ANDREW (1984). *Method of Social Science. A Realist Approach*. Hutchinson, London.

SAYER, DEREK (1979). *Marx's Method. Ideology, Science and Critique in Capital*. Harvester Press, Sussex, and Humanities Press, New Jersey.

SCHAFFER, BERNARD (1984). 'Towards Responsibility: Public Policy in Concept and Practice', in E.J. Clay and B.B. Schaffer (eds.), *Room for Manoeuvre. An Exploration of Public Policy Planning in Agricultural and Rural Development*. Heinemann Educational Books, London, pp. 142–90.

SCHAFFER, B. and G.B. LAMB (1974). 'Exit, Voice and Access'. *Social Science Information*, December 1974.

SCHAFFER, BERNARD and HUANG WEN-HSIEN (1975). 'Distribution and the Theory of Access'. *Development and Change*, 6, no. 2, pp. 13–36.

SCOTT, MAURICE and DEEPAK LAL (eds.) (1990). *Public Policy and Economic Development*. Clarendon Press, Oxford.

SEN, AMARTYA (1977). 'Rational fools: A Critique of the Behavioural Foundations of Economic Theory'. *Philosophy and Public Affairs*, 6.

—— (1981). *Poverty and Famines. An Essay on Entitlement and Deprivation*. Clarendon Press, Oxford.

—— (1986). 'The Causes of Famine. A Reply'. *Food Policy*, 11, no. 2, pp. 125–32.

—— (1993). 'The Causation and Prevention of Famines. A Reply'. *Journal of Peasant Studies*, 21, no. 1, pp. 29–40.

SEN, GEETA (1992). 'Social Needs and Public Accountability', in Marc Wuyts et al. (eds.), *Development Policy and Public Action*. Oxford University Press, in association with the Open University, pp. 253–77.

SENGUPTA, PRADYOT KUMAR (1984). 'A Few Thoughts on the Essential Commodities (Special Provisions) Act, 1981'. *Criminal Law Journal*, 90, pp. 41–6.

SHIVA RAMU, S. (1989). 'Problems of State Public Enterprises: a Karnataka Study', in Abdul Aziz (ed.), *Management Problems of State Public Undertakings*. Printwell Publishers, Jaipur, pp. 88–101.

SKOCPOL, THEDA (1979). *States and Social Revolutions*. Cambridge University Press, Cambridge.

—— (1985). 'Bringing the State Back in: Strategies of Analysis in Current Research', in Peter B. Evans, Dietrich Rueschemeyer and Theda Skocpol (eds.), *Bringing the State Back in*. Cambridge University Press, Cambridge etc., pp. 3–37.

—— (1995). 'Targeting within Universalism: Politically Viable Policies to Combat Poverty in the United States', in Theda Skocpol, *Social Policy in the United States. Future Possibilities in Historical Perspective*. Princeton University Press, Princeton, pp. 250–74.

SLATER, RICHARD and JOHN WATSON (1989). 'Democratic Centralization or Political Consolidation; the Case of Local Government Reform in Karnataka'. *Public Administration and Development*, 9, no. 2, pp. 147–57.

SRINIVAS, M.N. and M.N. PANINI (1984). 'Politics and Society in Karnataka'. *Economic and Political Weekly*, 19 no. 2, pp. 69–75.

SRINIVASAN, T.N. (1985). 'Neoclassical Political Economy, the State and Economic Development'. *Asian Development Review*, 3, no. 2, pp. 38–58.

—— (1991). 'Reform of Industrial and Trade Policies'. *Economic and Political Weekly*, 26, no. 37, pp. 2143–45.

STUIJVENBERG, P.A. VAN (1994). 'Structural Adjustment in India — What about Poverty Alleviation?', in *Structural Adjustment and Poverty in India: Policy and Research Issues*. Papers and Proceedings of IDPAD Seminar 29–30 November 1994, The Hague.

SUKHATME, P.V. (1981). 'Measuring the Incidence of Undernutrition'. *Economic and Political Weekly*, June 6, pp. 1034–1036.

—— (1981). 'On Measurement of Poverty'. *Economic and Political Weekly*, August 8, pp. 1318–24.

SURESH, C.P. (1986). 'Electoral Politics', in N. Jose Chander (ed.), *Dynamics of State Politics. Kerala*. Sterling Publishers, New Delhi, Bangalore, pp. 152–203.

SURYANARAYANA, M.H. (1995a). 'PDS Reform and Scope for Commodity-

Based Targeting'. *Economic and Political Weekly*, 30, no. 13, pp. 687–95.

—— (1995b). 'Some Experiments with Food Stamps'. *Economic and Political Weekly*, 30, no. 52, p. A 151–59.

SWAMINATHAN, MADHURA (1995). 'Revamped Public Distribution System. A Field Report From Maharashtra'. *Economic and Political Weekly*, 30, no. 36, pp. 2230.

—— 1996. 'Structural Adjustment, Food Security and System of Public Distribution of food'. *Economic and Political Weekly* 32, No. 26, pp. 1665–72.

THARAKAN, MICHAEL (1994). 'Social and Economic Lessons from Kerala'. Paper Presented at the Centre for Asian Studies Amsterdam, May 1994.

THOMAS, ISAAC T.M. and S. MOHANA KUMAR (1991). 'Kerala Elections 1991: Lessons and non-Lessons'. *Economic and Political Weekly*, 26 no. 47, pp. 2691–2704.

THOMAS ISAAC T.M. and P.K. MICHAEL THARAKAN (1995) 'Kerala: Towards a New Agenda'. *Economic and Political Weekly*, 30, no. 31/32, pp. 1993–2002.

TILLY, CHARLES (1984). *Big Structures, Large Processes, Huge Comparisons*. Russell Sage Foundation, New York.

TOYE, JOHN (1987). *Dilemmas of Development. Reflections on the Counter-Revolution in Development Economics*. Blackwell Publishers, Oxford etc.

—— (1988). 'Political Economy and the Analysis of Indian Development'. *Modern Asian Studies*, 22, no. 1, pp. 97–122.

TRIENEKENS, G.M.T. (1987). 'De Voedselvoorziening in de Jaren 1940–45'. *Spiegel Historiael*. February 1987, pp. 78–85.

TURK, A. (1976). 'Law as Weapon in Social Conflict'. *Social Problems*, 23, pp. 276–91.

TYAGI, D.S. (1990). *Managing India's Food Economy. Problems and Alternatives*. Sage Publications, New Delhi etc.

VAIDYANATHAN, A. (1983). 'On the Validity of NSS Consumption Data'. *Working Paper*, no. 183, Centre for Development Studies, Trivandrum.

VANAIK, ACHIN (1990). *The Painful Transition. Bourgeois Democracy in India*. Verso, London and New York.

VARKEY, OUSEPH (1984). 'The Rise and Decline of the Left and Democratic Front in Kerala', in John R. Wood (ed.), *State Politics in Contemporary India. Crisis or Discontinuity*? Westview Press, Boulder and London, pp. 103–38.

VARSHNEY, ASHUTOSH (1993). 'Self-Limited Empowerment: Democracy,

Economic Development and Rural India'. *Journal of Development Studies*, 29, no. 4, pp. 177–215.

VENUGOPAL, K.R. (1992). *Deliverance from Hunger. The Public Distribution System in India*. Sage Publications, New Delhi.

VIJAYASANBAR, P.S. (1986). *The Urban Casual Labour Market in Kerala. A Study of the Headload Workers in Trichur*. Centre for Development Studies, Trivandrum.

VIJVERBERG, MARION (1994). 'Poverty Debt and Food Security. The Price Paid by the Poor'. Unpublished Report. Wageningen Agricultural University, The Netherlands.

VITHAL, B.P.R. (1994). 'Evolving Trends in the Bureaucracy', in T.V. Sathyamurthy (ed.), *Social Change and Political Discourse in India. Structures of Power, Movements of Resistance. Vol. 1: State and Nations in the Context of Social Change*. Oxford University Press, Delhi etc., pp. 198–217.

VYAS, V.S. (1994). 'Agricultural Price Policy: Need for Reformulation', in G.S. Bhalla (ed.), *Economic Liberalization and Indian Agriculture*. Institute for Studies in Industrial Development, New Delhi, pp. 107–27.

—— (1996). 'State, Society and the Poor. Book Review of "The State and the Poor: Public Policy and Political Development in India and the United States" by John Echeverri–Gent'. *Economic and Political Weekly*, 31, no. 23, pp. 1394–95.

VYAS, V.S. and PRADEEP BHARGAVA (1995). 'Public Intervention for Poverty Alleviation. An overview'. *Economic and Political Weekly*, 30, no. 41–2, pp. 2559–572.

WADE, ROBERT (1982). 'The System of Administrative and Political Corruption: Canal Irrigation in South India'. *Journal of Development Studies*, 18, no. 3, pp. 287–328.

—— (1985). 'The Market for Public Office: Why the Indian State is not Better at Development'. *World Development*, 13, no. 4, pp. 467–97.

—— (1990). *Governing the Market: Economic Theory and the Role of Government in East Asian Industrialization*. Princeton University Press, Princeton.

WEBER, MAX (1968). *Economy and Society*. (Edited by Guenter Roth and Claus Wittich), Bedminster Press, New York.

WEINER, M. (1967). *Party Building in a New Nation: The Indian National Congress*. Chicago.

WHITE, GORDON (ed.) (1988). *Developmental States in East Asia*. Macmillan, London.

WHITE, GORDON (ed.) (1993). *The Political Analysis of Markets*. Special Issue of *IDS Bulletin*, 24, no. 4.

WOOD, JOHN R. (1984). 'Introduction: Continuity and Crisis in Indian State Politics', in John R. Wood (ed.), *State Politics in Contemporary India. Crisis or Continuity*. Westview Press, Boulder and London, pp. 1–19.

WOOD, GEOF (1985). 'The Politics of Development Policy Labelling', in Geof Wood (ed.), *Development and Change*, 16, no. 3, pp. 347–73.

WORLD BANK (1991). *India: 1991 Country Economic Memorandum*. Vol. II, Agriculture: Challenges and Opportunities.

—— (1994). *World Development Report 1994. Infrastructure for Development*. Oxford University Press, Oxford etc.

—— (1995). *Bureaucrats in Business. The Economics and Politics of Government Ownership*. Oxford University Press, Oxford.

Name Index

Subject Index

Oxford
5/4915
24/2/99